Roswitha Sieper

The Student's Companion to the U.S.A.

Max Hueber Verlag

Acknowledgements

Acknowledgement is made to the following for permission to reproduce maps in the appendix:

Figure 1: Physical Divisions – From: J. Wreford Watson, North America. Its Countries and Regions (Longman Group Ltd., London, 1963), p. 495. – © 1963 J. Wreford Watson

Figure 2: Agricultural Belts – From: J. H. Patterson, North America. A Geography of Canada and the United States (Oxford University Press, London, 4th edn. repr. 1971), p. 57. – © 1970 Oxford University Press

Figure 3: Physical and Topographical Map of the U.S.A. – From: The International Atlas (Rand McNally Co., Chicago, 1974), pp. 168–169. – © 1974 Rand McNally & Company

ISBN 3–19–00.2182–1
1. Auflage 1975
© 1975 Max Hueber Verlag München
Satz und Druck: Allgäuer Zeitungsverlag, Kempten
Printed in Germany

Contents

Preface

The present handbook on American Studies was written to complement my earlier book *The Student's Companion to Britain* (Hueber No. 2104). I firmly believe that students of English must include in their studies an examination of American life and American culture, as they cannot afford to ignore the dominant position of the U.S.A. in the world today. From my experience as a lecturer and examiner I know that this is the case in language and interpreters' schools, where language studies are orientated to practical application, but that this applies only to a lesser extent at universities and colleges of education. This book may also be used as a basis for instruction in the final school years (*gymnasiale Kollegstufe*) as well as for reference by teachers of English.

When the U.S.A. is discussed nowadays in our schools and in political groups, the arguments one hears are so frequently coloured by emotional attitudes that one is tempted to ask the question whether the opinions expressed have only been taken from the newspaper headlines or whether they are founded on factual knowledge of the country. True factual knowledge demands however not only insight into contemporary phenomena, but also into their origins. One must be guided by this insight when passing judgement.

I have endeavoured to present the reader with systematically organized facts and have therefore not aimed at journalistic "appeal". I have sufficient dealings with the preparation of papers and with examinations to be aware of how thankful students are when the basic information they need is presented in a clear and concise way.

It now remains for me to thank all those whose interest in the book and active assistance served as a constant encouragement to me; above all Mr. Scott Sebastian, who on account of his comprehensive knowledge of his country provided me with essential information. His acute judgement helped me in modifying my views where necessary, and enabled me to decide what was essential and what had to be pruned away. My thanks go also to Mr. Gary Seale, Mr. David Ganz and Mr. Jerry Roth for their stimulating comments on individual chapters of the book. Furthermore, I should like to express my indebtedness to Mr. Timothy Wilson and Mrs. Janine Heilbronner-Fitzpatrick, who, thanks to their superb command of the language, gave me advice on linguistic questions. I should also like to thank Mr. D. C. Flint for his assistance with the map in Figure 4 of the appendix.

Since the use of British English is current in English language teaching in most European countries, this book adheres to British usage.

Munich, May 1975   R. S.

1. Historical Outline

1.1. Colonial Period

1.1.1. Founding of the British Colonies

Two main factors contributed to the colonization of North America by British settlers: the trading initiative of commercial companies and the religious intolerance in the mother country, which compelled persecuted sects to find refuge in the New World.

Virginia* was the first permanent colony to be founded by the English in America. After an earlier attempt by Sir Walter Raleigh in 1584 had failed, a new colony was established by the London Company in 1607. Despite great hardship resulting from malaria, famine and from the hostility of the Indians, the colony gradually flourished as a result of tobacco culture and grants of land to individual colonists.

The northern Atlantic Seaboard, which was later to be known as New England, was first settled by Puritans who had been persecuted in England.

The first colony in this region was Plymouth. In 1620, 102 'Pilgrim Fathers' sailed in the *Mayflower* to the New World and landed on the coast of Massachusetts. The Mayflower Compact, drawn up for government in the new settlement provided for the first pure democracy in America. The colony grew slowly and was later incorporated into Massachusetts.

Massachusetts was colonized by the Massachusetts Bay Company, which had been formed by groups of Puritans in England. The first settlements were Salem (1628) and Boston (1630). Economic and cultural life developed rapidly. In 1636, the first American university, Harvard, was founded in Cambridge near Boston. However, religious intolerance in the Puritan Bible commonwealth caused many settlers to leave and found new colonies. These were Rhode Island, the first colony to establish full religious freedom, and Connecticut, with the settlements Hartford and New Haven. With its Fundamental Orders, Connecticut boasted 'the first written constitution in history'. Dissenting Puritan groups from Massachusetts founded settlements in New Hampshire. Maine, originally colonized by Anglicans, was soon incorporated into Massachusetts. Vermont was settled from Massachusetts as late as 1724.

---

* The thirteen colonies given in spaced print formed the United States of America after the War of Independence.

New York and Delaware were originally colonized by other countries. New York was founded in 1614 on Manhattan Island as a Dutch trading post called 'New Amsterdam'. Captured in 1664 by the Duke of York (later King James II), it was renamed New York. Delaware, settled by Swedes, was conquered by the English in 1682.

Later settlements to the south of New England were proprietary colonies granted by the English King to individuals.

Maryland, the first of these colonies, was granted to a Catholic, George Calvert, later Lord Baltimore, and was settled chiefly by Catholics. Pennsylvania, granted to a Quaker, William Penn, soon admitted the persecuted of all nations, particularly Quakers, and prospered greatly, especially after self-government was granted by Penn. Other proprietary colonies were New Jersey and Carolina. The latter was divided into North Carolina and South Carolina in 1729. The last of the English settlements, Georgia, was founded in 1733 by the philanthropist James Oglethorpe for English debtors released from prison and for persecuted Protestant sects of all nations.

1.1.2. Immigration

The first immigrants came chiefly from Britain. English colonists settled mainly on the coastal plains, Scottish and Irish settlers, who came later and had to move west, on the poorer soils of the Appalachian valleys. Persecuted sects from Germany, encouraged by Penn's agents, immigrated into Pennsylvania. The 'Pennsylvania Dutch' came from the German Palatinate. Georgia admitted Protestants from Salzburg.

1.1.3. Further Development of the Colonies

The Northern colonies became the cradle of American democracy. They were early granted home rule with wholly elected assemblies and even elected governors (otherwise appointed by the King). Since the poor soil and hilly terrain of this region did not favour large plantations with hired or slave labour, the normal social pattern was the democratic community of independent small farmers and tradesmen. Eventually shipping gave rise to a mercantile aristocracy, which later became influential in American politics with the development of banking, manufacture and land speculation.

The Middle Atlantic colonies enjoyed an even balance between farming on middle-sized farms, trade (New York and Philadelphia becoming major ports), and, later industry based on the iron ore of the Alleghenies.

The Southern colonies formed an aristocratic society supported by slave labour on large plantations. The profitable cultivation of staple crops (tobacco, indigo, rice, cotton) and the economic self-sufficiency of the individual plantations prevented the development of industry.

1.2. Independence

1.2.1. Conflict with the British Parliament

When the British government began to lay duties on the import of tropical products in order to meet the heavy debt incurred in the British colonial war against France, this policy was passionately resented in the colonies. On the principle of 'no taxation without representation' (i. e. in Parliament), the colonies opposed the *Stamp Act*, a tax imposed on newspapers and legal documents. In 1773, the cargo of an English tea ship in Boston harbour was thrown into the sea by colonists disguised as Indians, an incident which later became known as the 'Boston Tea Party'. When the British government answered by closing the harbour and curtailing the rights of the Massachusetts government, the First Continental Congress met in 1774 to discuss united resistance.

1.2.2. War of Independence, 1775–83

In New England, the colonists were victorious in engagements at Lexington and Concord, April 1775. British troops were successful in a skirmish on Bunker Hill, but suffered heavy losses and were finally forced by General Washington to evacuate Boston.

The Second Continental Congress representing all colonies met in May 1775 at Philadelphia. It appointed Washington Commander-in-Chief of the newly created army and navy. It issued the Declaration of Independence on July 4, 1776 (now celebrated as 'Independence Day'), and contracted a military alliance with France. The Congress drafted a formal plan of Union called the Articles of Confederation. Henceforth the colonial population was divided into Patriots and Loyalists. Many of the latter joined the British forces or emigrated to Canada ('United Empire Loyalists').

In their campaign in the Middle colonies the English under General Howe took New York and held it despite successful attacks by Washington at Trenton and Princeton. A British attempt to sever the Northern from the Middle colonies, however, failed when General Burgoyne was captured with 5,000 of his men at Saratoga.

Hoping to find less resistance in the aristocratic South, the British captured Charleston (South Carolina) and Savannah (Georgia). Aided by a French fleet,

Washington laid siege to Yorktown peninsula (Virginia), and forced General Cornwallis to surrender.
The Treaty of Paris, 1783, recognized the independence of the thirteen colonies.

1.2.3. American Constitution

When the earlier Articles of Confederation providing for a relatively loose union failed to co-ordinate the interests of the various states, a Constitutional Convention of 55 delegates including the most distinguished men in America (Washington, Franklin, Hamilton, Madison) met in 1787 to draft a constitution for a closer federation. The American Constitution (p. 121) came into force in 1789, when nine of the thirteen states, after hard negotiations to preserve their individual rights, had ratified it. It established the United States as a federal republic with a bicameral legislature and a President who is official head of state as well as leader of the government.

Fathers of the Revolution

Benjamin Franklin, 1706–90, was born in Boston. He was apprenticed in the printing trade and became a newspaper editor. Later he left the narrow Puritan atmosphere of New England for free-thinking Pennsylvania, where he became extremely active in public affairs. He organized a militia and established an academy, the first in which scientific subjects as well as the conventional humanities were taught. He made the famous kite experiments which led to the invention of the lightning rod. In the War of Independence, he was responsible for the alliance with France and took part in the peace negotiations. He was a member of the Constitutional Convention and became Governor of Pennsylvania. The best-known of his many publications is his uncompleted *Autobiography*.
George Washington, 1732–99, 'the best-loved American', a Virginian aristocrat, fought as a British officer in the British colonial war against France, after which he retired to his plantation, Mount Vernon in Virginia (now a national monument). In the War of Independence, he was appointed Commander-in-Chief of the Continental Army and led his country through initial failures to victory by his calm determination and the influence of his noble, disinterested character. After being unanimously elected first President of the U.S.A., he organized U.S. defence and administration, and established a policy of strict neutrality. He served two terms. His Farewell Address is the classic statement of American isolationist policy. He liberated his slaves in his will.
Thomas Jefferson, 1743–1826, a Virginian planter, was one of the most versatile men of his age. He was a farmer, architect, inventor, writer, philosopher and statesman, who finally determined the spirit of the Constitution by the sheer force of his idealism. He drew up the Declaration of Independence, one of the world's great political documents. Jefferson acted as Governor of Virginia and Ambassador to France and was finally elected President, serving two terms. He organized the Democratic Republican Party (ancestor of today's Democratic Party) to represent the rights of the individual states and the common man. Although at the time of the Constitutional Convention he was Ambassador to France, he was the real inspirer of American democracy, with its placing the control of government in the hands of the common man.

Alexander Hamilton, 1757–1804, was the great financier of the early republic and a brilliant writer. He served in the War of Independence as Washington's aide-de-camp, leading the New York troops in the assault at Yorktown. He studied law and became a member of the Constitutional Convention where he advocated an aristocratic centralized government. As Secreaty of the Treasury he strengthened the federal government by taking over the debts of the states, thereby giving the central government extensive taxing powers within the states. His 'Federalist Papers' have remained the best authority on the nature of the Constitution.

James Madison, 1751–1836, a member of the Constitutional Convention with extensive knowledge of political institutions, has been called 'the Father of the Constitution'. He was Secretary of State under Jefferson, whom he succeeded in 1809 as President, serving two terms.

1.2.4. Early Foreign Policy

Early foreign policy pursued isolationism by refusing to allow European intervention in the Western hemisphere.

1.2.4.1. The War with Great Britain, 1812–14, was caused by the British blockade of the Atlantic during the Napoleonic Wars. Despite some destructive naval engagements, no significant gains were made by either side. An American invasion of Canada failed. The British attacked Washington and burned the Capitol and the White House. When they invaded the Gulf region, they were defeated by Andrew Jackson in the Battle of New Orleans. The Peace of Ghent recognized the status quo.

1.2.4.2. *Monroe Doctrine*, 1823: The interference of European powers in the affairs of Latin America prompted President Monroe to recognize the independence of the former Spanish colonies which had revolted against the mother country, and to proclaim the *Monroe Doctrine* containing the following provisions: The U.S.A. would not interfere with internal affairs of Europe. Europe was not to interfere with existing governments in the Americas. Europe was not to colonize any further in the Americas.

1.2.5 Jacksonian Democracy

Life in the U.S.A. was soon determined by conflicts between Northern plutocrats and the democratic farmers of the newly settled territories, who opposed the high interest charged on land credits and protective tariffs preventing cheap imports. The militant frontier spirit was embodied by President Andrew Jackson (victor of the Battle of New Orleans), who became the popular hero of the egalitarian West. His two administrations (1829–37) initiated 'the era of the common man' freed from aristocratic leadership, fostering contempt of class distinction and of higher education. Jackson established the new type of democratic party which swept away surviving religious and property qualifications for voting and office-holding. On the other hand, the Jackson era introduced the 'spoils system', which substituted partisan appointees for experienced officials.

1.3. Continental Expansion

1.3.1. Territorial Expansion

Territorial Expansion was propagated by the nationalistic spirit of the age under the slogan 'Manifest Destiny'. The *Northwest Ordinance, 1787,* had provided for the settling of the West. New territories, at first to be administered from Washington, were to be admitted as states when their population reached 60,000.

1.3.1.1. The Mississippi Valley was settled by a new wave of uncontrolled immigration, which also brought Scandinavians and Germans. Within a few decades, the frontier (edge of civilized settlement) was pushed towards the 'American Desert'. Indians, despite repeated treaties, were steadily driven further west.
The *Louisiana Purchase, 1803,* secured the western part of the Mississippi Basin from Napoleon for $15 million. This doubled the area of the United States.

1.3.1.2. Florida war invaded during the Napoleonic Wars by Andrew Jackson and finally acquired through a treaty with Spain in 1819.

1.3.1.3. Texas, though part of Mexico, was chiefly settled by Americans. The revolt of American settlers against Mexican rule under the leadership of Sam Houston led first to independence and later to the admission of Texas to the Union (1845).

1.3.1.4. Mexican (or Texan) War, 1846–48: The conflict with Mexico concerning Texas and U.S. claims to the Spanish-settled Mexican territories California and New Mexico led to a successful invasion of both territories and northern Mexico. By the treaty of Guadeloupe-Hidalgo the U.S.A. received New Mexico, Aricona, Colorado, Nevada, Utah and California.

1.3.1.5. Alaska was bought from Russia in 1867 for $7,200,000.

1.3.2. Economic Development of the West

1.3.2.1. Mississippi Valley: The northern part was settled by farmers from the Northeast under the democratic Northern township system. The main occupations were lumbering, dairy farming and corn cultivation. In the southern part, Southern plantation owners introduced the plantation and slave system. The invention of the cotton gin, a machine which greatly speeded up the removal of seeds from the cotton fibre, made the Southern territories the 'Cotton Kingdom'.

1.3.2.2. Far West: Oregon and Washington were claimed for the U.S.A. by the American explorers Lewis and Clark, 1805, and by the American Fur Company. Utah was settled by the Mormons, a religious sect, who, after being persecuted in the East, migrated to the Great Salt Lake. They founded Salt Lake City, 1847, turning the desert into a flourishing region by irrigation.

In California, the discovery of gold in 1848, shortly after the acquisition of the new territory, resulted in the greatest gold rush in history. Within one year the population was large enough to secure statehood. After the decline of the gold yield, new prosperity was founded mainly on agriculture.

The 'mining states' in the Rockies were founded by the rapidly increasing mining population after the exhaustion of the Californian gold-fields.

1.3.2.3. The prairies between the Mississippi Valley and the Rockies were opened up between 1866 and 1890 in two stages: The earlier ranching era created the cowboy romance of the open range. Texas cattle were driven by cowboys on 'the long trail' to northern markets to fatten on the grass of the Great Plains. The subsequent settlement of farmers tilling and fencing in the land ended the cowboy romance. The *Homestead Act,* 1862, the greatest government contribution to free enterprise in farming, provided that public land be allotted free of charge in small parcels of 160 acres to intending settlers. After five years of farming, they would become the legal owners. With the settlement of the prairies, which was hastened by the building of transcontinental railroads, the frontier was closed.

1.4. Civil War (War of Secession)

Causes of the war were the economic servitude of the South in relation to the North and the slavery issue. Like the West, the financially weak South was dependent for the development of its industry on Northern capital, which was provided only at high interest, since the North did not want to endanger its industrial supremacy.

1.4.1. The Slavery Issue

Slavery was first introduced into the colonies in 1619 in Virginia. By 1860, slaves constituted 50 per cent of the Southern population.

In the War of Independence, the first strong anti-slavery feeling bore results: the New England states and the Middle colonies abolished slavery.

The admission to the Union of slave-holding territories in the Mississippi Valley threatened the balance of power between the slave-holding South and the free Northern staates. The *Missouri Compromise*, 1820, balanced admission of Missouri as a slave state with the admission of Maine as a free state, and forbade slavery in the territories north of the Missouri River.

A strong abolitionist movement soon became a crusade in the North and included among its supporters poets like Whittier and Longfellow. Harriet Beecher Stowe's novel *Uncle Tom's Cabin* was inspired by indignation at the *Fugitive Slave Law*, 1850, which required restoration of fugitive slaves to their owners. Abolitionist elements joined in a new Republican Party, which, because of a split in the Democratic Party, was able to get its candidate, Abraham Lincoln, elected President in 1860.

Violent anti-slavery agitation in the North, and fear in the Southern states that their economic and social system, which was dependent on slave labour, was to be destroyed, finally brought about the secession of the Southern states after the election of Lincoln.

Abraham Lincoln became the most celebrated statesman in the U.S.A. after George Washington. In contrast to Washington, he stands for the backwoods virtues of pioneer life. He was born in Kentucky and spent his youth in very poor circumstances, receiving altogether not more than six months formal schooling. He served as captain in an expedition against the Indians and was later postmaster in a frontier town, where he taught himself law. After practising in Springfield, Ill., he was elected to the House of Representatives, where he advocated the abolition of slavery. Lincoln was finally elected President in 1860. He brought the Civil War to a successful conclusion for the North. Soon after its close, he was shot by a Southern fanatic.

1.4.2. Resources of North and South

The Union of the 23 Northern states under President Lincoln was superior in manpower and equipment. The Southern Confederacy under its own president, Jefferson Davis, numbered only 13 states. The North had the federal fleet, banking capital and a far superior railway network. Its farming system was diversified, while the South had to shift to food crops. Northern troops outnumbered Southern troops four to one.

1.4.3. The Civil War

The Civil War, which lasted from 1861 till 1865, was the most devastating in U.S. history.

The Capture of Fort Sumter, South Carolina, by the Confederates, which marked the beginning of the conflict, constituted an initial Southern success, while the blockade of the Southern coast, which stopped cotton and tobacco exports, became a powerful weapon of the North. On the other hand, Lincoln's *Emancipation Proclamation*, 1862, declaring the freedom of all slaves did not succeed in preventing the slaves from supporting the Confederate cause by their work.

In the Virginia campaign, Northern hopes of conquering the Confederacy by striking a blow at its capital, Richmond, were thwarted by the superior defensive tactics of General Lee. Four Union generals were repulsed successively, twice at Bull Run, at Federiksburg and near Richmond.

The Mississippi campaign weakened the South by severing the Confederate states west of the Mississippi from the rest of the Confederacy. In a brilliant manoeuvre, the Union's ablest general, Ulysses Grant, advanced from Kentucky to Mississippi and conquered Vicksburg, Miss., while Admiral Farragut captured the key port New Orleans.

In the East, Lee's attempt to relieve pressure on Virginia by an offensive in Union territory failed. He was defeated at Antietam, Maryland, and in the bloody battle of Gettysburg, Pennsylvania, in which 40,000 soldiers were killed (cf. Lincoln's famous Gettysburg Address, 1863, on dedication of the battle-field as a burial ground). The almost simultaneous victory of Northern troops at Vicksburg sealed the doom of the Confederate cause. Grant took over the supreme command and opened an offensive against Lee in Virginia (the 'Wilderness Campaign'). Sherman advanced southeast through Georgia and captured the Southern factory and railway centre Atlanta. In a devastating march through the enemy's country, foraging on the newly gathered crops and destroying all railway lines, Sherman advanced to the sea and took Savannah. Four months later, Grant and Sherman surrounded Lee at Appomatox, where he surrendered.

1.5. The South in the Reconstruction Period

1.5.1. Northern Policy of Revenge

A policy of revenge was adopted by Congress although Lincoln had proposed a liberal plan to pardon the ruined Southern states. Ill-feeling caused by the 'reconstruction' policy has cast a shadow over relations between North and South ever since.

Amendments 14 and 15 to the Constitution, which gave Negroes citizenship and the right to vote, barred Southern participants in the 'rebellion' from state and federal offices, and declared that claims for payment of compensation for freed slaves were illegal.

When the Southern states rejected Amendment 14, the *Reconstruction Act*, 1867, provided for the military occupation of the states which had seceded. 'Carpetbaggers' (corrupt Northern adventurers) aided by 'scalawags' (Southern collaborators) acted as officials and leaders of the newly enfranchised blacks, who held state offices. In some legislatures, Negroes who could neither read nor write outnumbered whites.

The Ku Klux Klan, a secret association, was founded by embittered whites to frighten Negroes away from public life by terrorism, occasionally including outright murder.

1.5.2. Recovery of the South

Under the *Amnesty Act*, 1872, whites regained power. After the withdrawal of the occupation troops, 1877, new state constitutions legalized the virtual disfranchisement of Negroes through literacy and property tests, which were tacitly tolerated by the federal government.

Hopes of the freed Negroes for a life of ease did not materialize because, without opportunities for earning their livelihood, they were left to starvation. Many of them wandered rootlessly about and finally returned to the plantations to work as tenants for the landowners, who were too poor to hire labour. Under the new sharecrop system, landowners provided land and implements and received one half of the crop.

1.6. Industrial Revolution and Big Business

1.6.1. Industrial Development

The Industrial Revolution was accelerated by American inventions (e.g. Bell's telephone, Edison's electric bulb, Howe's sewing machine, Westinghouse's air brake), which founded American economic supremacy.

1.6.1.1. Transportation helped to open up the continent: Robert Fulton's steam boat, which made its first journey on the Hudson River in 1807, initiated a new era in navigation. The Erie Canal, 1825, which provided a direct connection between the East coast and the West hitherto impeded by the Appalachians, inaugurated the period of canal building. Railroad building beginning in 1829 opened up mountainous regions. Completion of the first transcontinental railway, the Union Pacific, facilitated the settlement of the Far West. Aviation was initiated by the first practical flying machine, constructed by the Wright brothers in 1903.

1.6.1.2. American agriculture became the most efficient in the world through American inventions. Ely Whitney's cotton gin revolutionized cotton culture; Newbold's cast-iron plough immensely improved ploughing. The wheat farmers' problem of growing more wheat than they were able to reap in the short harvesting season was solved by Cyrus McCormick's reaper, which was soon supplemented by binding and threshing machines, finally developing into enormous combines for the complete processing of the crop.

1.6.1.3. Industry developed as a result of declining imports during the Napoleonic Wars. The early iron industry was based on coal and iron ore mined in the Appalachians. The textile industry processed home-grown cotton with the water power of the New England streams. In the 20th century, Henry Ford established the principle of mass production in the automobile industry with his highly efficient conveyor-belt system.

1.6.1.4. Commercial life was revolutionized by Sholes's typewriter. By providing genteel jobs for women, the typewriter became one of the main factors in the emancipation of women.

1.6.2. Rise of Big Business

1.6.2.1. 'Captains of industry' rose to dominant positions in key industries and crushed competitors by ruthless methods. The most prominent men to apply the characteristic 'rugged individualism' of the frontier to the fields of financing and industrial production were Carnegie (steel), Rockefeller (oil), Pierpont Morgan (banking), Kaiser (heavy industry), Ford (automobiles), Du Pont (gun powder, later chemical industries), Vanderbilt and Harriman (eastern railroads), and Hill (transcontinental railroads).

1.6.2.2. Consolidation of business, merging smaller companies into large corporations, was favoured by the necessity for large amounts of capital to utilize the vast resources and span the huge distances of a gigantic continent. The Standard Oil Company, controlled by Rockefeller, combined the operations of producing, refining and transporting oil along pipelines. The Carnegie Steel Company owned iron-ore mines, maintained a fleet of carriers on the Great Lakes and established a railway line from Pittsburgh to Lake Erie. The U.S. Steel Corporation, created in 1901 by the merger of the Carnegie interests with other concerns, was the first billion-dollar corporation in the history of the country. General Motors merged a large number of automobile companies and eventually grew to control 50 per cent of the U.S. automobile market.

1.6.3. Import of Labour

Import of cheap labour for mines, factories and railroad building (10 million people between 1905–14) brought a new wave of immigration. From southern and eastern Europe came Italians, Greeks, Poles, Lithuanians, Galician Jews, from Asia Chinese and Japanese.

Immigrants from less developed countries were mostly illiterate, had no experience in self-government and were accustomed to a very low standard of living. Congregating in alien 'islands' of large cities, often with no intention of staying permanently and of learning English, they were difficult to integrate and often formed an element of unrest.

1.6.4. Influence of Economic Development on Party Politics

1.6.4.1. 'Solid South': Republican mismanagement during the Reconstruction Period and the necessity of protecting the Southern farmer from the Northern tariff policy created a 'solid South' for the Democratic Party in subsequent elections.

1.6.4.2. Third parties, usually short-lived, were formed as a consequence of distress in the farming West resulting from high railway rates, excessive interest rates (8–12 per cent) on mortgages and other farming debts. Most of their demands, considered radical at the time, have since been realized.

The *Granger Movement* (or 'Patrons of Husbandry'), which was founded in 1867, succeeded in getting legislation against ruthless railway practices passed. Such laws, however, were often made ineffective when appeals to the Supreme Court were decided in favour of the railways.

The *National Greenback Party* demanded resumed issue of inflated paper currency (which had been withdrawn after the Civil War) to allow farmers to meet their debts with cheaper money.

The *Populist Movement* in the 1890s added to this platform demands for an eight-hour day, a graduated income tax and government operation of big corporations and public services.

The *Progressive Party*, which was formed in 1912 by supporters of Theodore Roosevelt's progressive New Nationalism, advocated reforms of the election system, industrial legislation establishing minimum wages and prohibiting child labour, and a better control of large corporations.

Socialist parties demanded government ownership of means of production.

1.6.5. Trade Unions

The Trade Unions developed slowly, because the individualism and capitalistic inclination of the working classes, and the struggle of employers against workers' organizations (often supported by the courts) did not favour unionization.

The *Knights of Labour* were founded in 1869 to unite skilled and unskilled workers in a great national union, but failed because of radicalism and internal dissensions.

The *American Federation of Labour* (A.F.L.), founded in 1881, organized skilled trades. Under Samuel Gompers, its president for more than fourty years, it fought for moderate demands, especially for higher wages and the eight-hour day.
The *Congress of Industrial Organizations* (C.I.O.), which was founded in 1935, represented workers of mass-production industries.

1.6.6. Industrial Strife

Labour strove to enforce its demands through strikes in which non-strikers were prevented from entering the plants by picket lines, and through the boycott of products manufactured by hostile employers.
Employers answered by lockouts (closing of factories to force workers to accept the management's terms) and blacklists recording names of agitators, who were refused employment.
Strikes of railroad workers and miners led to violence and intervention by federal troops.

1.6.7. Anti-Trust Legislation

Anti-trust legislation to fight big business and its corrupt influence on politics was prompted by the agitation of 'muckrakers', social critics who revealed the cut-throat practices of big trusts, sometimes in a distinctly sensationalist manner.
The *Interstate Commerce Act,* 1887, laid down the principle of federal regulation of big business by establishing control over railway rates and monopolistic practices.
The *Sherman Anti-Trust Act,* 1890, declared illegal every trust or 'conspiracy in restraint of trade', but was, like many later acts, successfully evaded. Although some trusts were dissolved, newly formed 'holding companies' (controlling other companies by virtue of stock ownership in these companies) proved equally powerful.
The *Pure Food and Drugs Act* and *Meat Inspection Act,* 1906, forbidding adulterated food and impure meat products were enacted partly as a result of the sensational revelations about the shocking conditions in Chicago's meat industries by Upton Sinclair's novel *The Jungle.*
The *Clayton Anti-Trust Act,* 1914, forbade interlocking directorates between companies and the prohibiting of strikes, peaceful picketing, or boycotts.
The Department of Labour was established in 1913 as a separate ministry with a conciliation service for labour disputes.

1.7. Overseas Expansion

With an expanding industry seeking foreign markets and growing interest in the Pacific after settlement of the Far West, imperialism began to replace isolationism and reached its climax under presidents McKinley and Theodore Roosevelt at the beginning of the 20th century.

1.7.1.

Japan, which had excluded foreigners, was opened to American trade through an agreement in 1853. In 1863, a joint naval action by England and the U.S.A. opened the country completely to the outside world.

1.7.2.

China: After the opening of Chinese ports to foreign trade following the Opium War, 1842, foreign powers began to compete for political and commercial influence in China. When the Chinese Boxer Rebellion, 1900, was suppressed by Western powers, the U.S.A. pleaded for the preservation of Chinese independence and an 'open-door' policy. This made the U.S.A. the main supporter of Chinese territorial integrity until World War II.

1.7.3.

Hawaii: The steady influx of American traders and sugar planters had led to a preponderance of American interests, which resulted in Hawaii's annexation by the U.S.A. in 1898 as a means of establishing American naval and commercial predominance in the Pacific.

1.7.4.

Samoan Islands: The ceding of ports and commercial privileges to the U.S.A., Britain and Germany led to the establishment of a joint protectorate by Germany and the U.S.A. in 1899.

1.7.5.

Cuba and Puerto Rico (Caribbean), the Philippines and Guam (Pacific) were conquered in the Spanish-American War, 1898: Revolts in Cuba against Spain as a result of economic depressions threatened the considerable U.S. investments in Cuban sugar and tobacco plantations.

The U.S.A. sent the battleship *Maine* to protect U.S. citizens in Cuba. An explosion in the ship, which caused the death of 260 sailors, was attributed by popular U.S. propaganda to Spain.

Within four months, Cuba, Puerto Rico and the Philippines were invaded, the capitals Santiago (Cuba) and Manila (Philippines) conquered.

By the Treaty of Paris, 1899, the U.S.A. annexed Puerto Rico and Guam. Spain withdrew from Cuba and ceded the Philippines for $20 million.

1.7.6.

Panama Canal Zone: The war with Spain had demonstrated the need for an Atlantic-Pacific canal for more effective operations of the U.S. Navy, but a U.S. offer to Colombia to build a canal through the Isthmus of Panama was rejected. A revolution of foreign residents in Panama was supported by a U.S. gun boat. Panama declared her independence from Colombia, which was immediately recognized by the U.S.A. In return, the U.S.A. was granted a perpetual lease of a 10-mile strip of land across the Isthmus of Panama. The building of the canal, 1904–14, was a great engineering and sanitary achievement. Tropical diseases caused by the deadly climate were almost completely eliminated.

1.7.7.

Annexation of Nicaragua (1912), Haiti (1914) and Santo Domingo (1916): Political unrest in these countries induced the U.S.A. to intervene by landing marines and establishing protectorates under the Roosevelt Corollary to the Monroe Doctrine, 1904, which had assigned to the U.S.A. 'police power' in disturbed South American states.

1.7.8.

The Virgin Islands were bought from Denmark in 1917.

1.8. World War I

1.8.1. Causes of Entry into the War

U.S. interests in war production bound America to the Allies, who controlled the seas.

Unrestricted submarine warfare by the Germans led to the sinking of unarmed British vessels carrying munitions. The sinking of the *Lusitania*, 1915, and the

Sussex, 1916, caused the loss of more than a hundred American lives. In the Sussex Pledge, brought about by the intervention of President Wilson, the Germans agreed not to sink merchant vessels without warning and without saving human lives. However, they resumed unrestricted submarine warfare in 1917.

Allied propaganda, which alleged that German soldiers hat committed atrocities, appealed to the crusading spirit of the American nation. The national mood was expressed in President Wilson's War Message to Congress, which proclaimed: 'The world must be made safe for democracy'.

1.8.2.

American war efforts decided the war in favour of the Allies. The U.S. Navy took part in the war against submarines. An expeditionary force of two million men helped to halt the last German advance in France. American troops participated in Allied counter-offensives on the Marne. In 1918, an American force of 1,200,000 men broke through the German lines between Metz and Sedan.

1.8.3.

President Wilson's *Fourteen Points,* 1918, which helped to bring about the German surrender, proposed 'a peace founded upon honour and justice'. Apart from proposals for territorial readjustments, they demanded the abolition of secret diplomacy, freedom of the seas, removal of international economic barriers, reduction of armaments, establishment of a general association of nations, self-determination for the peoples in disputed areas, and impartial settlement of colonial claims.

1.8.4.

The *Treaty of Versailles,* 1919, determined by previous secret agreements and a desire for revenge, disregarded Wilson's Fourteen Points and was not ratified by the American Senate, chiefly for fear that responsibility for maintaining peace would draw the U.S.A. into new conflicts. Although Wilson succeeded in having the Covenant of the League of Nations written into the treaty, the U.S.A. itself did not join the League.

1.8.5. Effects of the War on the U.S.A.

The U.S.A. had become a naval power. Her economy had developed immensely through the export of arms and the opening up of new markets following the disruption of European trade. The U.S.A. became the principal creditor nation in the world.

1.9. Interwar Period

1.9.1. American Peace Efforts

Aid was granted to war refugees and war-shattered nations.
The Washington Conference, 1921, provided for a reduction of naval armaments. An agreement on the navies of the five great naval powers fixed the proportion of tonnage at 5 (U.S.A. and Britain), 3 (Japan), 1.67 (France and Italy).
A conciliatory attitude was taken towards nations unable to continue payment of war debts. The German reparations were scaled down by the Dawes Plan, 1924, and the Young Plan, 1929. A proposal by President Hoover, 1931, to postpone payment of reparations and intergovernmental debts for one year encouraged most nations to suspend payment altogether.
The Kellogg-Briand Pact, 1928, negotiated by France and the American Secretary of State, Kellogg, and formally approved by more than sixty nations, tried to put an end to war.
Neutrality Acts between 1935 and 1937 provided for an embargo on the shipment of arms, and the prohibition of loans to belligerents, and banned the arming of American merchant vessels. American citizens were forbidden to travel on belligerent ships.

1.9.2. Economic Crisis

In 1929, the U.S.A. suffered the most serious depression in its history, with world-wide repercussions. The crisis was caused by the reduced purchasing power of nations weakened by war, and by the failure of debtor countries to pay in gold or through exports, which were made impossible by the high U.S. tariffs.
The stock market crash, 1929, wiped out many fortunes, and bank failures destroyed savings. Unemployment reached staggering proportions (14 million), leading to hunger parades and rent strikes.

1.9.3. Restriction of Immigration

Hostility among American workers, particularly in California, towards the willingness of Asiatic immigrants to work for low wages led to Exclusion Acts barring Chinese labour, and an agreement with Japan. The Japanese government was to prevent emigration of Japanese labourers by refusing to issue passports.
Quota laws led to permanent restriction of immigration. In 1929, the total annual immigration was finally limited to 150,000. Immigration from each country was fixed at 2 per cent of the number of each nationality resident in the U.S.A. in the year 1920. Thus 'new immigration' (imported cheap labour from southern and

eastern European countries) was restricted in favour of the 'old' (prospective permanent settlers from northern and western Europe).
Anarchists and physically or mentally disabled persons were excluded.

1.9.4. Prohibition and Crime

The prohibition of the manufacture, transport and sale of intoxicating beverages had been demanded soon after the Civil War by the Prohibition Party, founded in 1869, the Women's Temperance Union and the Anti-Saloon League. By 1917, more than half the states had introduced Prohibition, but a flourishing smuggling trade from 'wet' into 'dry' states made legislation on a federal level necessary.
In 1917, Congress passed the 18th Amendment to the Constitution (enforced by the *Volstead Act*). From the start, Prohibition met with strong opposition on the grounds that it was an infringement of personal liberty. It was evaded by all classes of the population and led to a great deal of illicit distilling and smuggling, the profit going into the pockets of 'bootleggers' and criminals. Prohibition favoured the organization of crime on a large scale by notorious gangsters and 'racketeers' like Al Capone and Frank Costello, linked with the international crime organization, the Mafia, which had originated in Sicily. Although Prohibition was repealed in 1933, gangsters continued to control certain unlawful businesses (drug traffic, gambling, prostitution), and to terrorize trade unions, e. g. the long-shoremen (dock workers) and teamsters (lorry drivers), especially in Chicago, New York and San Francisco.

1.9.5. Roosevelt Administration and New Deal

The cry for a strong democratic leader, who would help the common man rather than big business, led to the election of Franklin Delano Roosevelt (Governor of the State of New York) in 1932, and to a full victory for the Democrats in Congress as well. The 'New Deal' which Roosevelt had promised the American people in his election campaign became a huge programme for internal reconstruction.

1.9.5.1. Banking and finance: The bank crash and financial panic of 1933 was met by the devaluation of the dollar (to meet the competition of European countries with devalued currencies), the insuring of bank deposits and the limitation of speculation.
1.9.5.2. Agriculture: The distress of farmers was to be relieved by the *Agricultural Adjustment Act*, 1933, which provided for the curtailing of farm production and the compensation of farmers by bounty payments. When the Supreme Court annulled the Act, a new law based on the principle of soil conservation introduced

benefit payments for farmers who shifted land from soil-depleting to soil-enriching crops (e. g. cereals to legumes). Other laws introduced marketing loans and insurance against the loss of crops by wheat farmers. Large sums of money were spent on drought relief, the resettling of farmers on better land, the supply of electricity to depressed rural areas and the buying up of surplus farm products for distribution among the unemployed.

1.9.5.3. Work relief: The *Federal Emergency Act*, 1933, appropriated funds for public works, which provided jobs for millions of unemployed men. $8 billion were spent on slum clearance and low-cost housing projects, reforestation, highway construction and land reclamation (p.).

1.9.5.4. Industry: The *National Industrial Recovery Act* (N.I.R.A.) 1933, authorized loans to industry to finance the projects of the work relief programme. Although N.I.R.A. was cancelled by a Supreme Court decision, the increased purchasing power resulting from work relief soon led to a recovery of industry.

1.9.5.5. Labour relations: The *Wagner Labour Relations Act*, 1935, the 'Magna Carta' of the trade unions, secured full recognition of trade unions and created a National Labour Relations Board for settling industrial disputes. The *Labour Standards Act (Wages and Hours Act)*, 1938, banned child labour and fixed minimum wages and maximum working hours.

1.9.5.6. Social security: The *Social Security Act*, 1935, established an unemployment insurance and old-age pension system. It authorized federal grants to states for poor-relief.

1.9.5.7. Roosevelt and the Supreme Court: After 1935, New Deal measures were annulled more frequently by Supreme Court decisions. To break the conservative majority in the court, Roosevelt, after his re-election in 1936, proposed the appointment of one additional member for each judge remaining in office beyond the age of 70. Although Roosevelt's measure was not carried because of general fear of executive influence on the court, Roosevelt was able to fill vacancies through retirement with new appointments and thus assure the success of his measures.

1.9.5.8. The New Deal met with increasing opposition. Its opponents pointed out the threat of inflation caused by over-spending, and it was not easy to justify measures for cutting back the production of food in the face famine in other countries.
Nevertheless Roosevelt was the first president in U.S. history to be re-elected twice (1940, 1944). He died in 1945, but Harry Truman, who succeeded to the presidency, continued the New Deal programmes.

1.9.6. Retreat from Imperialism

The Pan-American Movement originating in the 1920s advocated more harmonious relations among the American nations, which, however, did not materialize, owing to ill-feeling against U.S. imperialism. The announcement of a 'good neighbour policy' by President Franklin Delano Roosevelt in 1933 banned intervention and eased the tension.

The military occupation of Santo Domingo had already ended in 1924. The marines stationed in Nicaragua were withdrawn in 1933. In the same year, the *Platt Amendment,* 1901, which had reduced Cuba to a protectorate of the U.S.A., was cancelled, although one naval station was retained. The military occupation of Haiti was concluded in 1934. In most of these countries, however, American control of financial affairs continued.

Pan-American conferences formulated new principles for co-operation, especially in case of war. The Pan-American Conference at Lima, 1938, warned the totalitarian states that intervention or aggression would be resisted by 21 American countries.

1.10.   World War II

1.10.1. U.S. Policy Before Entry Into the War

Cash and Carry, 1939, repealed the arms embargo laid down in the *Neutrality Acts* of 1935–37: Belligerents were allowed to buy arms provided they paid in cash and carried them on their own ships.

The first peace-time conscription in U.S. history, 1940, ruled that all men between 21 and 36 were to be drafted for 12 months training.

A ring of defence was established through the military occupation of Iceland and Greenland, 1941, as well as the exchange of destroyers for naval and air bases in Newfoundland and the British West Indies.

The Atlantic Conference, 1941, between Roosevelt and Churchill laid down principles for the restoration of peace after the defeat of the Axis powers. The Atlantic Charter stated that neither the U.S.A. nor Britain would seek territorial aggrandizement after the war. It established the principles of self-government for all peoples, greater freedom of trade and 'freedom from fear and want'.

Under the *Lend-Lease Act,* 1941, the President received power to give all-out aid to democracies whose defence was held vital to the defence of the U.S.A. American merchant vessels were armed against submarines and allowed to sail into combat zones.

1.10.2. Entry into the War

The Japanese air attack on the American naval port of Pearl Harbour (Hawaii), December 7, 1941, followed by declarations of war from Germany and Italy, brought the U.S.A. into the war. Under the direction of the Department of Defence Mobilization and the War Production Board, the U.S.A. created 'the mightiest war-time arsenal' the world had ever seen. The drafting of all men between 20 (later 18) and 44 increased the army from 1.8 to 11 million. Under a Relocation Order, 1942, more than 100,000 Japanese Americans were evacuated from the West coast to inland 'relocation centres'.

1.10.3. European War

The U.S. and British invasion of French North Africa, 1942, under General Dwight Eisenhower, U.S. Supreme Commander in Europe, turned the tide of the European war in favour of the Allies. The collapse of Axis resistance in North Africa was followed by the conquest of Sicily, 1943, and the invasion of southern Italy.

In Germany, air bombings from English bases wiped out industrial centres and the inner core of larger cities. On D-Day, June 6, 1944, American and British forces began to invade Normandy. The landings were preceded by air and naval bombardment of the landing area. Paris was liberated on August 25. The last major offensive of German forces in the Ardennes was repulsed by January 1945. On March 7, the Allied troops crossed the Rhine. Six weeks later they made contact with the Russians on the Elbe River. On May 7, after Hitler's suicide, Germany declared her unconditional surrender.

1.10.4. Pacific War

In 1942, the Japanese had won rapid victories over the Allied forces and conquered Hong Kong, Guam, Singapore, the Dutch East Indies and later Burma. They advanced into New Guinea and the Bismarck and Solomon Islands.

An American counter-attack, 1942, succeeded in halting the Japanese advance in the naval battles of the Coral Sea off Australia and at Midway Island. Supported by Allied forces, the Americans reconquered important bases, including the American dependency Guam. In October 1944, General Mac Arthur's forces landed in the Philippines at Leyte Island, where Admiral Halsey won a decisive victory in the naval battle of Leyte Gulf. In January 1945, the largest of the Philippine Islands, Luzon, hat been conquered. The capture of Okinawa on the outskirts of Japan in June 1945 gave the American air forces advanced bases from which industrial centres on the mainland were subjected to destructive air raids. When Germany surrendered, the Americans, after an official ultimatum, dropped an atomic bomb on Hiroshima, and three days later on Nagasaki, virtually obliterating both cities. Japan surrendered and was occupied by American forces.

1.11. Postwar Leadership

1.11.1. Administrations of Harry Truman

The Democratic President Truman included in his administrations (1945–49, 1949–53) as Secretaries of State James Byrnes (–1947), Georg Marshall (–1949) and Dean Acheson (–1953).

1.11.1.1. Foreign Policy was determined by efforts to create a system of collective security in the cold war now beginning with Russia. A policy of 'containment' strove to contain Russian expansion within the 1947 boundaries. Vast sums were spent on rearmament and the stationing of military forces in friendly countries.

1.11.1.1.1. United Nations: The U.N. conference in San Francisco, 1945, ratified the U.N. Organization Charter drafted when the U.N. was founded in 1944. The U.N., with its seat in New York, was to consist of the following bodies:
The General Assembly was to be composed of delegates of all member states.
The Security Council was to maintain international peace, and had the power to intervene, if necessary, with an international armed force drawn from U.N. member states. It was to include the major nations (U.S.A., U.S.S.R., Great Britain, France and China), each with a right to veto any decision. The fact that this veto power was later constantly used by the U.S.S.R., diminished the effectiveness of the U.N. in resolving international issues and led to the formation of regional military alliances, such as N.A.T.O., S.E.A.T.O. and A.N.Z.U.S.
The Secretariat was to administer the various U.N. activities. Specialized agencies were the International Labour Organization (I.L.O), the World Health Organization ((W.H.O.), the Economic and Social Council, the U.N. Educational, Scientific and Cultural Organization (U.N.E.S.C.O.), the Trusteeship Council to deal with dependent areas of the world, the International Court of Justice at the Hague and the International Atomic Energy Commission. The U.N.R.R.A. (United Nations Relief and Rehabilitation Administration) was created to supply food to war-shattered nations, the major share being contributed by the U.S.A.

1.11.1.1.2. The Potsdam Conference, July–August 1945, between Truman, Stalin, Churchill and Attlee, provided for a four-power occupation of Germany (under U.S. General Lucius Clay). Industries were to be dismantled, Germans in Poland, Czechoslovakia and Hungary to be repatriated. The ensuing Nuremberg trials of war criminals were presided over by Justice R. H. Jackson of the U.S. Supreme Court.

1.11.1.1.3. The Philippines were granted independence in 1946. This first retreat from colonialism in Asia (followed by the withdrawal of Britain from India and Burma in 1947) encouraged national risings in all colonial areas.

1.11.1.1.4. The Paris Peace Conference, 1947, drafted treaties with Italy and the Axis satellites Hungary, Rumania and Bulgaria. However, no agreement could be reached on a peace treaty with Germany.

1.11.1.1.5. Truman Doctrine, 1947: Soviet efforts to expand Communist control in the Balkans and the Middle East were prevented by financial aid to Turkey and Greece, where the Communists had provoked a civil war. American aid helped the Greek government to restore its authority.

1.11.1.1.6. Marshall Plan and G.A.T.T.: After dissolution of U.N.R.R.A., 1947, U.S. Secretary of State Marshall offered war-shattered European countries economic aid to prevent economic depression, which was felt to favour Communist subversion. Sixteen European nations not under Communist control responded to the offer, which led to the European Recovery Programme (E.R.P.), 1948–52. $ 17 billion were spent on European reconstruction.
G.A.T.T. (General Agreement on Tariffs and Trade), 1947, between 23 nations (already excluding the U.S.S.R. and her satellites) provided for the relaxation of international trade barriers in order to revive trade.

1.11.1.1.7. U.S.A. and Latin America: The Inter-American Treaty of Rio de Janeiro, 1947, provided for reciprocal assistance and defence between North and South American states. The Conference of Botoga, Colombia, in 1948, established the Organization of American States (O.A.S.).

1.11.1.1.8. Berlin airlift, 1948–49: When Russia responded to the union of the American, British and French occupation zones with a blockade of Berlin, the Western powers kept up an airlift for ten months to bring supplies to the two million inhabitants of their sectors of Berlin.

1.11.1.1.9. The Point-Four Programme of Truman, 1949, provided technical assistance to underdeveloped countries in Asia, Africa and Latin America.

1.11.1.1.10. N.A.T.O.: The North Atlantic Treaty Organization was founded in 1949 by twelve nations on both sides of the Atlantic, including the U.S.A., Canada, Great Britain, France, Norway and, later, Turkey and Greece (1953) and West Germany (1955). The alliance, based on a 50-year mutual defence treaty, provided for reciprocal military aid in case of aggression.
The N.A.T.O. defence force in Europe includes U.S. soldiers and is largely equipped with American weapons. The European Headquarters, S.H.A.P.E. (Supreme Headquarters of Allied Powers in Europe), is in Brussels.

1.11.1.1.11. China: Until the Japanese surrender, the U.S.A. had supported the Chinese government against Japan and Chinese Communists, but finally withdrew, not wishing to commit itself further to supporting an unpopular and largely corrupt government which was rapidly losing support. Civil war in China in 1949 brought the Communists under Mao Tse-tung to power on the mainland, while the Nationalist regime under Chiang Kai-shek withdrew to Formosa. Red China was at that time neither recognized by the U.S.A. nor admitted to the U.N.

1.11.1.1.12. The Korean War, 1950–53, was the first effect of the U.S policy of containment. The invasion of South Korea by North Korean forces equipped with Russian arms was repulsed by U.N. troops (chiefly U.S. units formed in Japan) under General MacArthur. Mac Arthur's powerful counter-offensive into Manchuria (Chinese territory) was thwarted by his dismissal and by the ensuing truce with Truman, which arose from Truman's fear of another world war.

1.11.1.1.13. A.N.Z.U.S.: A treaty between Australia, New Zealand and the U.S.A. in 1951 established a policy of mutual support for security in the Pacific.

1.11.1.1.14. Japan: After the war, Japan was occupied by U.S. forces under General MacArthur, who instigated democratic reforms. A new constitution provided for a parliamentary government, land reforms and female suffrage. Under a peace treaty signed in 1951 by 48 nations despite Russia's objections, Japan lost her former empire but regained sovereignty and the right to rearm for self-defence. The U.S.A. retained military bases in Japan.

1.11.1.2.   Internal Affairs

1.11.1.2.1. Labour management relations: Extensive strikes in 1946 caused considerable losses to industry. A strike in the coal mines was answered by a temporary seizure of mines by the government.
The *Labour Management Relations Act (Taft-Hartley Act)*, 1947, passed by a Republican Congress over Truman's veto revised former legislation favouring trade unions. The Act made it possible to suppress strikes if they threatened to become national emergencies. It made unions liable for breach of contract, outlawed 'the closed shop', under which only union members may be employed, but allowed the 'union shop', which may require a worker to join the union after employment. The law prohibited 'featherbedding' (hiring of more men than needed) under union pressure, and strikes without a 60-day 'cooling-off period'. It required labour leaders to sign an affidavit declaring non-membership of the Communist party.
1.11.1.2.2. National security: The *Atomic Energy Act*, 1946, created an Atomic Energy Commission (A.E.C.) to control ownership and production of fissionable materials and to conduct atomic research. It placed the power of decision about the use of atomic bombs in warfare solely in the President's hands. Rearmament

was speeded up after the explosion of the first Russian atom bomb. The U.S.A. exploded the first hydrogen bomb in 1952.

1.11.1.2.3. The detection of Communist espionage rings resulted in investigations against, and dismissal of persons suspected of Communist sympathies. Within one year, three million federal employees were checked by the Loyalty Board. 200 were dismissed. The physicists Mr. and Mrs. Rosenberg, who had betrayed atomic information to the Russians, were executed in 1953.

1.11.1.2.4. Amendment 22 to the Constitution, 1951, prohibited the election of a president for more than two terms.

1.11.2. Administrations of Dwight D. Eisenhower

The Republican President Eisenhower included in his administrations (1953–57, 1957–61) Richard Nixon as Vice-President and John Foster Dulles as Secretary of State.
Eisenhower's great popularity as a national hero secured a sweeping victory over his opponent Adlai Stevenson in two successive elections. Eisenhower's two administrations initiated a short period of political moderation and complacency at the achievements of an affluent society.

1.11.2.1. Foreign Policy was determined by the cold war between East and West. Dulles, who took up a very active stand against Communism, strove to exchange the concept of containment for that of 'roll-back' of Russian power.

1.11.2.1.1. Korea: The Korean armistice at Panmunjon, 1953, fixed the demarcation line between North and South Korea along the front line, which favoured South Korea. The armistice had been delayed for two years chiefly because no agreement could be reached on the U.N. pledge to prisoners of individual freedom of choice with regard to repatriation.

1.11.2.1.2. In South America, the U.S.A. supported military regimes suppressing demands for social improvements, in order to protect U.S. business interests. A rebellion in the South American 'banana state' of Guatemala against social reforms, introduced by the elected government in 1954, was supported in order to uphold the interests of the American-controlled United Fruit Company.

1.11.2.1.3. S.E.A.T.O.: The Southeast Asia Treaty Organization was a collective defence treaty between the U.S.A., Great Britain, France, Australia, New Zealand, Pakistan, the Philippines and Thailand. It was formed in 1954 under U.S. leadership, after the civil war in French Indo-China had resulted in North Vietnam's becoming a Communist state. S.E.A.T.O., which issued a Pacific Charter against

Communist subversion, was opposed not only by Communists, but also by non-aligned countries in Asia.

1.11.2.1.4. A defence treaty with Nationalist China was drawn up in 1954, guaranteeing U.S. protection of Formosa and the adjacent chain of the Pescadore Islands. In 1955 and 1958, Red China attacked the two islands Quemoy and Matsu not covered by the treaty, to prepare an invasion of Formosa, which, however, was repulsed with military aid from the U.S.A.

1.11.2.1.5. U.S. military bases were established under bilateral agreements in Greece, Spain and the Portuguese Azores in 1953, in return for economic and military aid. The American-Iberian security treaty, 1956, incorporated Spain and Portugal into the West-European defence system.

1.11.2.1.6. Middle East: The U. S. endeavour to maintain control of Middle East oil resources and prevent Russian infiltration in the Middle East led to agreements with Saudi Arabia, 1951, Ethiopia and Libya, 1954, for the maintenance of military bases. The Eisenhower Doctrine, 1957, offered economic and military aid for safeguarding the independence of the Middle-Eastern nations against Communist subversion.
A Communist revolt in Iraq led to a temporary occupation of the Lebanon in 1958 by U.S. troops, at the request of the Lebanese government, and to the signing of bilateral defence agreements with Turkey, Iran and Pakistan.

1.11.2.1.7. 'Peaceful coexistence', proposed by Russia after Stalin's death, initiated the era of summit conferences on disarmament, to discuss the feasibility of stopping atomic tests, with a system of inspection and control of underground tests. Krushchev's policy spelled a short era of good will through personal diplomacy, reaching a climax in Krushchev's meeting with Eisenhower at Camp David in 1959. The Summit Meeting in Paris, 1960, however, was thwarted by Krushchev, after the crash of a U.S. reconnaissance plane over Russian territory had disclosed U.S. espionage.

1.11.2.1.8. Cuba, where the rebellion of Fidel Castro had overthrown the regime of General Batista in 1959, came increasingly under Soviet influence. Castro, who engaged in fierce agitation against U.S. imperialism, carried out land reforms amounting to partial confiscation of American sugar plantations. When Castro concluded trade agreements with Russia and Red China, the U.S.A. answered by cutting purchases of Cuban sugar.

1.11.2.1.9. O. E. C. D.: The U.S.A. became a member of the Organization for Economic Co-operation and Development, founded in 1960, and contributed $4 billion for foreign aid.

1.11.2.1.10. Indochinese War, 1946–54: Indochina had been a French protectorate since 1884. In the twenties, Communism began to infiltrate into the country; in 1930, Ho Chi Minh founded the Communist Party of Indochina. After the surrender of France in World War II, the country was invaded by the Japanese, who were finally defeated by Ho Chi Minh with the help of the Allies. After the Japanese surrender, Ho Chi Minh proclaimed the Democratic Republic of Vietnam. De Gaulle's attempt to regain a footing in the country started the Indochinese War, in which the French, despite U.S. financial support, were defeated. The *Geneva Settlement*, 1954, divided Vietnam into North and South Vietnam, pending reunification through elections scheduled for 1956.

The U.S.A., fearing that the loss of Indochina to Communism would lead to the whole of Southeast Asia falling under Communist control ('domino theory'), committed itself to supporting the non-Communist South Vietnam regime under Ngo Dinh Diem. Although the *Geneva Settlement* had forbidden the introduction of troops or the establishment of bases, the U.S.A. launched a programme of economic aid and assistance with military training. In 1956, resistance to the increasingly oppressive and corrupt regime in South Vietnam led to a rebellion of the Communist-led Vietcong; from 1959, they received active support from North Vietnam.

1.11.2.2.   Internal Policy

1.11.2.2.1. Measures against Communist infiltration were intensified.
People could be dismissed without even knowing who their accusers were or what the exact accusation was, and without the possibility of legal defence. During this period, 863 federal officials were dismissed. The 'red-hunt' reached its climax when Senator Joseph McCarthy (Wisconsin) accused the State Department of protecting more than 200 'card-carrying' Communists. McCarthy's considerable influence on public opinion ended when he was censored by the Senate in 1954.

1.11.2.2.2. Trade Unions: The A.F.L. (American Federation of Labour) and the C.I.O. (Congress of Industrial Organizations) were merged in 1955.
Under its Code of Ethical Practices, the A.F.L.-C.I.O. expelled corrupt union officials and also its largest member-union, the International Brotherhood of Teamsters with its president Hoffa.
The *Landrum-Griffin Labour Act (Labour Management Reporting and Disclosure Act),* adopted in 1959, was the first labour act to control the internal operations of unions, after a Senate Committee had revealed corrupt and despotic practices among union officials. It guaranteed union members the right of secret election of union executives and free speech at union meetings. It forbade illegal picketing, boycotting of strike breakers and misuse of union funds.

1.11.2.2.3. Segregation of Negroes raised the problem of equality of civil rights for minorities and inflamed a vehement nation-wide controversy.

Racial discrimination in the armed services was forbidden in 1958.

A Supreme Court decision, 1954, required public schools to admit Negro children, reversing an earlier decision of 1896 in favour of 'separate but equal educational facilities'. The ruling was largely evaded, and challenged on the ground that it impaired the authority of the individual states in a field reserved to them by the Constitution.

The *Civil Rights Act*, 1957, was the first federal attempt since the Civil War to safeguard the Negro's right to vote: The Federal Government was empowered to seek court orders, if necessary, against infringements of the individual's right to vote.

Segregation in Little Rock, Arkansas, in 1957 became a test case: Governor Faubus used the Arkansas National Guard to bar from high school Negro students who were to be admitted under a federal court order. Eisenhower sent federal troops to protect the students during the school year.

The *Civil Rights Act*, 1960, provided for the registration of Negro voters under the protection of the federal courts in areas where Negroes were denied the right to vote.

1.11.2.2.4. *Social Security Act*, 1958, raised old-age and disability benefits, and extended them to additional categories of workers.

1.11.2.2.5. Admission of new states: Alaska (pop. 200,000) and Hawaii (pop. 600,000) became American states in 1959. Both states are of great strategic importance.

1.11.2.2.6. National security: The launching of Sputnik I in 1957 by Russia was a shock to the U.S.A. and led to a race in space development with Russia. In 1958, the U.S.A. initiated a space programme under N.A.S.A. (National Aeronautics and Space Administration) and launched its first satellite, Explorer I. In 1959, the government submitted the highest peacetime budget in U.S. history to speed missile development.

The first American nuclear submarine, *Nautilus,* launched in 1954, sailed under the polar ice cap to the North Pole. In 1960, the submarine *George Washington* fired a Polaris missile while submerged.

1.11.2.2.7. Farm programme: After World War II, the falling demand for farm products necessitated new price supports establishing a minimum price level. If market prices fell below this level, the government took over the excess produce and used it for constructive purposes, such as school lunch programmes and relieving famines in other countries.

1.11.3. Administration of John F. Kennedy

The Democratic President Kennedy included in his administration Dean Rusk as Secretary of State, his brother Robert Kennedy as Attorney-General, and McNamara as Secretary of Defence.

Kennedy, at 43 the youngest president in U.S. history, defeated the Republican candidate, Vice-President Nixon, by a narrow margin. In his vigorous election campaign, conducted partly in television debates with his rival, Kennedy had called for a more energetic policy to strengthen the Western cause under U.S. leadership. Kennedy introduced an era of intellectualism in politics, turning for advice to university professors rather than to big businessmen.

1.11.3.1. Foreign Affairs

1.11.3.1.1. Cuban crisis: In 1961, exiled Cubans attempted to invade Cuba in the Bay of Pigs. The failure of this invasion, which had been supported by the U.S.A., led to a considerable loss of U.S. prestige.

When the Soviet Union began to establish military bases in Cuba, Kennedy announced that ships carrying offensive weapons to Cuba would be captured. Despite Communist protests alleging that the U.S.A. was aiming at war, Krushchev yielded in a note promising the removal of missiles and jet planes from Cuba under U.N. supervision.

1.11.3.1.2. South America: Kennedy's concept of an 'Alliance for Progress', proclaimed as a generous programme for aid and development, was resented in Latin America as 'trade not aid' because it allegedly supported countries subservient to the U.S.A. rather than nationally minded, progressive governments. The National Liberation Movement of the Tupamaros in Uruguay was founded in 1962 to help the workers in the American-controlled sugar plantations.

1.11.3.1.3. Vietnam: Kennedy's 'broad commitment' to South Vietnam instead of the 'limited risk gamble' of the Eisenhower administration foreshadowed the longest war in U.S. history, which diminished U.S. prestige in the whole world. Although Kennedy resisted pressures for sending American ground-combat forces to Vietnam, he significantly expanded advisory and military support missions in order to strengthen South Vietnamese operations against the insurgent Vietcong. The number of American personnel involved and killed in action increased steadily. In 1963, the U.S.A. supported a military coup against the corrupt and inefficient regime of President Diem and prepared for covert operations against North Vietnam.

1.11.3.1.4. Kennedy's visit to Berlin, Britain, and Ireland – the home of his ancestors – met with a wave of popular enthusiasm.

1.11.3.2.   Internal Affairs

1.11.3.2.1. Space travel: In 1961, the first American astronaut Shephard was rocketed into space. In 1962, America's first manned satellites were put in orbit; in 1963, Cooper circled the earth 22 times. In 1962, N.A.S.A. launched the world's first commercial communications satellite.

1.11.3.2.2. Kennedy Round: Under the *Trade Expansion Act*, 1963, the President was given power to liberalize trade by a further reduction of U.S. tariffs and by multilateral agreements.

1.11.3.2.3. Racial integration in the South: Federal troops were sent to protect from arrest Negroes demonstrating against segregation. Negro students were no longer to be barred from schools and universities. A Supreme Court decision, 1963, voided sentences of Alabama courts against Negro demonstrators.

1.11.3.2.4. Kennedy's assassination: On November 22, 1963, Kennedy was shot by a Southern fanatic, Lee Harvey Oswald, when visiting Dallas, Tex. The death of the President, who had become to many people, not only in America, a symbol of youthful idealism, was received with genuine dismay throughout the world.

1.12.   National Unrest

1.12.1. Administrations of Lyndon Johnson

The Democratic President Johnson included in his administrationss (1963–65, 1965–69) Hubert Humphrey as Vice-President, Dean Rusk (Secretary of State), R. S. McNamara (–1968) and C. M. Clifford (Defence).
Vice-President Johnson was sworn in as President on the night of Kennedy's assassination, and became President in his own right in 1964 after an overwhelming victory over the Republican candidate, Barry Goldwater of Arizona, who had rallied the conservative and racist forces of the South.

1.12.1.1.   Foreign Affairs

1.12.1.1.1. Vietnam: In 1964, Johnson ordered covert military operations against North Vietnam in order to force Hanoi to put an end to support of insurrections of Vietcong guerillas in South Vietnam and Communist Pathet Lao in Laos. As the Vietcong rebellion gathered strength, the U.S.A. increasingly supported the government with bombing and the use of defoliants and Napalm. In August 1964, a North Vietnamese attack on a U.S. destroyer in the Gulf of Tongking was followed by an escalation of airborne and maritime operations after the Senate had adopted the

Tongking Gulf Resolution. This escalation was later exposed in the *Pentagon Papers* as planned five months in advance of the Tongking assault. In 1965, the U.S.A. began to bomb North Vietnam and Laotian infiltration routes in order to prevent 'a collapse of national morale' in South Vietnam. When the sustained air attacks of the Operation Rolling Thunder proved ineffective, the U.S.A. finally assumed the major burden of the ground war with an increase of the U.S. military support forces under the command of General Westmoreland. By 1968, U.S. troops in Vietnam totalled 469,000.

Late in 1966, doubts about the effectiveness of American policy in Vietnam began to split the Johnson Administration. While the Joint Chiefs of Staff and General Westmoreland proposed a significant escalation of war with a call-up of reserves, Secretary of Defence, McNamara became the leader of a group of disillusioned 'doves' recommending a halt in bombing, which had killed far more civilians than fighting men, and an attempt to negotiate. Other leading advocates of a withdrawal from military commitments (also in Europe) were Senators Fulbright, Mansfield, Eugene McCarthy, and, in the ensuing presidential campaign of 1968, Robert Kennedy. The President held a middle course and was criticized by the 'hawks' as well as the 'doves'. In January 1968, McNamara, who had even advocated a government in Saigon including members of the Vietcong, was replaced by Clifford as Secretary of Defence. By 1968, 800 draft resisters were serving average sentences of 32 months in federal prisons.

In 1968, the Vietcong launched the Tet offensive, beginning with an attack on the U.S. embassy in Saigon, and spreading to almost every town in South Vietnam. Aware of nation-wide opposition to his Vietnam policy, Johnson, in March 1968, announced his decision to limit American operations in Vietnam and to renounce a second term as President. In May 1968, the U.S.A. entered into negotiations with Hanoi in Paris conducted on the American side by W. A. Harriman and, later, Henry Cabot Lodge.

1.12.1.1.2. Maritime Air Forces Mediterranean (MARAIRMED): Russia's increasing naval activities in the Mediterranean caused N.A.T.O. to establish a new command at a base near Naples for a better co-ordination of air control. Apart from its participation in MARAIRMED, the U.S.A. has its 6th Fleet operating in the Mediterranean.

1.12.1.1.3. In South America, U.S. policy continued to support the interests of American corporate business. Military coups against socialist regimes were often supported through secret operations of C.I.A. agents (who tracked down the Bolivian guerilla leader Che Guevara in 1966). Under strong U.S. pressure, most O.A.S. (Organization of American States) countries broke off diplomatic relations with Communist Cuba in 1964 and joined the U.S. blockade of Cuban exports. The *Sugar Act* of 1962, providing that sugar purchases should be suspended if a

Latin American country violated U.S. private interests, was extended to cover other goods.

In Santo Domingo, which had become a major sugar supplier of the U.S.A. since the blockade of Cuba, the U.S.A. intervened in internal conflicts to prevent a Communist takeover.

Anti-American riots in Panama, 1964, to bring about the nationalization of the Panama Canal were suppressed.

1.12.1.2. Internal Affairs

1.12.1.2.1. 'War on Poverty': Johnson's ambitious programme of social and civil rights legislation, referred to as the Great Society programme, could not alleviate the misery of the 15 per cent of the population living below the poverty line. In May 1965, more than 1,200 marchers of the Poor People's Campaign trekked to New York. In 1968, thousands of Negroes, Indians and Puerto Ricans flocked to Washington under black leadership and built 'Resurrection City' on a meadow in front of the Lincoln Memorial. The climax of the Poor People's Campaign was Solidarity Day (June 28), which brought 55,000 people, both black and white, to Washington. Although Resurrection City was finally demolished by the government, the campaign resulted in a speeding up of food relief programmes, plans to create new jobs, and funds for the head-start school programme and health care.

1.12.1.2.2. The Negro problem developed into open warfare when agitation of the Black Muslims for a total separation of the two races in different states, and the Black Panthers' call to violence under the slogan of Black Power led to riots in many American cities. Nevertheless, civil rights legislation continued. In 1964, the poll tax widely used to deprive Negroes of their vote was prohibited. The *Civil Rights Bill* of 1968 improved housing conditions.

1.12.1.2.3. Unrest in cities: In 1966, the misery of the poor led to severe riots in twenty four cities, especially in Negro ghettos. In 1967, Johnson had to send regular troops to Detroit to put down a riot, in which seventy people were killed. Strikes of teachers, policemen, dockers and garbage collectors paralyzed life in New York, which was also haunted by a rising crime rate, drug addiction and the continuing terror exercised by gangster bosses within trade unions.

1.12.1.2.4. Space travel: In 1965–66, the two-man Project Gemini demonstrated in ten manned flights that man can control his spacecraft, leave it, link it with another in space, and endure a prolonged space flight in good physical condition. Surveyor 1 performed the first soft moon landing. Mariner 4 took pictures of Mars from a distance of 9,000 miles.

1.12.1.2.5. Economics: In order to cut the continued deficit in the balance of payments, Johnson, in March 1968, outlined a five-point programme in support of the dollar, providing for a curtailment of U.S. investment and tourism abroad, a 10 per cent surcharge on the income tax, and cuts in government spending overseas by the Pentagon, embassies and G.I. dependants.

1.12.1.2.6. Assassinations: In April 1968, the Negro leader Dr. Martin Luther King was shot at Memphis, Tenn., by an escaped convict. His murder caused an unprecedented wave of looting and violence in the country's black ghettos. In Washington, a force of regular troops had to be called in to put an end to three days of pillaging. Two months later, Senator Robert Kennedy was assassinated by an Arab nationalist, Sirhan Sirhan.

Gun-control laws, demanded by Johnson to end 'the trade in mail-murder', were defeated largely through the efforts of the National Rifle Association, which claimed to be standing up for the American citizen's right to self-defence in a state of threatening anarchy.

1.12.1.2.7. The 1968 election campaign became one of the most hectic demonstrations of the nation's problems. On the Democratic side, the contest for nomination was fought between Vice-President Hubert Humphrey and the Senators McGovern, McCarthy and Robert Kennedy. The latter, who had fought for desegregation already as Attorney-General under his brother, President John F. Kennedy, won the enthusiastic support of the young anti-war generation by his plea for peace in Asia and civil rights for Negroes. Robert Kennedy was assassinated just after he had won the California primary election in the contest for the Democratic presidential nomination. The National Democratic Convention in Chicago, in which Humphrey won the final contest against McCarthy, turned out a major battle between anti-war demonstrators and the Chicago police (enforced by the Illinois National Guard), which indiscriminately attacked a crowd of some 3,000 with clubs and chemical stun gas.

On the Republican side the candidates running for nomination were the Governor of New York, Nelson Rockefeller, the Governor of California, R. Reagan, and Richard Nixon.

In the presidential election, November 1968, Richard Nixon won a narrow victory over Humphrey. Alabama Governor George Wallace, who was running for his own American Independent Party, won 14 per cent of the national vote, taking five states in the South, in which a majority of whites were opposed to desegregation.

1.12.2. Administrations of Richard Nixon (1969–73, 1973–74)

Richard Nixon, who had been Vice-President under Eisenhower and was narrowly defeated by J. F. Kennedy in the presidential election of 1960, had won the votes of the middle-class majority by promising to restore law and order, and, in foreign affairs, to seek negotiation instead of confrontation. Although Nixon had to deal with a Democratic Congress and a Supreme Court largely staffed with old-time Liberals, his Cabinet was formed of personal friends with conservative leanings: William Rogers as Secretary of State, John Connally (Treasury), Melvin Laird (Defence). In his second administration, his chief adviser, the German emigrant Henry Kissinger, who had acted as his representative in most foreign negotiations, replaced Rogers as Secretary of State. James Schlesinger was appointed to take the place of M. Laird as Secretary of Defence.

When, in October 1973, Vice-President Agnew was threatened with court proceedings for tax evasion and corruption during his terms as Governor of Maryland and as Vice-President, he resigned, and Nixon appointed Gerald Ford, Republican Whip in the House of Representatives, Vice-President in his place.

1.12.2.1. Foreign Affairs

1.12.2.1.1. Vietnam and Cambodia: Continued failures in Paris to negotiate an agreement with Hanoi thwarted hopes of the disengagement promised by Nixon in his election campaign. The gradual withdrawal of ground forces initiated the announced Vietnamization of the war. The bombing, however, continued. Crops were destroyed through the use of defoliants. In May 1970, Nixon ordered the invasion of neutral Cambodia to hit Vietcong operation centres.

The attack gave new momentum to the anti-war agitation in America. Publication, in 1971, of the *Pentagon Papers* (secret government study on the war in Vietnam) by *The New York Times* and *The Washington Post* revealed U.S. plans for a war against North Vietnam, at a time (1964) when Johnson had been conducting his election campaign against Goldwater as a peace president. Although Nixon demanded a court order to forbid further publication as detrimental to U.S. security, a Supreme Court ruling allowed publication of the material. The former Defence Department official Daniel Ellsberg, who was to be arrested as the source of documents classified as top secret, disappeared. On his return from Vietnam, Ellsberg had resigned his government post and had begun demonstrating and writing against the war.

Atrocities committed by the Special Forces, the 'Green Berets', and by U.S. troops under Lieutenant Calley at My Lai, 1968, had aroused alarm and disgust throughout the world. Drug addiction in the army and draft resistance began to endanger military efforts. The P.E.A.C.E. (People Against Corrupt Establishment) movement, made up of U.S. servicemen, conducted a vigorous anti-war campaign.

In April 1972, North Vietnam started a vigorous offensive against South Vietnam, conquering provincial cities and advancing on Saigon. The South Vietnam counteroffensive relying on heavy U.S. bombing and mining of North Vietnamese ports was spurred on by a newly awakened nationalism.

After repeated failures of the negotiations in Paris, Nixon ordered a new escalation of bombing. Carried out during the Christmas period, the bombing aroused violent criticism throughout the world. Finally, in January 1973, a peace was concluded, providing for the withdrawal of American troops and the repatriation of American soldiers. Despite the cease-fire, which came into force on 28th January, Vietnamese soldiers on both sides continued fighting in order to gain as much territory as possible before a final peace. The war, which had never been declared and had lasted more than a decade, had taken a toll of 46,000 American lives. Although American troops were withdrawn from Vietnam, hostilities continued. North Vietnam kept considerable forces in Laos, the U.S.A. in Thailand. In Cambodia, the war continued unabated. Communist troops besieging the capital Phnom Penh were mercilessly attacked by U.S. bombers stationed in Thailand. Congress, in serious opposition to Nixon's policy of continuing the war, set August 15, 1973 as a deadline for a halt to the bombing. Consequently, in August 1973, the last American troops were withdrawn from Cambodia.

1.12.2.1.2. Middle East: Continued American support of Israel despite her refusal to return Arab territory annexed in the Seven Days War against Egypt, Syria and Jordan, induced Russia to expand technical and military aid to the Arab countries. To counteract an expansion of Russian influence in the Mediterranean and the Middle East, the U.S. Sixth Fleet in the Mediterranean was reinforced by the Seventh Fleet.

1.12.2.1.3. Commitment in Europe: The Nixon administration rejected the plan of Senator Mike Mansfield to reduce U.S. forces in Europe from 300,000 to 150,000. Greece received military support as 'essential to the defence of Israel' despite world-wide criticism of American co-operation with a totalitarian regime. American troops were stationed on Greek soil and American ships in Greek waters.

1.12.2.1.4. South America: Anti-American agitation continued unabated. The visit of Nixon's special envoy, Governor Nelson Rockefeller, who, as the owner of large interests in the Venezuelan oil industry, is considered to be a major exponent of U.S. dollar imperialism, gave rise to violent demonstrations (as had Nixon's own visit to South America in 1958, when he was Vice-President), causing several deaths. Between 1968 and 1970, four members of U.S. embassies in South America were kidnapped as hostages, and one of them was killed. Several American-controlled industries were nationalized (oil in Peru, copper in Chile).

When, in September 1973, the socialist regime of Allende in Chile was overthrown by a military junta, the U.S.A. was suspected of having had a hand in the coup d'état. The government admitted that it had been informed beforehand, but claimed that the American embassy had been ordered to take a strictly neutral attitude. Such official statements, however, did not allay criticism directed against the intrigues of C.I.A. and I.T.T. agents in support of Allende's Chilean enemies (see also p. 97).

1.12.2.1.5. India: In a war between East and West Pakistan, the U.S.A., under commitments arising from the S.E.A.T.O. and C.E.N.T.O. treaties, supported West Pakistan. When East Pakistan (with Indian and Russian aid) won its independence, the new state of Bangladesh was finally recognized by the U.S.A. in April 1972.

1.12.2.1.6. Arms limitation: Nixon's alleged aim of disengagement from land wars and Breshnev's growing readiness for closer co-operation with the U.S.A., in view of Chinese ascendancy, heralded a new era of willingness to substitute 'parity' for superiority in the field of armament.

The Nuclear Non-Proliferation Treaty ratified by the Senate in 1969 restricted the right to possess nuclear weapons to the nations already in possession of nuclear arms (U.S.A., Russia, Britain). Red China and France did not sign.

S.A.L.T. (Strategic Armament Limitation Talks) held in Vienna, Helsinki and at the Moscow summit, May 1972, led to a treaty with Russia: both super-powers limited their nuclear arms and deployment of their A.B.M. (anti-ballistic missile) system, and agreed on a five-year freeze on the development of offensive missiles.

America's bacteriological and chemical war stocks were destroyed. The centres were changed into medical research institutes.

1.12.2.1.7. China: Throughout the postwar period, the U.S.A. had supported the government of Generalissimo Chiang Kai-shek, which, since the emergence of Red China, had been restricted to the island of Taiwan. The U.S.A. recognized nationalist China as the only legal representative of the whole country.

In 1971, Red China was admitted to membership of the U.N. (including a permanent seat on the Security Council), while Taiwan was excluded by a vote of the General Assembly. The admission of Red China to the U.N. led to the 'ping-pong diplomacy' of gradual mutual rapprochement between the Republic of China and the U.S.A. A Chinese invitation to an American table tennis team to compete in China was answered by the easing of the long-standing U.S. embargo on trade with China and a secret visit of Nixon's special adviser, Henry Kissinger, to Peking. In February 1972, Nixon reversed former anti-Communist policy with his sensational visit to Peking to normalize relations with the Republic of China.

1.12.2.1.8. Japan: An agreement with Japan, January 1972, revised the security treaty of 1960 by restoring Okinawa to Japan with the promise that all nuclear weapons on the island would be removed. The fact that military bases were retained, however, led to serious anti-American campaigns in Japan against the revised treaty. Moreover, Nixon's visit to Peking dealt a blow to America's Far Eastern allies Taiwan and Japan, which the U.S.A. had committed itself to protect against Red China. In September 1972, Japan established diplomatic relations with Peking, at the same time maintaining its trade relations with the U.S.A.

1.12.2.1.9. Oil crisis: The renewal, in October 1973, of the Middle East conflict in a war between Israel and the Arab states Egypt, Syria, Jordan and Iraq brought on the greatest oil crisis in history. Although U.S. Secretary of State, Henry Kissinger, played a prominent part in bringing about a truce between the belligerents, U.S. transport and industry were severely affected by the oil shortage caused by the reduction of oil supplies from Arab countries (p. 89).

1.12.2.2. Internal Affairs

1.12.2.2.1. Space travel: With the flight of Apollo 11 on 20 July 1969, the U.S.A. succeeded for the first time in landing men on the moon. Five other moon landings during the next three years brought further scientific knowledge. Project Mariner to explore Mars was continued. In 1971, Mariner 9 took pictures of the planet while orbiting it several months. In 1972, Pioneer 10 was launched on a 620-million mile journey to Jupiter.

1.12.2.2.2. Law enforcement: The growing hostility between various groups in American society (Negroes against whites, New Left against the Establishment) resulted in an alarming increase in violence and crime. Although the federal government and the Supreme Court pursued a liberal civil rights policy, both the federal and state courts undertook rigorous prosecutions of Negro student militants. Some law enforcement agencies were accused of increasingly repressive tactics.
Chicago Trial, 1969: Under federal anti-rioting laws, eight leaders of the New Left were accused of conspiracy, following riots at the Democratic Convention in Chicago, 1968 (p. 41). The harsh trial, in which the Black Panther leader, Bobby Seale, was chained to his chair and gagged, heralded the end of the 'student revolution'.
A Crime Act, 1970, giving federal authorities greater powers to fight terrorism and organized crime, was adopted by a large majority in Congress. It provided among other things that bombings causing casualties be capital offences.
My Lai trials, 1970/71: In the longest and most publicized court-martial in U.S. history, six U.S. officers and soldiers were accused of premeditated murder of hundreds of Vietnam civilians in a massacre at the village of My Lai, 1968. The only defendant convicted was Lieutenant William Calley, whose life sentence with hard labour was later reduced to 20 years. He was released from his confinement at Fort Benning on the orders of President Nixon, awaiting a review of the verdict against him. General Koster, then commander of the division, was accused of having suppressed information and was demoted to the rank of brigadier general.
Manson trials, 1970/71: Charles Manson, leader of a Californian hippie commune, and five members of his 'family' were found guilty on charges of murder, after nine

persons, including the film star Sharon Tate and four guests in her villa, had been killed in an orgy of ritual murder.

Massacre of Attica: A revolt in the New York state prison of Attica resulted in a massacre of many prisoners and of several guards being held as hostages.

Angela Davis Trial, 1972: The young black philosophy teacher, Angela Davis, who made herself the spokesman of the black cause, was tried on a charge of conspiracy for murder, because she had purchased the guns used in a court-room shoot-out attempt to free the black defendants. She was acquitted on all charges (see also p. 135).

1.12.2.2.3. 'Busing', i. e. the transport in school buses of both white and black children to schools in other neighbourhoods in order to achieve integration, became an important issue in the election year. It was greatly exploited by the racist George Wallace to stir the voters' emotions against integration. Nixon also proposed a moratorium on further court orders for busing, demanding instead a liberal aid programme for poor families and better education in city centres (where the population is predominantly Negro).

1.12.2.2.4. Environmental measures: The American supersonic transport programme was defeated by the environmentalists in the Senate, 1971, on the grounds of noise and possible stratospheric pollution as well as its extremely high cost. A *Clean Air Law,* 1972, required the automobile industry to produce virtually non-polluting cars by 1975.

1.12.2.2.5. Economics: Strongly tied to big business, Nixon favoured private business and discontinuance of public control. Nevertheless, inflation caused by the Vietnam War continued, and large corporations were increasingly criticized for causing environmental pollution and encouraging expenditure on armaments rather than on social reform. The 1971 monetary crisis, which was caused by the U.S. balance of payments deficit resulting from the Vietnam War und by the massive capital outflow for the acquisition of large parts of European industry, upset the international balance of payments. It became necessary to realign the exchange rate of the dollar with drastic protectionist measures designed to stabilize the dollar and to improve the competitive chances of U.S. industry. In pursuance of a 'Buy American' policy, Nixon introduced a ten per cent tariff on imports, and ordered a three-month freeze on wages and prices. In December 1971, he agreed to a practical devaluation of the dollar. At the same time, the government endeavoured to fight unemployment by encouraging investment with an easy-money policy, low interest rates and tax incentives, while trying to induce Europe and Japan to make trade concessions. In January 1973, Nixon abolished the wage and price controls, reserving the right of the government to intervene if increases were deemed excessive.

1.12.2.2.6. The voting age for the federal elections was reduced to 18 in 1971, adding a 'youth vote' of 11.3 million to the electorate.

1.12.2.2.7. Presidential election campaign of 1972: On the Republican side, Nixon was renominated; on the Democratic side Hubert Humphrey, who had already run in the 1968 election, was defeated by George McGovern. McGovern was acclaimed especially by the young people for his integrity and his uncompromising stand against the Vietnam War and for social justice at home. His programme for heavier progressive taxation, a juster incomes policy and for a quota system to open up jobs for the underprivileged secured him the support also of the black population and the more progressive groups of the middle classes. In the course of the election campaign, however, his radical social platform, which added extremist groups to his supporters, estranged many of the more moderate voters, while Nixon commanded the votes of the large conservative middle class and big business, which liberally financed his campaign.

Nixon's appeal rested not so much on personal popularity as on his prestige as an experienced statesman, and his foreign policy of 'negotiating from strength'. He was able to win support from various groups of the traditional Democratic coalition: from Jewish voters by a record of support for Israel, from Catholics by an offer of federal aid to private schools, from trade unions by his protectionist policy and silence on laws against the closed shop. His rejection of busing won the racist supporters of the independent candidate George Wallace, who had dropped out of the presidential campaign after he was shot and paralyzed during his campaign.

In November 1972, Nixon won an overwhelming victory over McGovern.

1.12.2.2.8. Watergate Scandal: On June 17th, 1972, five men were arrested for breaking into the Democratic Party Headquarters at Watergate in Washington D.C. to install surveillance devices. The fact that connecting links between the burglary and the Committee to Re-elect President Nixon and even the White House were soon established, led to the greatest constitutional crisis in recent U.S. history. An ex-C.I.A. agent, who was sentenced, alleged that political pressure had been brought to bear on him to plead guilty in order to protect White House officials involved in the Watergate Affair. A Senate Select Committee on Presidential Campaign Activities under the chairmanship of Sam Erwin was formed to investigate charges of political espionage, sabotage, illegal fund-raising practices, and the involvement of White House officials and even the President. Its investigation was hampered by the fact that President Nixon invoked executive privilege to withhold from the committee secret recordings of political conversations taped on hidden recorders in the White House. When tapes were finally produced, evidence derived from them corroborated the suspicion that Nixon himself was involved, and led to impeachment investigations by the Judiciary Committee of the House of Representatives.

When even strong supporters of Nixon voted for impeachment, the President resigned (August 1974).

1.12.3. Administration of Gerald Ford

The Republican President Ford, who as Vice-President succeeded Nixon, included in his cabinet H. Kissinger as Secretary of State. He selected Nelson Rockefeller (pp. 41, 43) as his Vice-President.

1.12.3.1. Watergate: Only ten days after assuming office, Ford pardoned Nixon for his involvement in the Watergate Affair. This met with strong criticism in view of the forthcoming trials against his aides, many of whom were later found guilty of serious crimes. Although Nixon's resignation had rendered the matter irrelevant, the House of Representatives, by a vote of 412 to 3, accepted the report of the Judiciary Committee which had recommended that Nixon should have been impeached for obstructing justice in trying to cover up the Watergate Affair.

In February 1975, three of Nixon's principal advisers (Mitchell, Haldeman and Ehrlichman) were sentenced to imprisonment for terms of $1^1/_2$ to 8 years on the charges of conspiracy and obstruction of justice. Minor sentences followed later.

1.12.3.2. A clemency programme for draft evaders and Vietnam deserters was announced by Ford in September 1974. The programme required all returnees to perform 'alternative service' for a period of up to 2 years.

1.12.3.3. When it was revealed that the C.I.A. (Central Intelligence Agency) had kept 10,000 files on American politicians despite the fact that its statutes confined it to activities in foreign countries, Congressional committees were called on to investigate the C.I.A.'s domestic activities and its involvement in the overthrow of Allende's government in Chile and in political assaults.

1.12.3.4. Economy: By the beginning of 1975, the American unemployment figure had reached a peak of 8.2 per cent. Hardest hit was the automobile industry in Detroit, which came near to collapse. In February the President submitted his long-expected Budget Message proposing a $16 billion tax cut and a tariff on imported oil. The oil tax and Ford's general tight-money policy were strongly opposed by Congress, which proposed to stimulate the economy by an increase in public borrowing and a more generous tax cut. In late March a compromise was reached.

1.12.3.5. South Vietnam and Cambodia: In February/March 1975, the U.S.A. maintained an airlift to the Cambodian capital, Phnom Penh, which was besieged by the Khmer Rouge. President Ford's proposal to send $222 million in additional emergency aid to the Cambodian government was rejected by Congress. The Cambodian issue became a new test case in the struggle between the executive and Congress for political supremacy.

After the fall of Phnom Penh and Saigon in April 1975, Cambodia and South Vietnam surrendered to the Communists. The U.S.A. evacuated its personnel and about 80,000 South Vietnamese who fled from the Communist regime.

The full withdrawal of the U.S.A. from Cambodia and South Vietnam after a 15-year disastrous commitment on behalf of non-Communist countries meant an immense loss of U.S. prestige throughout the world.

1.13. Presidents of the United States

1789–97	George Washington	(Fed.)
1797–1801	John Adams	(Fed.)
1801–09	Thomas Jefferson	(Dem.-Rep.)
1809–17	James Madison	(Dem.-Rep.)
1817–25	James Monroe	(Dem.-Rep.)
1825–29	John Quincy Adams	(Coalition)
1829–37	Andrew Jackson	(Dem.)
1837–41	Martin Van Buren	(Dem.)
1841	W. H. Harrison	(Whig)
1841–45	John Tyler	(Whig)
1845–49	James K. Polk	(Dem.)
1849–50	Zachary Taylor	(Whig)
1850–53	Millard Fillmore	(Whig)
1853–57	Franklin Pierce	(Dem.)
1857–61	James Buchanan	(Dem.)
1861–65	Abraham Lincoln	(Rep.)
1865–69	Andrew Johnson	(Rep.)
1869–77	Ulysses S. Grant	(Rep.)
1877–81	Rutherford B. Hayes	(Rep.)
1881	James A. Garfield	(Rep.)
1881–85	Chester A. Arthur	(Rep.)
1885–89	Grover Cleveland	(Dem.)
1889–93	Benjamin Harrison	(Rep.)
1893–97	Grover Cleveland	(Dem.)
1897–1901	William McKinley	(Rep.)
1901–09	Theodore Roosevelt	(Rep.)
1909–13	William H. Taft	(Rep.)

1913–21	Woodrow Wilson	(Dem.)
1921–23	Warren G. Harding	(Rep.)
1923–29	Calvin Coolidge	(Rep.)
1929–33	Herbert Hoover	(Rep.)
1933–45	Franklin D. Roosevelt	(Dem.)
1945–53	Harry Truman	(Dem.)
1953–61	Dwight D. Eisenhower	(Rep.)
1961–63	John F. Kennedy	(Dem.)
1963–69	Lyndon Johnson	(Dem.)
1969–74	Richard Nixon	(Rep.)
1974–	Gerald Ford	(Rep.)

2. Physical Geography and Natural Resources

The U.S.A. ranks fourth in area among the countries of the world, after the Soviet Union, Canada and China.

It consists of fifty states – forty eight continental states covering the central part of the North American continent, the peninsula of Alaska and the island group of Hawaii.

The U.S.A. is a compact land mass with largely natural frontiers: the Pacific, the Atlantic, the Gulf of Mexico, and the Rio Grande. The extensive Atlantic and Pacific coastlines with their excellent harbours have stimulated commercial and cultural contact with the rest of the world.

2.1. Climate

The climate is prevailingly continental, characterized by wide variations and sudden changes in temperature.

2.1.1. Temperature

Temperatures range from subtropical to temperate, but, in contrast to Europe with its Alpine mountain barrier, there is no sharp division between a cold North and a warm South. Even the subtropical Gulf coast can experience spells of frost. The size of the land mass causes extremes and abrupt changes in temperature. In England, the difference between the mean temperature of the coldest and hottest months is 12° C; in Minneapolis it is 32° C. The Great Lakes, which lie on the same latitude as Italy, are ice-bound for several months of the year. The mean temperature of New York is 6° C lower than that of Naples which is on the same latitude. This is largely due to the influence of the cold Labrador Current on the temperature of the northern Atlantic coast. Climatically the most favoured region is southern California, which has a Mediterranean climate, tempered by the prevailing westerlies and the cool California Current.

2.1.2. Winds

The absence of a mountain barrier between North and South allows an unrestricted exchange of warm air masses from the Gulf of Mexico and cold from the polar regions, giving rise to hot and cold waves. Hurricanes striking the Southern states and the east coast, and tornadoes sweeping across the plains at a terrific speed can cause loss of life and immense material damage. Cold northern winds in the Great Plains sometimes bring sudden drops in temperature by as much as 30° C, and blizzards are lethal to cattle wintering outdoors. Chinoks, sudden hot winds on the eastern slopes of the Rockies, can parch crops and melt the snow cover which protects the crops from frosts.

2.1.3. Rainfall

The U.S.A. is divided into a moist eastern and a dry western half:
In the West, rain-bearing westerly winds from the Pacific lose their moisture over the high mountain ranges near the coast. While the northern Californian Coast Range receives heavy rainfall averaging more than 80 in., which favours rich forest vegetation on the mountains, the region between the Sierra Nevada and the 100th meridian ('American Desert') is very dry. The annual average rainfall in the plateau region between the Sierra Nevada and the Rockies is less than 10 in.
The East is relatively moist, having large bodies of water on three sides (Gulf, Atlantic, Great Lakes). The humid subtropical Southeast, which receives onshore trade winds, has the heaviest rainfall (60 in.). The lower Mississippi and the lower Tennessee River were once subject to disastrous floods, but these are now largely under control.

2.2. Physical Divisions
(see appendix, figure 1)

The basic structure of the North American Continent is relatively simple. The Mississippi Basin, one of the world's largest plains, is bordered by two mountain ranges, in the east by the Appalachians, followed by the Atlantic Coastal Plain, or Atlantic Seaboard, in the west by the Rockies, followed by the Pacific Slope.

2.2.1. The Atlantic Seaboard

The Atlantic Seaboard extends 1,000 miles from north to south and thus has a wide variation in climate.
The northern part has a cool climate producing crops of the temperate zone. Its coastline is deeply indented by drowned river valleys and bays with excellent harbours (New York, Philadelphia, Baltimore), which early encouraged shipping and trade. As the natural point of entry for immigrants from Europe, who formed an inexhaustible labour reserve, it has become the country's major industrial centre and thus the most populated part of North America.

The broader southern section, which is sandy and swampy along the coast and fertile farther inland, has favoured the production of staple crops requiring a warm climate (tobacco, cotton, rice).

2.2.2. The Appalachians

The Appalachians are ancient, densely wooded mountains stretching 1,300 miles north and south, which, for 150 years, formed a barrier to western migration. The low foothills on the Atlantic side (Piedmont Belt) fall steeply down to the plain. This 'fall line', which was the head of river navigation, gave rise in the early days to settlements as suitable points for unloading goods from ship to wagon, and, later, to industrial centres using its water power. The northern section, covering the mountainous parts of New England and New York State, consists of rolling, wooded upland with scattered ranges of higher mountains, such as the Catskills, the Adirondacks, the Green and the White Mountains. The thin glacial soil is suited to grazing rather than to arable farming.

The central and southern sections make up what is called the Alleghenies (an Indian name meaning 'endless mountains'). They comprise, from east to west, the Piedmont, the Blue Ridge, the Great Valley and the Cumberland and Allegheny Plateaux. The Blue Ridge forms a practically uninterrupted mountain barier rising to 6,000 ft., which gave the adjoining Great Valley its importance as the only feasible western route for early pioneers. Daniel Boone's famous Wilderness Road of the 1770s left the valley at the Cumberland Gap, the only point where a wagon could be driven up onto the deeply dissected plateau. The Cumberland Gap thus gained historic importance as the earliest route across the montains for migration to the west.

The Alleghenies contain the world's largest coal fields.

2.2.3. Central Plain

The Central Plain, extending 1,300 miles east and west, includes, from north to south, the Great Lakes region, the upper Mississippi Basin, the Gulf coast region, and, to the west, the Great Plains rising to the Rockies.

2.2.3.1. The *Great Lakes*, including, from east to west, Lakes Ontario, Erie, Huron, Michigan and Superior, constitute the world's largest fresh-water surface, which the St. Lawrence River links with the Atlantic, providing a seaway into the middle of the continent. Linking the chief U.S. iron ore and coal deposits, this transport route has given rise to great industrial cities.

2.2.3.2. The *Mississippi Basin* is a fertile plain drained by the immense, largely navigable river system of the Mississippi and its tributaries, the Ohio and Tennessee rivers (east), the Missouri and Arkansas rivers (west). Once largely covered by dense forests, it is today one of the world's main grain producing areas. The vast level expanse is broken south of the Missouri by the Ozark Mountains, which rise to heights of 2,000 ft. and contain important mineral deposits. The Ouachita Mountains south of the Ozarks contain the country's main bauxite field.

2.2.3.3. The *Gulf Coast Region* is low-lying alluvial land with luxuriant vegetation and tree-filled swamps. Its subtropical climate has made the region, especially Florida, the principal winter resort of the country.

Under proper drainage the fertile muck soils of the Gulf coast produce rice and the country's only tropical crop, sugar cane. Moreover, subtropical fruit and early-season vegetables have made the Gulf coast, particularly Florida, the winter garden of the East.

In the dry western part of Texas, the sparse grass cover has for a century been utilized for extensive ranching, while irrigation has made possible intensive cultivation of rice and winter vegetables in certain areas, especially along the Rio Grande.

The region west of the Mississippi, extending through Oklahoma, Texas and Louisiana, has the country's richest oilfields.

2.2.3.4. The *Great Plains,* rising from the Mississippi Basin towards the Rockies to a height of 5,000 ft., were originally covered by prairie grass supporting vast herds of buffalo. Their utilization today depends on the distribution of rainfall. The moister area in the east forms the Wheat Belt, the drier parts in the west are chiefly used for extensive grazing. The monotony of the plains is broken by the eroded dome of the Black Hills in South Dakota, which are rich in minerals – gold, tin and lead. The southern plains have vast petroleum and natural gas resources.

2.2.4. The Cordilleras

The Cordilleras, which continue the South American Andes, constitute a mountainous region of great variety and beauty, and are rich in minerals. They consist of three parallel mountain ranges, separated by the Plateau Region between the Rockies and the Sierra Nevada, and the Central Valley of California between the Sierra Nevada and the Coast Range.

2.2.4.1. The *Rocky Mountains,* which rise to heights of more than 14,000 ft., are rugged and wild. Their chief assets are their magnificent scenery, which stimulates a lively tourist trade, and their minerals. The Rockies are rich in silver, lead and zinc, and have vast reserves of copper, uranium, phosphate rock and oil shale. They have also gold and coal deposits.

As they lie in the rain shadow of the Sierra Nevada, the Rockies receive little rainfall. Arable farming is possible only where mountain streams are used for irrigation. The semi-arid basins provide pasture during winter and spring; in summer the animals are driven to mountain pastures.

2.2.4.2. The *Plateau Region* includes the Great Basin (500 miles wide) with the Great Salt Lake – all that is left of a large ancient inland sea – the Wyoming Basin and the Colorado Plateau to the south. These plateaux at the height of several thousand feet are cut by deep canyons. Grand Canyon, Ariz., with its many-coloured rock layers cut by the Colorado River, is the world's deepest gorge, averaging 6,000 ft. deep, and is 217 miles long. It allows a study of every period of geological history.

The plateaux are the driest part of the country, and vast sections are covered only with desert scrub. In the states of Arizona and New Mexico, lying south of the mountain barrier of the Sierra Nevada, precipitation is sufficient to produce semi-desert grassland suited for year-long grazing. Here are the reservations of the Navajo Indians, whose sheep roam the ranges. The highlands of Arizona are a weird landscape of mesas, volcanic peaks and sand dunes.

2.2.4.3. The *Sierra Nevada* and its continuation to the north, the *Cascade Range*, are as high as the Rockies and famous for their varied natural wonders. Within 100miles of the country's highest peak outside Alaska, Mount Whitney (14,495 ft.), lies the country's deepest point, Death Valley, sinking to 282 ft. below sea level. The Sierra Nevada is famous for its gorges, mountain lakes and waterfalls, the most beautiful being in Yosemite Valley. The Cascade Range, which is only broken by the Columbia Basin, has glaciers and ice-covered volcanoes.

2.2.4.4. The *Central Valley*, the heart of California, lies between the Sierra Nevada and the Coast Range. It is an alluvial plain 450 miles long and 50 miles wide, which is watered by the Sacramento and San Joaquin rivers joining to reach the sea in San Francisco Bay. The valley's chief crops are grapes and cotton.

2.2.4.5. The *southern lowland* of California is extensively irrigated by the Colorado River, whose waters are stored by a number of dams. The Hoover Dam has created the country's largest reservoir, Lake Mead. The irrigated lowland of Los Angeles contains extensive orange groves. It is also rich in oil.

2.2.4.6. The *Coast Range*, which is composed of rolling hills two to three thousand feet high sloping directly down to the coast, is broken by the 'Golden Gate' of San Francisco. The northern part is densely wooded, the southern part, stretching through semi-desert country, has sparse vegetation.

2.2.5. Alaska

Alaska, a peninsula in the extreme northwest of the American continent, is separated from the rest of the U.S.A. by Canada. Lying in a sweeping curve along the southern coast is the Alaska Range, which contains the country's mightiest glaciers and highest elevation, Mount McKinley (20,000 ft.). Behind the mountains, the peninsula, from south to north, consists of the Yukon Plateau, the Brooks Mountains, and the Arctic coastal plain.

The frozen tundra of most of Alaska is not suited to agriculture. But the rugged 'panhandle' in the south, which shares the milder climate of the Pacific Northwest, has heavy rainfall and is therefore densely wooded.

Apart from its forests, the state is rich in fishing grounds and minerals. At the beginning of the 19th century, it provided a new frontier for gold prospectors. Recently rich oil finds in the remote north have attracted the big petroleum companies.

3. The Regions

From a geographical and historical point of view, the U.S.A. can be divided into a number of regions, each having its own economic and cultural patterns.

Although America is today becoming an increasingly homogeneous land, the phenomenon of 'regionalism' has played an important and often decisive role in its development.

From the historical point of view, the U.S.A. is divided into the 'East', the narrow Atlantic Seaboard colonized in the 17th century, and the 'West', the vast land stretching from the Appalachians to the Pacific coast. The earliest settlements along the Atlantic coast developed into three distinct regions: the commercial and industrial Northeast, the agricultural and aristocratic South, and the cosmopolitan Middle Atlantic states, which were later to become the workshop of the nation.

The West was opened up in various stages. The Mississippi Basin, the northern part of which is generally referred to as the 'Midwest', was settled during the first half of the 19th century. In 1848, news of gold in California sent tens of thousands of settlers across the continent to the West coast. When the Californian gold was exhausted, many of these 'forty-niners' moved east to exploit the mineral resources of the Rockies and founded the 'mining states'. Only later were the vast dry plains west of the Mississippi settled by farmers under the *Homestead Act* (1862). The frontier was officially 'closed' in 1890.

3.1. New England (Northeast)

New England, which consists of six small states on the northern Atlantic Seaboard (cf. p. 9) was the stronghold of Puritanism and the cradle of American democracy. The descendants of the Pilgrim Fathers lived in a rugged land with poor soil little suited to agriculture and derived their living from farming on a small scale, fishing, shipping, and various specialized trades. The rural towns, whose steepled churches and white wooden houses seemed to embody the Puritan ideals of integrity and sober austerity, are still a characteristic feature of New England.

The independence of thought and the responsible way of life that had brought the Pilgrim Fathers to the New World soon gave their descendants cultural predominance and political leadership in the establishment of a democratic society. The capital of Massachusetts, Boston (p. 72), was the British colonies' earliest intellectual centre and had the country's first university; it was also the birthplace of the Revolution. New England philosophers and writers became the leaders in the golden age of American literature. Puritan energy and thrift laid the foundations of American trade and industry. New Englanders became the first American shipbuilders, and their clippers soon dominated trade on the Atlantic coast.

The inventions of ingenious Yankee mechanics had an important influence on the development of American economy. Ely Whitney's cotton gin revolutionized agriculture in the South. Morse's telegraphic code and Bell's telephone laid the foundations of telecommunication. Thus the manufacture of machinery also became important in New England.

When the centre of industrial activity shifted to Pennsylvania and the Great Lakes, New England lost its industrial lead.

Today it concentrates on industries requiring specialized skills. However, the many early fortunes made through shipping and industry established a financial aristocracy, whose capital became a determining factor in opening up the West. The 'Atlantic Establishment' in Boston and New York held the western farmer in financial servitude for almost a century.

New England's cultural tradition survives in its publishing industry and its renowned institutions of learning.

3.2. Middle Atlantic States

The Middle Atlantic region includes, from north to south, New York State, Pennsylvania, New Jersey, Delaware and parts of Maryland.

As the region was settled by peoples of diverse nationalities and creeds, the resulting cosmopolitan character of the population tended to breed a liberal spirit; this has been a special feature of the Middle states ever since the Quakers established the ideal of tolerance in colonial Pennsylvania. Philadelphia, 'the city of brotherly love', became the home of the liberal-minded Benjamin Franklin and the birth place of the Declaration of Independence.

In colonial times, these middle colonies soon developed a flourishing economy based on the commercial advantages of a long waterfront and an intermediary position between North and South. It was only natural that America's first great cities would grow up, here. The ports of New York, Philadelphia and Baltimore developed rapidly into manufacturing and trading centres.

Pittsburgh, America's major steel-producing city grew up in the vast coal-fields of western Pennsylvania. The opening of the Erie Canal through New York State to the Great Lakes accelerated the growth of a whole series of industrial cities along its course.

The Middle Atlantic states have nowadays become America's most industrialized and therefore most highly urbanized area. In addition to the continuous stream of immigrants from foreign countries, the cities of this region have absorbed millions of black Americans, who left the South in the hope of economic betterment. Thus racial and ethnic tensions, as well as America's most obvious imbalance of wealth, have made these cities the focus of cultural disintegration and social unrest (see New York, pp. 71–72).

3.3. The Middle West

The American Middle West is a vast level expanse stretching for hundreds of miles to the south and west of the Great Lakes. The region is favoured by a remarkable balance between a sound farming system and well distributed industries. The rich soil of the southern part supports America's Corn Belt, while the Great Lakes region is the country's Dairy Belt.

The Great Lakes system, which provides cheap transport, has given rise to important cities: Chicago (p. 72), the heart of the nation's railway and air network, Cleveland with its oil refining and steel production, and Detroit, the centre of the American car industry. In the east, this broad industrialized belt eventually joins the urbanized Middle Atlantic states to form America's Manufacturing Belt.

The many medium-sized cities scattered across the rest of the Midwest, which developed as centres for processing meat and grain, have today a wide range of industries. Like the states of the region, they are rather similar in character, lacking the social tensions of America's great cities.

The invigorating, youthful atmosphere of the Middle West finds its expression in the character of the population. It was here that the new kind of American arose, for the modern world the typical representative of Americanism – practical, unsophisticated, vigorous, democratic, believing in individual effort, unhampered by old cultural ties to Europe. In the early decades of the Union, it was this region which upheld Jefferson's belief in the common man against the Eastern plutocracy and the Southern planter. When the conflict between slave and non-slave states threatened to disrupt the Union, the mere existence of the Mississippi Basin tended to check a permanent cleavage between North and South. Abraham Lincoln, a native of this region, has become the great symbol of this fusion.

Today, this heartland of the Union with its stable economic development has become the mainstay of American conservatism, constituting once more a stabilizing force in an age of disruption and national unrest.

3.4. The Great Plains

The arid plains east of the Rocky Mountains, which early explorers called 'the American Desert', were the last area to be settled, when the tide of gold prospectors in the Far West began to flow back through the mountains into 'the great open spaces'. The treeless prairies once supported vast herds of buffalo, which were the main source of subsistence for the nomad Indians. Their meat provided food, their pelts were used for clothing and wigwams, their trails showed the Indians the way to the sparse water holes.

From the seventies onwards their numbers (estimated at 60 million) were decimated by ruthless buffalo hunters, whose main exponent, 'Buffalo Bill' became famous as the typical 'Wild West' hero. The Indians, deprived of their subsistence, were confined to government reservations, which are still most numerous in those areas least coveted by the white man.

During a short transitional period, the Great Plains were used as an open range for Texan cattle. This era of cowboy romance contributed to the American legend of the 'Wild West', which continues to be glorified in America's chief film export to the world, the Western.

When, in 1862, the federal government issued the *Homestead Act,* which gave to any family willing to settle on the land 160 acres free of charge, the rancher had to give way to the farmer, at least in the immensely fertile eastern part of the Great Plains. This region, which received just enough rainfall to support grain, became America's Wheat Belt.

Yet the climate remained a fearful hazard. As long as summers were moist, the Wheat Belt enjoyed reasonable prosperity, but, during the thirties, continuous droughts, followed by dust storms, turned ploughed land into a 'dust bowl'. Thousands of farmers were ruined. Abandoning their farms, they increased the number of unemployed or trekked to California (cf. John Steinbeck's novel *The Grapes of Wrath*).

Today, modern methods of soil conservation have rehabilitated much of the eroded land (p. 80). But in many respects the Great Plains have remained the land of the vast open spaces, where hot and parching winds in summer and blizzards in winter strain the nerves of the people. The few small towns, which consist of a single sun-burned street with small stores, a farm-implement agency and a bar, are no longer the same as the towns of the Westerns with their pioneer atmosphere but instead preserve the monotonous atmosphere of Sinclair Lewis' novel *Main Street.*

The landscape has a majestic monotony. The eastern states resemble an ocean of billowing grain, with the tall elevators along the railway tracks and the balloon-like water tank the only landmarks breaking the endless vistas. In the western part, great herds of cattle roam the prairies. The cowboy – 'the last and most brilliant flash of colour in our varied ways of making a living' is more often seen riding in a jeep than on a horse.

3.5. The South

The South, which extends from Maryland in the Northeast to Texas in the Southwest, is the largest of the regional sections.
The original 'South' is the southern part of the Atlantic Seaboard. It was in Virginia, Carolina and Georgia that a distinctively aristocratic culture developed. This civilization, based on slave labour, was cultivated in the graceful white-pillared mansions of the big planters. It was this land-owning class, which, before the Civil War, gave ten presidents to the U.S.A., including Washington and Jefferson.
With the opening-up of the West, the slave-owning South extended its culture into the Gulf Plains, just as the North had extended its democratic society into the Lake Plains. In contrast to the organic development of the North, however, the Southern way of life came to an abrupt end through the devastations of the Civil War and the abolition of slavery. For almost a century, the South was a depressed area, in which illiterate sharecroppers (p. 18) grew the traditional staple crops on largely exhausted soils. There was almost no industry, because the region's raw materials were processed in the North. Not until the 20th century was the South discovered as a profitable field of investment, and its impoverished population as a source of cheap labour – there being no need for such living expenses as warm clothing, solid housing or heating. Industries, which now grew up rapidly, especially after World War II, greatly contributed to a recovery of the region. The Tennessee Valley Authority has made Tennessee, once the poorest part of the region, the leading state in terms of economic development. Almost fully bypassed by this recovery process was the sub-region known as Appalachia. The backwoods inhabitants of this mountainous central area of the South ('hillbillies') have a standard of living far below that of the rest of the country. Only since 1965 has Appalachia become the primary target area in the American war on poverty.
By far the greatest factor contributing to instability in the South is the racial problem, the legacy of slavery. The Negroes, who constitute one fifth of the population (almost twice as many as the national percentage), are still subject to discrimination and smouldering hatred. The fact that the South has also the largest number of 'poor whites' has worsened the problems of illiteracy and social unrest.
Certain Southern states have retained traces of other foreign cultures introduced by earlier settlers. The history of Florida dates back to 1565 when a Spanish conquistador founded St. Augustine, the oldest town in North America. Florida has something of the atmosphere of the Deep South, but also a tremendous number of visitors from the North, who come to enjoy its subtropical climate, the fascination of the Hemingway country near Key West or the luxury hotels of Miami Beach. Louisiana, especially the city of New Orleans, is today still quite conscious of its history as a French colony.

The most 'modern' and buoyant of the Southern states, which is popularly known for judging the value of everything in terms of size, is Texas, the largest continental U.S. state. The eastern part with its cotton and rice fields, its white and Negro sharecroppers, recalls the economy of the Old South, while the orange groves and palms of the Rio Grande delta resemble America's winter garden, Florida. All its own, however, is Texas' oil boom since the discovery in 1901 of the country's richest oil and natural gas reserves. These have given rise to petrochemical industries, to which the city of Houston owes its spectacular development. The western part of Texas is the land of the open range, where ranches boasting the country's best cowboys cover thousands of acres. San Antonio, once the centre of Spanish missionary activity, later became the starting point of the old Chisholm Trail, along which thousands of cattle were driven every year to railheads in distant Kansas. The conflict between the old-time cattle king and the prospector gaining enormous wealth from his oil claims is described in Edna Ferber's novel *Giant*.

Texas, where flat-roofed adobe pueblos jostle luxurious hotels and commercial buildings, gives some indication of the Indian and Spanish past as well as of the wealth of modern America.

3.6. The Southwest

The Southwest, which includes mainly New Mexico and Arizona, is a land of immense variety or landscape and strange flora. It has glacial mountain peaks, the country's largest canyon and sun-parched deserts studded with sagueros cacti, whose branches point upwards like candelabras, and yucca plants with their long pointed leaves stretching out over the dusty soil.

Three cultures – Indian, Spanish and American – meet in the Southwest, not only in archeological remains, but in the contemporary lives of the people. Well-preserved cliff-dwellings in canyon walls are remains of the early Indian tribes, whose varied cultures were superseded by new patterns of life when Spanish warriors, explorers and missionaries filtered into the region. In the 19th century came the Yankees – scouts, trappers, Indian fighters. Traders from Missouri established a trail to New Mexico's ancient capital, Santa Fe, where even today the three cultures mingle without losing their identity. Indians grind corn on their mesas, Spanish Americans lead their donkeys along the sun-baked plazas of somnolent villages, American painters and writers enjoy the Southern atmosphere of freedom and repose. This is now increasingly broken by thousands of visitors every year, who find recreation in the fine climate and enjoy the cowboy atmosphere on 'dude' ranches, watching rodeos and Indian dances. Phoenix, the capital of Arizona, is the scene of the annual World Rodeo Championships.

Arizona boasts of some of the country's greatest natural wonders. In the multi-coloured rock strata of the Grand Canyon and the Painted Desert, the violent colours of the southwestern landscape are intensified; in the Petrified Forest there are tree trunks a million years old.

One third of Arizona is Indian land, on which some 55,000 Indians live in reservations containing fifteen tribes. Nomadic Navajo Indians pasture their sheep and cattle on a reservation of 16 million acres on the Colorado Plateau. Tribes of Pueblo Indians living in adobe towns still grow crops by ancient irrigation methods.

3.7. Rockies and Plateau Region

The Rocky Mountains, the 'Scenicland' of the tourist folders, contain much of the most striking mountain scenery in America and have most of its national parks. The snow-covered, wind-swept peaks reach heights up to 14,000 feet.

The minerals of the Rockies attracted the first settlers, chiefly 'forty-niners', who, after exploiting the Californian gold fields, came to tap the rich deposits of copper, silver, lead and gold in the rugged wilderness. Many deserted 'ghost towns' in the 'mining states' give evidence of the shifting character of the industry.

Besides mining, the region's main industry is stock-raising in the semi-arid basins. In recent times, many cattlemen have added to their income by running 'dude ranches' for tourists.

The Plateau Region between the Rockies and the Sierras contains the Great Salt Lake and the monotonous flats of the Great Basin. Vast areas of the region are virtually unpopulated wasteland. The first settlers in what is now Utah were the Mormons, who irrigated the desert and founded Salt Lake City, which has become the industrial and cultural centre of the region. With its six-spired Temple, it has remained the heart of Mormonism.

The neighbouring state of Nevada, which once produced more gold and silver than all the other states put together, is still a major mining region. Despite its monotony and barrenness, Nevada, too, has its share of tourism. Lake Mead behind Hoover Dam offers good sailing facilities. The state's few towns attract people with their convivial frontier atmosphere. Las Vegas is one of the country's most glamorous gaming centres, Reno is sought by couples from all over the world for rapid divorces, which are made possible by the state's liberal divorce laws.

3.8. California

California, the third largest state in the Union, with its two great cities, San Francisco and Los Angeles, further apart than New York and Montreal, offers a greater variety and sharper contrasts than any other state. It has mountains whose snowfall is one of the heaviest in the world and deserts as hot and dry as the

Sahara. Its vegetation ranges from the country's tallest conifers to palm trees and cactus.

California's main asset is that it is a land of sun. The greater part of the ocean rim has a Mediterranean climate, which attracts two million visitors every year. Retired people from all parts of the country settle in California. The film and aircraft industries profit from the reliable weather.

Until 1848, when California was first under Spanish, then under Mexican rule, the vast region contained only about 7,000 Europeans – Spaniards living on scattered ranches, at missions and military presidios. In the same year in which California became part of the U.S.A., the discovery of gold in the Sacramento River started one of the greatest migrations of the 19th century, the gold rush of 1849. When California became a state in 1850, its population already numbered 90,000.

By the 1870s, California had become the country's second wheat growing state (cf. Frank Norris's novel *Octopus*). When refrigerator cars and commercial canning (cf. John Steinbeck's *East of Eden*) enabled fruit growers to sell their fresh fruit to the faraway Eastern markets, agriculture turned to the cultivation of fruit and vegetables, whose yield repaid the cost of artificial irrigation.

Nature and history have made California a land of great paradoxes and keen fascination. It has a colourful old heritage of graceful Spanish missions, Mexican fiestas and rodeos, and possesses the world's greatest young metropolis, Los Angeles. It has the nation's highest per capita income and at the same time the problem of low-paid migrant labour, which is strikingly illustrated by a comparison between the shabby wood and adobe dwellings in city slums and the showy mansions of Hollywood's film stars in Beverly Hills.

California contains the nation's most varied religions and life styles. As the gateway to Asia it has become the land of exotic cults. Here also was the birthplace of the hippie movement and of the Jesus People. It was here that the Berkeley Free Speech movement led to the first university demonstrations in the student revolution. California has the largest and fastest growing population of any state, and with its exuberance and *joie de vivre* it is generally considered as America's land of the future.

3.9. Pacific Northwest

The Pacific Northwest, which consists of the states of Oregon and Washington, is divided by the Cascade Mountains into two distinct climatic and economic areas: the rain-drenched, densely wooded coastal slopes, and the dry but fertile Columbia Plateau east of the mountains. The Columbia River, which breaks through the Cascades, links the inner regions with the sea. While the coast region lives on its salmon fisheries and its vast forests, the plateau produces wheat and fruit.

The Pacific Northwest was first opened to immigration when, shortly after 1800, the expedition of Lewis and Clark crossed the Continental Divide and followed the Columbia River to its mouth, thus charting a gateway to the new West. On their heels came the first hunters, miners and lumberjacks, who were finally followed by families crossing the prairies in their wagons over the Oregon Trail to settle as farmers and stock-breeders.

In the 1930s, the hydroelectric system of the Columbia River gave rise to new industries. The Grand Coulee Dam turned much of the arid eastern region into an important farming area. The Bonneville Dam, nearer the coast, gave rise to electrometallurgical industries and aluminium plants, which, during the Pacific War, supplied the shipbuilding and aeroplane industries of the West.

Seattle, the chief city of the Northwest, is the country's greatest lumber market and the centre of the industrial concentration around Puget Sound. It is America's nearest harbour for commerce with Asia, and the main port for traffic with Alaska.

3.10. Alaska

Although Alaska is by far the largest American state, it is the least populated because of its climate and geographical isolation. Alaska was bought from Russia in 1867 for $7.2 million, but did not become a state of the Union until 1959. Originally inhabited by Indians and Eskimos, it was at first only visited by New England whalers rounding Cape Horn and agents of New York fur traders. However, the discovery of gold started the Klondike gold rush of 1898, which made Alaska America's 'last frontier'.

The Alaskan towns of Fairbanks, Nome and Juneau grew up as mining communities, as more discoveries of gold and, later, copper were made. In 1968, the discovery of oil on the North Slope attracted the attention of the world's big oil companies, who made million dollar bids for tracts of land in what had until then been regarded as a polar bear patch. The dense forests on the lower Pacific slopes support a lumber industry which has given rise to pulp and paper manufacturing.

Alaska's main industry, however, is fishing. Anchorage on the Pacific coast is a thriving fishing centre, and the chief port for trade with the continental U.S.A. The Alaska Highway, which was built in World War II to make Alaska a base for defense operations in case of a trans-polar attack from Japan, has begun to bring a flood of tourists every summer. But Alaska's geographical isolation and arctic climate remain a handicap.

The state has a mobile population – traders, prospectors, military personnel, technicians with short-period contracts. There are 50,000 Eskimos (p. 110) living in the North on seal and reindeer.

4. National Parks

When the unhampered exploitation of natural resources began to threaten the scenic beauty of the country, the states and the federal government set aside special areas as National Parks in order to preserve scenery and wild life 'unimpaired for the enjoyment of future generations'.

The world's first National Park, Yellowstone Park, was created in 1872. Today the National Park system, administered by the National Park Service, consists of National Parks and Monuments, Seashores and Recreation Areas. Forty per cent of these are found in the Rocky Mountain states.

Yellowstone National Park is famous for its geysers, its hot springs, steaming pools, its terraced formations and the Yellowstone Canyon, into which the river rushes down 417 ft. in two beautiful waterfalls. Other attractions are its black bears, buffalo, antelope and herds of elk.

Three other famous National Parks preserving high mountain scenery are *Grand Teton* N.P. south of Yellowstone, *Glacier* N.P. in Montana, and *Rocky Mountain* N.P. in Colorado.

Mount Rushmore National Memorial in the Black Hills has been made into a Shrine of Democracy, and shows 'the world's largest sculptures' of four great American presidents, Washington, Jefferson, Lincoln and Theodore Roosevelt, carved in the rock of 6,000 ft. high Mount Rushmore.

Badlands National Monument shows the weird effects of erosion in the fantastically shaped peaks and gullies of completely barren rocks. Utah contains several of the most spectacular Canyon National Parks, e. g. *Bryce* N.P. with its sandstone pillars eroded out of a high plateau in all shades of pink, red and orange, and *Zion* N.P., which got its name of 'Heavenly City' from the Mormons.

The same coloured formations, on a still grander scale, are found in *Grand Canyon* N.P. in Arizona. The Grand Canyon (p. 55) has been described as 'a jagged mountain range with some peaks taller than any found in the Appalachians set in a trench so deep that you are above the loftiest summit when standing on the rim'.

The tourist folder's 'Frontier of Enchantment' south of the Colorado River is a land of dry high plateaux sprinkled with sagebrush and low evergreens, interrupted by sudden towering mesas and other scenic attractions. *Mesa Verde* N.P. preserves cliff houses of an ancient people under the rim of Mesa Verde ('green table'), a flat-topped pine-covered mountain, which rises 1,000 ft. above the surrounding terrain. These extensive one-to-four storey dwellings, in which entire villages were housed, are protected by the overhanging cliffs. Similar prehistoric dwellings with 35 rooms are preserved in *Gila Cliff Dwellings* National Monument.

Arches National Monument contains one of the greatest concentrations of natural stone arches in the world (88) and a maze of red sandstone pillars, spires and monoliths. *Carlsbad Caverns* N.P. contains caves 23 miles long, filled with stalagmites and stalactites. On the lower reaches of the Rio Grande is *Big Bend* N.P. Jagged, volcanic mountains rise from desert land gouged by deep, brilliantly coloured gullies. The river cuts its way through the mountains, forming canyons with walls up to 1,500 ft. high.

Everglades N.P. in Florida occupies flat, subtropical swampland filled with mangrove forests and bizarre cypress trees, covered with Spanish moss and teeming with wild life: exotic birds, snakes, alligators.

California, with the striking contrasts of its landscape, has the greatest variety of scenic features. In the Sierra Nevada lies *Yosemite* N.P. with glacial lakes and waterfalls. Upper Yosemite Falls, nine times as high as Niagara Falls, is the highest waterfall in the world.

In the *Sequoia* N.P. between San Francisco and Los Angeles are the country's tallest trees, some up to 3,000 years old, and Mount Whitney, the highest mountain in the continental U.S.A. A hundred miles to the south is *Death Valley* National Monument, 282 ft. below sea level, with the country's highest temperatures.

5. List of Staates of the Union

State	Abbreviation(s)	Population 1970 (in thousands)	Capital
Alabama	Ala.	3,444	Montgomery
Alaska	Alas.	300	Juneau
Arizona	Ariz.	1,771	Phoenix
Arkansas	Ark.	1,923	Little Rock
California	Calif. (Cal.)	19,953	Sacramento
Colorado	Colo.	2,207	Denver
Connecticut	Conn.	3,032	Hartford
Delaware	Del.	548	Dover
Florida	Fla.	6,789	Tallahassee
Georgia	Ga.	4,590	Atlanta
Hawaii	–	769	Honolulu
Idaho	–	713	Boise
Illinois	Ill.	11,114	Springfield
Indiana	Ind.	5,194	Indianapolis
Iowa	–	2,825	Des Moines
Kansas	Kans.	2,247	Topeka
Kentucky	Ky.	3,219	Frankfort
Louisiana	La.	3,641	Baton Rouge
Maine	Me.	992	Augusta
Maryland	Md.	3,922	Annapolis
Massachusetts	Mass.	5,689	Boston
Michigan	Mich.	8,875	Lansing
Minnesota	Minn.	3,805	St. Paul
Mississippi	Miss.	2,217	Jackson
Missouri	Mo.	4,677	Jefferson City
Montana	Mont.	694	Helena
Nebraska	Nebr.	1,483	Lincoln
Nevada	Nev.	489	Carson City
New Hampshire	N.H.	738	Concord
New Jersey	N.J.	7,168	Trenton
New Mexico	N.Mex.	1,016	Santa Fe
New York	N.Y.	18,191	Albany
North Carolina	N.Car. (N.C.)	5,082	Raleigh

State	Abbreviation(s)	Population 1970 (in thousands)	Capital
North Dakota	N.Dak.	618	Bismarck
Ohio	–	10,652	Columbus
Oklahoma	Okla.	2,559	Oklahoma City
Oregon	Oreg.	2,091	Salem
Pennsylvania	Pa.	11,794	Harrisburg
Rhode Island	R.I.	947	Providence
South Carolina	S.Car. (S.C.)	2,591	Columbia
South Dakota	S.Dak.	666	Pierre
Tennessee	Tenn.	3,924	Nashville
Texas	Tex.	11,197	Austin
Utah	Utah	1,059	Salt Lake City
Vermont	Vt.	444	Montpellier
Virginia	Va.	4,648	Richmond
Washington	Wash.	3,409	Olympia
West Virginia	W.Va.	1,744	Charleston
Wisconsin	Wis.	4,418	Madison
Wyoming	Wyo.	332	Cheyenne

6. Great Cities

6.1. Washington

Washington, D.C., with a population of 2.8 million*, is the capital of the U.S.A. It occupies the District of Columbia, which is not a part of any state. Founded under President Washington to avoid mutual competition between state capitals, it is an example of a completely planned capital.

Washington is beautifully laid out according to plans by L'Enfant, an 18th-century French architect, who intended to make it the Paris of the New World. With its neo-classical colonnaded government buildings, its broad avenues named after states of the Union, its parks and beautiful vistas, it is the most distinguished city in the U.S.A. As it has virtually no industry, Washington is said to lack the vitality of industrial cities.

The most important buildings are the imposing Capitol on Capitol Hill, in which Congress holds its sessions, the Library of Congress opposite the Capitol, and the White House in Pennsylvania Avenue, in which the President lives and holds office. One of the largest buildings in the world is the five-sided Pentagon, completed during World War II, which houses the Department of Defence.

The most imposing of the city's many monument are the obelisk of the Washington Monument and the Lincoln Memorial. On the west bank of the Potomac River is Arlington National Cemetery with the Tomb of the Unknown Soldier. Art galleries, museums, theatres, a symphony orchestra and the world-famous Smithsonian Institution for research and publication make Washington an important cultural centre. In spring, the blossoms of the Oriental cherry trees attract thousands of tourists.

Since the Civil War, Washington has attracted a large number of Negroes, who today constitute 70 per cent of the city's entire population.

In 1971, Washington, which used to be ruled exclusively by the federal government, achieved a measure of local sovereignty, including a non-voting member in Congress.

6.2. New York

New York City has 8 million inhabitants, its metropolitan area 18–20 million. Opening directly on to the Atlantic, with a long waterfront, it has outstripped all

---

* Population figures of the cities mentioned refer to metropolitan areas.

other Atlantic ports. With its command of the main routes to the interior, it has become the world's greatest immigration and commercial port. It is the principal industrial metropolitan area of the country.

Manhattan, the original site of the city, which Dutch settlers bought from Indians for trinkets and cloth worth $24, is only two miles wide and is separated from the shores of the mainland by the Hudson and the East River. The entrance to the harbour is dominated by the Statue of Liberty, a gift from France to the U.S.A. in commemoration of their alliance during the American Revolution.

The problem of utilizing the limited space on overcrowded Manhattan Island, where land values soon became exorbitant, was solved by building the world's first skyscrapers, which create an imposingly beautiful man-made landscape, especially at night when lit by millions of electric lights. The two towers of the World Trade Center have 110 storeys.

New York is America's trade and banking capital. As the leading city for the manufacture of clothing, it sets the standard for the country's fashions. While most industries have been driven out to suburban areas on the New Jersey shore (Newark and Hoboken), Manhattan has retained its commercial importance. Wall Street, with the Stock Exchange, is America's financial centre. The famous Broadway is the leading street for general business and entertainment.

New York's excellent theatres, news agencies and radio networks have established its fame as the cultural metropolis of the U.S.A. It is the nation's publishing, film distribution and broadcasting centre. In the 'roaring twenties', the Broadway theatres and music establishments set the standard for art and criticism throughout the continent. This 'Broadway myth' is still alive today in the theatres, cinemas and night clubs in the Times Square area.

The modern trend towards establishing large cultural centres started in New York with the creation of Lincoln Center for the Performing Arts on Broadway. The Rockefeller Center, which was built in the thirties by John D. Rockefeller, is a business and entertainment area consisting of seventeen buildings with exotic restaurants, shops and tree-shaded promenades. It includes galleries, a theatre and the TV and radio headquarters of the Radio Corporation of America.

New York's principal museums are the Metropolitan Museum of Art, the Museum of Modern Art and the Whitney Museum of American Art. Since World War II, New York has gained political importance as the headquarters of the United Nations.

As the world's greatest immigration port, New York has a cosmopolitan population. One in every four inhabitants is of foreign origin. The various racial and national groups congregate in distinct quarters: e. g. Negroes in Harlem, Italians in 'Little Italy'.

With its concentration of industries and its mixed population, New York is plagued by social unrest. It has become the scene of violent illegal practices, a hotbed of crime and race hatred perpetuated by the terrible conditions of its slums. Citizens are openly robbed in the streets without any of the spectators daring to intervene. Since gangs have directed much of their violence at schools, white middle-class families have moved out from the city. In 1970, New York held a record in crime with 117 murders, 74,000 robberies and 180,000 cases of burglary. Drug addicts cause 70 per cent of thefts. An investigation ordered by Mayor Lindsay brought to light considerable corruption among the New York police, some of whom were accepting bribes and turning a blind eye on vice and crime.

Mayor Lindsay has tried in vain to lessen the constant threat to life and property in the ghettos. His policy of decentralized community control has encouraged demagogical activity by inexperienced leaders, resulting in boycotts and riots.

New York has in many ways replaced Paris and London as the metropolis of the Western world. It has become the leading representative of cultural and social trends: modern art and theatre, underground and pop culture, fashion, social and racial conflicts, disintegration of public morale.

6.3. Boston

Boston, Mass., with 2,8 million inhabitants, is the American port nearest to Europe, and long handled a large part of the European trade. Today, Boston has lost much of its importance to New York, and its excellent deep-water harbour is now chiefly of importance for Canadian trade in winter when Canadian ports are ice-bound. Boston is still a centre of banking, and the largest manufacturing city in New England.

Its main asset, however, is, as in colonial times, its cultural importance. It is the seat of over 40 institutions of higher learning, including Harvard University and the famous Massachusetts Institute of Technology, and is a centre of publishing, education, science, technological and business research.

6.4. Chicago

Chicago, Ill., with a population of 6,9 million, is the country's third largest city and manufacturing centre, and the 'capital' of the Middle West. Its situation on the southernmost point of Lake Michigan, where the canalized Chicago River links the Great Lakes with the Mississippi, and its central position within the continent have made it the focus of the U.S. air and rail routes, with a big rolling-stock industry.

Lying in the middle of the world's greatest wheat-growing and livestock-raising belts, it has become the principal U.S. livestock and grain market. It contains the world's largest stockyards and meat-packing plants, and its leading farm machinery concern (McCormick harvesters). As the natural distributing centre between the industrial Northeast and the agricultural West, Chicago is the home of the great mail order firms (e. g. Sears, Roebuck and Co.) which cater for a large, prosperous farm population.

Chicago plays an important part in the cultural life of the West. It is a great publishing centre and contains several large universities, excellent theatres, art galleries and museums. It is 'the convention city' of the West.

Chicago has experienced a stupendous growth from 350 inhabitants in 1833 to seven million today and has the typical features of the modern American metropolis: sordid ghettos lie in the industrial parts, while the beautiful shore drive along Lake Michigan with its imposing skyscrapers and abundant parkland reflects the city's wealth and taste. In the 1920s, Chicago became the centre of New Orleans and Dixieland jazz, in the thirties, it gained notoriety as the city of Big Crime.

Even today, Chicago has a reputation for crime, perpetrated mainly in Southside, the black ghetto, which has a population of one million. 90 per cent of murders, committed largely in ghetto street fights between individual gangs, happen in Southside, revealing the complexity of the city's social problems.

6.5. New Orleans

New Orleans (1 million) is the main port in the Gulf of Mexico. Although it lies 100 miles from the mouth of the Mississippi, it has, ever since it was founded by the French in 1718, enjoyed a unique position as the continent's natural outlet for goods from the interior. Although its predominance as a Southern port has recently been challenged by the booming Texas ports, its foreign trade is still twice that of its greatest rival, Houston.

The 'Crescent City' on a curve of the river is one of the most distinctive in the U.S.A. Its picturesque French Quarter, with its alleys and the elaborately wrought railings of its balconies, recalls French colonial culture. Its carnival is one of the country's major tourist attractions. The gay, informal river-boat era added river-boat excursions to its many festivities. The dancing entertainments in the marine quarter of Storyville gave birth to jazz.

Lying below river level and protected only by levees of silt thrown up by the river, the city has always been threatened by dangerous floods. These have, however, been mitigated by the river control system instituted since the 1930s.

New Orleans commands the import trade for tropical products and exports grain and cotton. It has sugar and oil refineries and a considerable petrochemical industry.

Because of its history and its situation on the threshold of the Caribbean Sea, its population, though largely American-born, is very heterogeneous. It has a large

Creole population, descendants of whites or Negroes of the French colonial era, who have French names and speak a colonial variety of the French language.

6.6. San Francisco

San Francisco, Cal., has a population of 3,1 million. Lying on a narrow, hilly peninsula between the Pacific and San Francisco Bay, it has one of the world's largest natural harbours opening to the sea through the Golden Gate, which allows sea-going vessels to go as far inland as the Great Valley. Only a small Franciscan mission station until 1848, San Francisco rapidly developed into America's main gateway to Asia, with sailings and flights to all the Pacific countries. The city's industries, which have spread to Oakland on the opposite side of the bay, are steel, aeroplanes, shipbuilding, food industries, oil and sugar refineries. In the big metropolitan bay area, San Francisco is still the main port and business centre, Oakland the rail terminal, Berkeley the university town.

San Francisco, for many years a port of entry for immigrants from Asia, has many foreign quarters, the best-known of which is Chinatown, the largest Oriental community outside Asia. Though the Asiatic influx has been stopped, the city with its beautiful urban setting, pleasant climate and informal outdoor way of life attracts many new citizens from the eastern U.S.A.

Some of San Francisco's unique attractions are the Golden Gate Bridge, the colourful night life with night clubs and restaurants serving fish delicacies, with musical entertainment ranging from opera to jazz, and the old-fashioned cable cars climbing the steep hills, which afford magnificent views.

In 1906, San Francisco suffered a devastating earthquake. Today it has become the cultural heart of one of America's most rapidly growing and progressive metropolitan areas. It is served by the fully computerized Bay Area Rapid Transit System, which has set the pace for modern mass transport developments.

6.7. Los Angeles

Los Angeles, with 7 million inhabitants America's second largest city, has outgrown San Francisco despite its less attractive inland position in the southern lowlands of California. It is separated from its port on Long Beach by a belt of suburban development interspersed with oil derricks which caused the city's first boom in the 1920s. The urban area, the biggest in the U.S.A. (because largely composed of single-unit dwellings), has been described as 'a huddle of suburbs looking for a city'.

The inhabitants are engaged in a great variety of manufactures: steel, petrochemical industries, missile production, aircraft, the processing of South Californian citrus fruits, and the famous film industry in the suburb of Hollywood.

While film companies profit from the diversity and scenic beauty of the Californian landscape and the dependable climate, Los Angeles itself suffers from an irritating, unhealthy smog caused by the exhaust fumes of its two million vehicles and the moist air trapped by the mountains behind the town.

All the more important for recreational activities are neighbouring coastal cities, such as Long Beach and Santa Monica, which serve as starting points for the popular pastime of deep-sea fishing. Palm Springs, the desert vacation oasis, is the main winter golf resort of the U.S.A. In Pasadena is the Rose Bowl Parade in connection with the Rose Bowl Football Game on New Year's Day, which is viewed by millions on television every year. Other popular attractions are Disneyland in Anaheim and the elegant homes of film stars in Beverly Hills. The most important art collection in the Los Angeles area is to be found in the Huntington Library in San Marino.

The three great Californian university systems have campuses in Los Angeles and the surrounding communities. Yet, despite its cultural importance, America's youngest metropolis prides itself on being less sophisticated than San Francisco.

7. Economy

The U.S. economy is based on the capitalist system, which has always been favoured by the nation, including the working classes, perhaps because free enterprise, with its hazards as well as its possibilities, appeals more to the character of a pioneer nation than the restrictions of a controlled economy.

The U.S. economy is the world's most advanced in automation and leads in the most important fields of production.

7.1. Historical Development

Until the middle of the 19th century, the U.S.A. was predominantly an agricultural society exporting its staple primary products, tobacco, cotton and wheat. With the discovery of immense mineral resources in the newly explored West and South, the U.S.A. became a major supplier of copper, silver and oil. Its coal and iron ore deposits became the basis of the world's greatest steel industry.

By 1900, powerful magnates of industry and finance had built up industrial empires, taking advantage of the continuous stream of immigrants from eastern and southern Europe, China and Japan, who offered an inexhaustible reservoir of easily exploited cheap labour.

Since their monopolies threatened the cherished American ideal of free competition, anti-trust legislation, first enacted in 1890, aimed at splitting up large trusts. These, however, usually re-emerged as holding companies controlling the majority of stock in other concerns. Unionization of the workers, which had begun in the 19th century among the skilled trades, was accelerated by the Great Depression in the early thirties, when the workers of the mass industries established the Congress of Industrial Organizations. Henceforth the trade unions played a major part in securing for the working population a living standard which created for American industry the world's largest and most prosperous consumer market.

7.2. Big Business and the 'Corporate State'

The concentration of business, has, despite anti-trust legislation, proceeded almost unchecked. Big business continues to be encouraged by the gigantic capital requirements of a technological society. It is capable of financing industrial research and automation, and of creating environmental improvements to attract workers and increase their efficiency. All these advantages have allowed big businesses to expand further in spite of the public indignation aroused by their monopolistic and often corrupt practices, and the environmental pollution they cause. While horizontal expansion through the acquisition of firms with similar production was restricted in order to prevent monopolies, vertical concentration through the control of supplier and customer firms was not covered by anti-trust legislation, being considered even desirable in times of crisis.

More recently, the appearance of so-called conglomerates, owning a large number of unrelated firms, added new dimensions to the problem. For example, petroleum corporations have not only taken over the laying of pipe lines and the establishment of refineries, but also almost the whole fertilizer industry. Textron, once a declining New England textile factory, has bought 70 firms outside the textile industry producing electric equipment, dyes, furniture, boats, aircraft and many other items. The American-owned International Telephone and Telegraph Corporation (I.T.T.) has become the biggest conglomerate in the world. It controls the Sheraton hotel chain, Avis car hire, Lewitt houses, canteen food services, Continental Bakeries, Rimmel Cosmetics, Bobbs Merrill publishers and the huge Hartford Insurance Company.

Today, the 200 largest corporations control 58 per cent of American production. Taking advantage of less restrictive legislation in other countries, many concerns have established or bought firms overseas which yield 25–50 per cent of their net profits. National governments as well as supra-national communities like the European Communities have so far tried in vain to check the influence of the "multinationals". The absence of an international business law favours a development which may ultimately lead to a few corporations controlling not only national economies but also the world market.

In the thirties, the federal government entered the field of business for the first time by selling the electricity produced by the Tennessee Valley Authority. This aroused severe criticism among the apostles of a free economy based on private initiative. Today, forty years later, the bestseller *America Inc.* (by Mintz and Cohen) points out that, although we have been warned against a state functioning like a super-enterprise, we have not been warned enough against a super-enterprise functioning like a state. In spite of massive anti-trust legislation, the American ideal of a democracy guaranteeing individual rights is again in danger of being destroyed by a few giant corporations which are already beginning to control the government as well as the economy.

The financing of election campaigns by big business plays a considerable part in the outcome of elections, and the subsequent dependence of politicians on their backers often leads to outright corruption. In 1972, a Washington columnist exposed a memorandum of the principal I.T.T. lobbyist revealing that a case against I.T.T. conducted by the Anti-Trust Division of the Department of Justice concerning the control of the Hartford Insurance Company had, under its new head appointed by Nixon, been settled in favour of the corporation in return for a promise from I.T.T. of $400,000 towards the costs of the Republican Convention in San Diego.

In some cases, electronic data records of the private lives of undesirable rivals have been used to prevent appointments to positions on government committees. Members of anti-trust boards have been known to change over to top positions in the corporations they had been responsible for regulating, a phenomenon which has been called deferred corruption.

Even official government policy often works to protect big business against competition from new enterprises. Federal aid for industrial research favours the large concerns, which are able to afford research departments. Big armament corporations receive patents for armaments developed with government subsidies. Since the beginning of the Vietnam War, criticism has focused on the 'military industrial complex', i. e. the assumption of policy control by the Pentagon's industrial backers, who are made responsible for the increasing militarization of America.

7.3. The Consumer

In his books *The Affluent Society* and *The New Industrial State,* the notable economist J. K. Galbraith analyzes the functioning of an affluent civilization, whose standards are material needs and consumer products. This has given rise to the slogan 'consumer society', i. e. a society directed to nothing but material values and thus manipulated by industries and services profiting from them. In his book *The Hidden Persuaders,* 1957, Vance Packard drew attention to the fact that decisions as to what the public consumes are no longer determined by individual needs but by the manipulations of advertising agents. Advertising has become a science of exploiting people's pockets, just as public relations and management consultation are felt by many to be designed to exploit people's work. Apart from the enormous expenditure advertising requires, it also creates an inflated market of people persuaded into instalment buying, which may collapse in times of recession.

In recent years a young attorney, Ralph Nader, has made himself the spokesman of the consumer public. He has exposed offensive practices in American industry in some much-acclaimed publicity campaigns, whose chief targets so far have been the automobile and meat packing industries. The sensational revelations in his book: *Unsafe at Any Speed* produced the first car safety regulations in 1966. With relentless candour, he continued the fight against contaminated meat which Upton Sinclair had begun in his book *The Jungle,* in articles like 'We Are Still in the Jungle' or 'Be Careful with Hamburgers'. Far from being admitted to control boards established as a consequence of his exposures, Nader has been the target of open hostility on the part of the industries concerned. However, he has speeded up the emergence of a powerful consumer movement, which seeks to publicize corrupt practices in production, advertising and labelling. This has already compelled the government to enact a number of laws for the protection of the consumer against contaminated food, misleading packaging, cars not complying with safety regulations, and better information on interest to be paid on credits.

The fact that the American market is largely controlled by big business has also brought the consumer some advantages. With its standardized system of supermarket chains and mail-order firms, the U.S.A. has given modern society an economical form of marketing, which saves the consumer's time and, by reducing the number of employees and business establishments, ultimately works for the reduction of prices. The world's biggest mail-order firm is Sears Roebuck, Chicago.

7.4. Agriculture

Until the Civil War, the pattern of U.S. agriculture was monoculture on large plantations in the South, and diversified farming on family farms in the Northeast and Middle West. The agricultural system of the South was ruined by the Civil War, which resulted in the disintegration of large plantations into small tenant farms. The importance of arable farming in the Northeast declined as a result of industrialization and the growing importance of the West with its unexhausted soils as a supplier of wheat.

From the middle of the 19th century, the Midwest became the country's main grain-producing area. The vast expanse of the Central Plain favoured mechanization, which established new agricultural patterns. The large, tractor-size farm requiring little man power, which replaced the family-size farm, led to considerable concentration and deruralization. Whereas in 1800 the farmer produced food for only four people, today one person employed in agriculture provides for 55.

Although U.S. agriculture employs only 6 per cent of the working population, mechanization and scientific methods of farming and breeding have made the U.S.A. the world's leading agricultural nation. U.S. agriculture produces crops of all climatic zones except the tropical, and has been the pioneer in the development of new, more productive crops to suit special conditions.

Nevertheless, farming was for many years a major problem of U.S. economic policy.

7.4.1. Problems of U.S. Agriculture

Soil exhaustion through monoculture had been no problem as long as the abundance of fertile virgin soil allowed farmers to abandon their land when it had lost its productivity, but it became a serious issue when most of the arable land had been occupied. The area most affected was the South, where the land was rapidly depleted by the exclusive cultivation of soil-exhausting cotton. Methods of restoring the fertility of the soil include the reduction of the acreage planted with cotton, crop rotation and reforestation of marginal land.

Soil erosion is caused mainly by wind or excessive rainfall in conjunction with the clearing of forests for farming. The ploughed-up soil is carried away by dust storms or by water running off denuded hills.

In the Tennessee Valley, seven out of eight million acres were damaged as a result of excessive rainfall; one million acres were completely deprived of their topsoil. The Tennessee Valley Authority (T.V.A.), which was founded in 1933 and involves parts of seven states (an area approximately the size of Britain), was the greatest soil conservation scheme ever undertaken. Dams across the Tennessee River and its tributaries have reduced floods down to the mouth of the Mississippi. Reforestation of steep slopes and the terracing of cultivated slopes have prevented the soil from being washed away. Fertilization of tilled land with nitrates produced by T.V.A. plants has restored the productivity of the eroded soil. Farmers were encouraged through demonstration farms to make adequate use of their soil.

The Great Plains had suffered serious erosion from dust storms after the ploughing up of land had destroyed the balanced ecology of the prairies. From 1936 onwards, the government took action under the Farms Rehabilitation Act. It planted forest belts as windbreaks, and encouraged farmers to transfer from the staple crop of wheat to diversified farming including cattle-raising, in order to restore the grass cover.

Aridity and Reclamation: Dry areas are irrigated by the Reclamation Service, founded in 1902. The U.S.A. has millions of acres of irrigated land lying chiefly west of the 100th meridian. Most rivers in this area have water conservation schemes, and maps indicate the strings of artificial lakes along their courses.

In the Pacific Northwest, the Grand Coulee Dam (twice as high as Niagara Falls) provides water for the million-acre Columbia Basin Irrigation Project. The lower Columbia Basin is irrigated by the Bonneville Dam.

In California, the Shasta Dam on the Sacramento River serves the Central Valley. The Hoover and Parker Dams on the lower Colorado irrigate the southern deserts of California. The Hoover Dam has become the mainstay of South California's economic system (irrigation, power, civic water supply). It has turned the desert of Imperial Valley on the mouth of the Colorado into a fertile area which produces crops all the year round.

The deserts of Arizona are watered by the Roosevelt and Coolidge Dams.

7.4.2. Agricultural Belts (see appendix, figure 2)

Agricultural belts are still clearly discernible, although the depression of the thirties has led to a pronounced change-over from monoculture (which is more easily affected by climatic hazards and crises in the world market) to a greater diversity in farming. Agricultural belts follow climatic zones. They are, from north to south:

The *Dairy Belt* extends through New England and the Great Lakes area, where the short growing season and thin glacial soil are less suited to arable farming, and where the moist climate keeps pastures green. Regions near urban centres (e. g. Chicago and New York) produce fresh milk for the market. The less urbanized western portion of the Dairy Belt provides milk products (Wisconsin one half of U.S. cheese, Idaho, Minnesota and western Wisconsin butter). Another important dairy region is the Puget Sound lowland in the Pacific Northwest.

The *Corn (Maize) Belt* occupies the country's largest continuous body of fertile, level land, stretching from the Allegheny Mountains to Missouri. Iowa and Illinois are the chief corn producing states.

The Corn Belt has a genuine mixed farming system, in which the combination and rotation of corn with other grains and hay preserve the fertility of the soil. The corn itself occupies only 30–40 per cent of the farmland. Farmers of the Corn Belt use much of their corn as feed to fatten pigs and beef cattle before shipment to the meat-packing plants of the Corn Belt cities.

The *Wheat Belt,* which is one of the world's chief granaries, lies in the Great Plains west of the Mississippi. It is divided into the spring wheat area, stretching from west of Lake Superior into the Dakotas and the Prairie Provinces of Canada, and the winter wheat area, an irregular belt extending from northern Texas to Missouri. Kansas is the chief producer of winter wheat (see also p. 82).

The *Cotton Belt* extends through the south of the eastern U.S.A. from North Carolina to Texas. It does not reach down to the Gulf coast, where soils are sandy and poorly drained, and where excessive rainfall damages bolls.

The Cotton Belt was for many years a depressed area, where inefficient farming methods exhausted the soil and led to considerable migration among the rural population. Today, agricultural reforms have considerably improved conditions. Fertilization and rotation with other specialized crops like peanuts and rice, and pasture have revitalized the soil. While cotton acreage has dropped from 40 to 14 million acres, the output of cotton per acre has doubled.

7.4.3. Arable Farming

The U.S.A. is the world's largest producer of corn, tobacco and cotton, and ranks second to the U.S.S.R. as a producer of wheat.

Corn (maize): The U.S.A. produces more corn than the total from the rest of the world. The irregular growth of the corn plant (stalks bent, ears growing at different heights) normally requires a considerable amount of work. However, more recently the cultivation of hybrid corn with straight stalks and ears uniformly at waist height has made mechanization easier, and has cut working hours per acre from 14 to 6. Moreover, hybrid corn has a greater yield and a shorter growing season. Corn has also become a major industrial raw material. Alcohol extracted from corn plays a part in the manufacture of synthetic rubber, lacquers and explosives, cobs in the production of plastics. Corn starch is used in adhesives and sweets, stalks are used for making coarse paper.

Wheat: Spring wheat, which is sown after the cold winters, is grown in the northern section of the Wheat Belt with its shorter growing season. It has a smaller yield than winter wheat, which can be sown in September. The semi-arid half of the Winter Wheat Belt specializes in the hard wheat of Turkish origin which was introduced by Russian farmers.

In the Columbia Basin, wheat is grown partly on irrigated land, partly by dry farming methods.

Wheat production is highly mechanized. Harvesting is done by crews travelling with combines for cutting and threshing the wheat in one operation. This has greatly reduced the number of farmhands required. Since the two other seasonal operations, ploughing and sowing, also take little time, wheat farmers have developed a tendency to absentee ownership, preferring to reside in cities or pleasanter regions during the greater part of the year.

Cotton: Despite curtailment of acreage in the Cotton Belt (p. 81), the U.S.A. still produces one third of the world's cotton crop. Competition from the better quality Egyptian cotton grown under irrigation has led to production of irrigated cotton. The area west of the Mississippi, including irrigated land in Texas, Arizona and California, already accounts for one half of the U.S. cotton crop, Texas being the main producer. Complete mechanization has reduced working hours per bale of cotton from 155 by hand labour and mule to 12. After the oil has been extracted, the seeds are ground into meal for cattle feed.

Tobacco: The U.S.A. is by far the world's biggest producer of tobacco, which was the first staple crop of the British colonies in America. Tobacco needs a temperate warm climate and is consequently grown in the traditional Southern tobacco-growing states of Virginia and North Carolina, and in the hilly regions of Kentucky and Tennessee which are less suitable for the more mechanized cotton cultivation. Farmers usually plant only a fraction of their land with tobacco, since the crop wears out the soil and requires immense labour. The centres of tobacco manufacturing are in the producing regions: Richmond, Va., Durham and Winston Salem, N.C., Jackson and Tampa, Fla.

Vegetables (truck farming): Vegetables are generally grown near their markets to avoid long-distance hauling of the highly perishable products. Particularly suitable are the sandy soils of the Atlantic Coastal Plain, which get warm early in spring and dry quickly even after heavy showers.

Early vegetables are grown in Florida and the area irrigated by the Rio Grande. Other big vegetable producers are the southern part of the Great Lakes region, the Columbia Basin, and California, where irrigated land, especially in the Imperial Valley, yields several crops a year.

Fruit: Temperate-climate fruit is chiefly grown in the Pacific Northwest (esp. Willamette Valley, Oreg.) and near the Great Lakes, where the cool climate prevents early blossoming before the last frosts. Lakes Erie and Ontario produce mainly grapes, the area east of Lake Michigan cherries, Wisconsin huge crops of apples, peaches and grapes. Citrus fruits grow in Florida, along the Gulf coast and near the lower reaches of the Rio Grande. The introduction of the process of freezing has extended former seasonal marketing over the whole year. California, with its long north-south extension, grows fruits of all climatic zones, from apples, grapes, peaches and citrus fruits to figs and dates. Strawberries from the Imperial Valley are ready for marketing in December and January.

Californian fruit cultivation is a pattern of modern large-scale operations in production, processing and marketing. Production is controlled by a few processing or canning industries, which may themselves be principal producers of the crop. Marketing agencies and co-operatives guarantee safe packaging and cheap transport to the highly competitive Eastern markets. Even the picking of the fruit by seasonal workers moving north with the season is organized by large agencies. On the other hand, the high productivity of irrigated land allows small holdings of a few acres, which are encouraged by the government.

Bananas are not grown in the U.S.A., and so large plantations in the West Indies and Central America are controlled by the United Fruit Company, whose influence on Latin-American economy has been one of the chief targets of agitation against U.S. 'dollar imperialism'.

Sugar: Tropical cane sugar is grown only in Louisiana. The output, however, is small because the growing season is only eight, instead of the normal twelve, months. The wish to secure a dependable sugar supply was one of the ultimate reasons for the temporary annexation of Cuba and the Philippines in 1899. Now the demand can be at least partly met through sugar beet, which requires only a five-month growing season. Sugar beet is grown in the West, chiefly on irrigated land (Idaho, Colorado, Utah, California).

Rice: When the physical conditions of rice cultivation by hand were still very unhealthy, rice was only grown by slave labour, chiefly in the swamps of Carolina. Today, new techniques, such as sowing and fertilizing from the air, have reduced labour requirements to one man per acre (as opposed to 100 per acre in Asia). Mechanization has thus made possible rice cultivation in other areas as well, particularly Louisiana, Texas and California.

7.4.4. Livestock

The U.S.A. is the world's leading meat-producing country.

Cattle: Whereas dairy cows are raised on farms in the moist Dairy Belt near big population centres, beef cattle are kept on open ranges on the Great Plains, chiefly in Texas, Kansas and Nebraska. In these arid regions, where each head of cattle requires 100 acres of grazing land, and pastures have to be changed frequently, ranches are enormous (up to 300,000 acres). Herds roam wild over open ranges and are rounded up once a year by cowboys to be sold to the packing plants of the West. Cross-breeding with Brahman cattle from India has made the original European breeds hardier and more adapted to a subtropical climate. Cattle reared on the Great Plains and in the Rockies during the summer are often fattened in the Corn Belt during the winter.

Sheep, which need less water and graze closer than cattle, are reared chiefly in the arid West. Being good climbers, they are pastured in the summer in the national forests of the Rockies, in the winter they are taken down to the Plains. Their wool is shipped to be processed in Eastern textile centres.

7.5. Fishing

The Newfoundland Bank, stretching from Canada south along the New England coast, is one of the world's most productive fishing grounds. Its chief yields are cod, haddock and lobster. The fishing industry made the New Englanders the first shipbuilders in America, and they ventured upon long whaling voyages. The literary symbol of New England's whaling trade is Herman Melville's novel *Moby Dick*, which became an American classic. Today, New England provides 60 per cent of the U.S. catch.

The southern Atlantic coast yields mackerel, mullet and oysters. Tourists staying in luxury hotels in Miami Beach fish for tarpon, sailfish and marlin. The Gulf coast produces oysters, shrimps and sponges.

The southern coast of the Pacific yields tuna fish and sardines, the northern part, from San Francisco to Alaska, salmon. The Bonneville Dam, 200 miles inland from the mouth of the Columbia River, has special 'ladders' for salmon, which swim inland to spawn. The coastal fjords of Alaska have the world's largest salmon runs and halibut fisheries, and, farther north, the world's chief sealing grounds in the Pribilof Islands.

Lately the fishing industry has suffered severely from several factors. Over-fishing has begun to diminish salmon runs on the continental Pacific coast. In one of the most productive areas of the New England coast, a quota system has had to be introduced to limit the catch of haddock. Moreover, U.S. fishing suffers serious competition from other countries, esp. Russia and Japan, whose more modern fleets operate within the 12-mile offshore limit of U.S. territorial waters, while U.S. tuna fishing in South American waters is handicapped by a 200-mile limit established by Peru and Ecuador. Recently, marine pollution has become a further threat to fishing.

In 1971, 70 per cent of the fish consumed in the U.S.A. had to be imported. Both the government and private industry are conducting research on fish farming, which has already begun to revive the industry, by raising fish in pens tended by aquatic cowboys.

7.6. Forestry

About half the North American Continent was once covered by immense forests. Uncontrolled felling, first for farming and later for building and export, destroyed an extensive part of the eastern forests, but is now being fought by the National Forest Service. The cut-over areas in the Northeast and the South now provide second-growth timber for use in paper and chemical industries, while the virgin forests of the Northwest provide high-quality timber for building.

7.6.1.

The Pacific Northwest is the most productive area. The softwood forests of Alaska and Washington State produce Douglas fir, spruce and pine, which are exported from Seattle and Portland.

7.6.2.

The Californian Redwood Belt, stretching from the coast near San Francisco eastward to the Sierra Nevada, is covered with trees towering up to 300 ft. and having a life span of up to 3,000 years. This area produces more timber than the British Isles.

7.6.3.

Northeastern Forests: More than three quarters of New England is heavily forested with pine and spruce. These are used for milling and pulping. The chief importance of these forests, however, lies today more in tourism than in industry. Their southern fringes have beech, birch and maple trees, whose golden foliage in autumn produces the 'Indian summer' colours often featured in literature.

7.6.4.

Southeastern Forest Belt: The Appalachians are the main reserve of hardwoods (oak, beech, chestnut). The southern pine barrens stretching along the Atlantic coast from North Carolina to Texas provide slashpine, which has become the basis of the chemical industries, since it is ready for felling in about ten years. These forests are the chief suppliers of naval stores (tar and turpentine) from the resin.

7.6.5.

Gulf Coast and Florida: Fresh-water swamps produce cypresses, whose water-resistant wood is valuable for shingles, fence posts etc.

7.7. Minerals and Fuels
(see appendix, figure 4)

The U.S.A. is the world's leading producer of all major energy resources: hydro-electricity, petroleum, natural gas, coal. Moreover it ranks first in the production of copper, lead and vanadium, in sulphur and phosphate rock, and in uranium and aluminium.

Most of America's minerals are found in the Cordilleras, but her fuels and iron ore come primarily from east of the Continental Divide. Utah is the leading state in volume and variety of production.

7.7.1. Iron Ore

The U.S.A. is the largest producer of iron ore after the U.S.S.R. About 70 per cent of U.S. output comes from iron deposits near Lake Superior. The Mesabi Range in Minnesota, where high-grade ore near the surface has been mined from open pits since the end of the last century, is the largest deposit of iron so far worked in any country. Iron ore has been mined near Birmingham, Ala., since the middle of the 19th century. As high-grade ores are gradually being exhausted, one-third of current U.S. consumption is imported, above all from Canada. Deposits in Labrador, first discovered in 1945, have been made available largely by U.S. capital.

7.7.2. Copper

With 23 per cent of the world's reserves, the U.S.A. is the leading copper producer. Utah has the world's largest opencast copper mine in Bingham Canyon, which also produces silver, lead and gold. The mines of Butte, Montana, have become the centre of a great mining district.

7.7.3. Gold

The first gold found in California, which caused the gold rush of 1849, was washed from river sands in placer mines by indvidual gold prospectors. Since the exhaustion of these mines in 1860, gold has been dug from quartz veins in the Sierras. Recently, placer mining has been revived with huge dredges scooping up sand from the river beds. Although the U.S.A. is the third largest producer of gold, its output is comparatively small, about 6 per cent that of South Africa. The main producing areas are Alaska, South Dakota, Utah and California.

7.7.4. Silver

After the discovery in 1859 of the rich Comstock Lode in Nevada, the U.S.A. remained the leading producer until the thirties. Now Virginia City, which grew up on the Comstock Lode, has become one of the most famous 'ghost towns' of the West. Today, U.S. production, chiefly in Idaho and Utah, ranks second to Canada.

7.7.5. Uranium and Radium

Uranium and radium are mined in Colorado and Utah, where the carnotite ore also yields rare vanadium. Uranium production is strictly controlled by the Atomic Energy Commission (A.E.C.), which issues licenses to private mining companies. The U.S.A. is the world's leading uranium producer, with 51 per cent of the non-Communist world's output. To supplement its own resources, the U.S.A. has secured the greater part of Canadian production through long-term contracts.

7.7.6. Sulphur

The U.S.A. produces 44 per cent of the world output. The Gulf coast states of Texas and Louisiana account for practically the whole of North America's production.

7.7.7. Phosphate Rock

Phosphate rock, the basis of the American fertilizer industry, is chiefly concentrated in Florida, which provides a quarter of the world's phosphates.

7.7.8. Coal

In the 19th century, the U.S.A. had already replaced Britain as the world's leading coal producer. Today it still has vast unexploited coal reserves. Most of U.S. coal is mined in the East.

The Northern Appalachian field, extending from West Pennsylvania into eastern Ohio, yields 70 per cent of the continent's bituminous coal. The Pennsylvania Field, which has made the Pittsburgh district the most important steel-producing region in the world, is 50 miles long and 50 miles wide. Its thick, unbroken seams allow fully mechanized mining. Most U.S. anthracite coal comes from Pennsylvania.

In the Middle Appalachian Field, which extends from West Virginia into eastern Kentucky, the seams come to the surface on the sides of the valleys, from where the coal is easily mined and carried by gravity to railway carriages on the valley floor.

The Southern Appalachian Field around Birmingham has been worked for a century. Together with considerable iron deposits it has given rise to an important iron industry. The coal is sometimes so near the surface that the soil is stripped off and the coal mined in open pits.

The western coal-fields in Illinois and Missouri have an expanding market in the fast growing industries of the Midwest.

7.7.9. Oil

The U.S.A. produces more than a quarter of the world output. The richest deposits are in southern California (exploited since the 1890s), and in Texas, Oklahoma and Louisiana. These Mid-Continental Fields have been exploited since 1901. In the Gulf of Mexico drilling has been carried out many miles offshore; one well is over 1,000 ft. deep. Oil discovered in Alaska has added sizable resources to the economy.

Formerly, oil production involved enormous wastage. The sinking of too many wells in a given area, for instance, reduced the natural pressure forcing up the oil and made pumping necessary. This wastage has been curbed by a quota system introduced during the Depression. Furthermore, formerly wasted by-products are now used in petrochemical industries.

The U.S.A. has more than 200,000 miles of oil pipelines. Trunk lines carry both crude and refined oil from the Mid-Continental Fields to the Middle Atlantic region, the Chicago-Detroit area and the Pacific and Gulf coasts.

Throughout American history, the oil industry has been the prototype of big business. The early independent 'wild-cat' drillers have been replaced by the giant corporations. American anti-trust legislation resulted largely from the conflict of the oil magnate John D. Rockefeller with the federal government.

In 1911, Rockefeller's Standard Oil empire was split up into 34 individual companies, which soon grew faster than the parent trust. The Standard Oil Company of New Jersey, now renamed Exxon, has, with its subsidiary outside the U.S.A., Esso, become one of the world's greatest corporations with an annual product larger than that of Turkey. The other principal oil corporations are Texaco and the Gulf Company.

The international power wielded by the huge American oil concerns, which, between them, control $^3/_4$ of U.S. refinery capacity and natural gas production, and more than 50 per cent of uranium reserves, has become a major target of anti-American agitation. The acute petroleum shortage in the U.S.A. after the renewal of war between Israel and the Arab countries in September 1973 resulted as much from manipulations by the oil companies trying to derive profits from the general crisis as from a reduction of oil supplies from the Middle East.

As the U.S.A. is the world's largest consumer, anxiety for the nation's reserves has led U.S. oil companies to develop considerable interests abroad. Aramco (Arabian-American Corporation) and the Bahrein and Kuweit companies, which are largely controlled by American corporations, have become major producers in the Middle East, the International Petroleum Company operates in Latin America. However, the growing trend towards anti-colonialism in these areas has led in recent years to the nationalization of American-controlled companies in countries like Peru, Venezuela and Bolivia. This threatened U.S. imports even before the great oil crisis of 1973/74, and has consequently speeded up the development of domestic atomic power plants. Moreover, the immense reserves of oil shale in the Rockies await the time when oil can be economically produced from the shale.

7.7.10. Natural Gas

Natural gas, which was for a long time allowed to escape as a useless by-product, is now used as fuel and piped to factories and homes throughout the country. Since 1925, production has increased immensely. The major producers are the oil states of Texas, Louisiana and Oklahoma, which contain 75 per cent of the known U.S. gas reserves. Oil and natural gas now account for 77 per cent of the energy produced in the U.S.A.

7.8. Electric Power

The U.S.A. produces almost one third of the world's electric power. The first hydroelectric plants were built along the North Atlantic fall line (p. 53) and at the Niagara Falls, giving rise to the industrial cities in New England and along the Mohawk-Erie route. In 1933, the water of the Tennessee River and its tributaries began to be utilized by the Tennessee Valley Authority, which has made possible a new type of rural industrialization throughout a large area in the Southeast.

The Columbia and Missouri Valley Authorities harnessed the water resources of the West (p. 80). The Columbia Basin system has been the basis of the industrial development of the Pacific Northwest.

The development of nuclear power stations has been slow, due to the general fear of environmental pollution. The U.S.A. has now some 20 nuclear energy plants, which account for less than one per cent of U.S. power. The best known are Oak Ridge, Tenn., and Los Alamos, N.M., both linked to important research centres.

The fact that the country's power consumption doubles every ten years, combined with the diminishing world oil reserves now poses the serious threat of a power shortage. The oil crisis of 1973–74 has shown that the difficulty of securing sufficient fuel for continued economic growth has become one of the world's major political problems.

The first attempt to tap the great reserves of energy stored in hot granite deep in the earth's crust is now being made near Los Alamos. At a depth of 5,000 feet, to which the drilling rig is sunk, the rock is expected to be 200 degrees centigrade hotter than at the surface. If cold water pumped down into a hole which is drilled into the hot granite circulates through the fractured rock, it is expected to come up a second hole several hundred degrees hotter. At the surface, the steam produced can be used to generate electricity. If the team of the Los Alamos Scientific Laboratory succeeds, the experiment will open up a new source of almost unimaginable size producing very cheap power. Another project plans to gather energy from the sun through a satellite in space, which sends it down to stations on the earth.

7.9. Industry
(see appendix, figure 4)

The strength of American industry is based on the abundant natural resources of a large continent and a consumer market of more than 200 million. The U.S.A. has vast power resources and is one of the world's chief suppliers of the primary products processed by its own leading industries: iron ore for its steel, oil for its oil refining and petrochemical industries, cotton for its textiles, grain, meat and fruit for its food manufactures.

American industry leads the world in large-scale production, automation, technological, managerial and marketing research. In his book *The American Challenge,* the French journalist and politician Jean-Jacques Servan-Schreiber analyzes the factors constituting the superiority of American industry: 'Technological innovation has now become the basic objective of economic policy. In America today, the government official, the industrial manager, the economics professor, the engineer and the scientist have joined forces to develop co-ordinated techniques for integrating factors of productivity. These techniques have stimulated what amounts to a permanent industrial revolution ... This takes us a long way from the old image of the United States – a country where business was not only separate from government but constantly struggling with it, and where there was a chasm between professors and businessmen. Today, on the contrary, this combination of forces has produced the remarkable integrated entity that John Kenneth Galbraith calls a "techno-structure"'.

7.9.1. General Development

American industry is mainly concentrated in the Manufacturing Belt stretching from New England through New York and Pennsylvania to Lake Superior. Since World War II, there had not only been an immense increase in industrial capacity, but also an expansion into other areas of the country. The Southeast with its large cheap labour force and hydroelectric power from the Tennessee Valley Authority, and the oil-producing states of Texas and California have become new industrial centres. Moreover, cheaper transport of new power resources (electricity, oil, gas) has resulted in a dispersal of industry, now no longer dependent on coal and railroad sites. This dispersal makes for rural industrialization and is for social and security reasons encouraged by the government.

It has been pointed out that American industry, which was originally built up on the principle of individual initiative and free competition, is today largely dominated by a small number of giant corporations. In each of the fields of chemical, electrical and automobile manufacturing, the world's three largest concerns are American.

Since World War II, U.S. industry has not only tried to gain control of foreign markets, but also of industries abroad. With its flexibility and innovating dynamism, it captures those sectors of the economy which are most technologically advanced and have the highest growth rates.

U.S. industry has introduced into Europe the new science of marketing and a new giant of American business in its management consultancy organizations. J. J. Servan-Schreiber maintains that 'already, in the ninth year of the Common Market, this European market is basically American in organization ... Thus, much beyond massive U.S. investments, it is American-style management that is, in its own special way, unifying Europe'.

European industries have thus, along with the Japanese, become competitive in a number of American markets. Moreover, in the coming years U.S. industry will have to face the immense problem of stopping industrial environment pollution, which, it is estimated, may cost the country up to $ 30 billion annually.

7.9.2. Major Industries

7.9.2.1. *Steel:* The world's greatest iron and steel producing industry is handicapped by the fact that the two basic raw materials, iron and coal, come from areas lying 800 miles apart (Lake Superior and Pennsylvania), though the enormous distance is partially offset by the cheapness of water transport on the Great Lakes. The principal steel industries are consequently situated in cities along the Great Lakes (e. g. Cleveland), and in the Appalachian coalfields, esp. in Pennsylvania. Birmingham, Ala., with its own nearby sources of coal and iron is another important centre of steel production. As one fifth of the iron ore processed in the U.S.A. comes from overseas, steel mills are now increasingly built on the Atlantic Coastal Plain.

However, the centre of the U.S. steel industry is still Pittsburgh, Pa., which owes its development to its situation in the Pennsylvanian coal-field, local iron (now exhausted), and the early application of the Bessemer process by Andrew Carnegie, whose steel concern dominated the industry. Today, it is the seat of the U.S. Steel Corporation.

A major city which was planned as a steel town is Gary, Ind., whose founder, the U.S. Steel Corporation, took advantage of the cheap swampy land south of Chicago to make use of the water and transport facilities of Lake Michigan and the labour force of Chicago.

7.9.2.2. The *automobile industry* is centred round Detroit, where Henry Ford introduced the principle of assembly-line mass production at the beginning of the 20th century. The automobile industry is highly concentrated: 95 per cent of U.S. automobiles are produced by 'the Big Three': G e n e r a l   M o t o r s, (the world's biggest corporation with an annual product larger than that of Brazil), F o r d and C h r y s l e r. Automobile firms were among the first to expand their activities to other countries. General Motors bought British Vauxhall (1928) and German Opel (1932), Chrysler more recently French Simca and British Rootes. Ford has already transferred half of its production to Europe. The big car-hire firms Hertz and Avis have introduced the hiring system on a large scale to Europe. On the other hand, foreign producers, particularly German and Japanese firms, have begun to expand into the American market. The sucessful competition of smaller foreign cars, above all the Volkswagen, has however been met recently by the development of American 'compact' cars.

As the 110 million cars in use in the U.S.A. are the major source of air pollution, the automobile industry faces the problem of producing 'clean cars' by 1975 as required by the *Clean Air Law* of 1972).

7.9.2.3. The *aircraft industry* has immensely developed as a consequence of the Pacific and Vietnam wars and the Moon Project, which made it the Pentagon's and N.A.S.A.'s chief supplier. The largest firms are Lockheed (Burbank, Cal.) and Boeing (Seattle). This industry, heavily supported by the government, was the first to suffer from the effects of the economic recession, when the government was forced to curtail its space programme and to cut $ 7 billion in defence expenditure. Boeing, which was most severely affected when Congress in 1971 voted to end its costly supersonic transport (S.S.T.) development, had to cut its work force from the 1968 peak of 100,000 to 40,000. When inflation, in Europe as well, made it impossible for Rolls-Royce to deliver aircraft engines for Lockheed's Tri-Star Airbus project at the agreed fixed price, the Pentagon's biggest supplier was almost bankrupt. Lockheed could continue its programme only through emergency financing by the government. However, the sale of Boeing machines to China has begun to improve the industry's situation.

7.9.2.4. Electrical and electronic industries: The U.S.A. has, for a century, been a leading country in the development of electrical equipment. Thomas Edison invented the electric bulb, A.G. Bell the telephone.
By far the biggest producer of electrical equipment is General Electric, followed by Western Electric and Westinghouse. The giant firm I.B.M. (International Business Machines) owed its development to the fact that it led in a newly developed technological field, the computer. It has satellite plants in many countries with a billion-dollar turnover in Europe alone. When the French firm Machines Bull was threatened by bankruptcy, General Electric acquired most of the stock in the new merger Bull General Electric, which established time-sharing computer services in most European countries. The expectation that the computer, by replacing and speeding mental processes, would influence every aspect of human life (including teaching, translating and futurology) has not materialized. Moreover, the necessary investments for development and programming have confined the computer's economic value to the large institutions. All this has led to a serious recession in the industry.

7.9.2.5. The *chemical industry* is one of the most rapidly expanding modern industries. It centres chiefly on areas which provide power and the necessary raw materials: petrochemical industries (plastics, synthetics) in the Texas oilfields, the fertilizer industry, based on Florida phosphates, in the South, aluminium production with its high power requirements in Tennessee and the Pacific Northwest. The leading firms are Du Pont, Union Carbide, Monsanto and Dow Chemical. The world's largest chemical concern, Du Pont de Nemours, changed between the two World Wars from the manufacture of munitions to plastics and artificial fibres, expanding from its original headquarters in Delaware particularly into the South. Du Pont has invested millions of dollars in research to develop new products, the most revolutionary being the nylon fibre. Since the fifties, it has established new industries overseas. Du Pont's satellite plants in Europe already account for more than 10 per cent of its turnover.

7.9.2.6. The *textile industry* was formerly concentrated in New England, where it took advantage of the water power of the Piedmont streams, the capital accumulated by Atlantic commerce, and the expert skill developed earlier in its crafts. The first textile mill was started by Samuel Slater, a textile machinist who immigrated from England and built from memory the machines whose export was strictly forbidden.

Now a large segment of the textile industry has shifted to the cotton-growing states of the South. Second-growth timber of the Southeast provides the raw material for the rayon industry. The woollen industry is still concentrated in New England, the manufacture of clothing chiefly in the New York metropolitan area.

7.9.2.7. *Foodstuffs* are processed largely in the agricultural areas of the Midwest. Flour-milling centres are mainly situated in the Wheat Belts – in St. Louis, Kansas City, Minneapolis. Meat is processed in immense meat packing plants, which are situated in the chief livestock markets – Chicago, Kansas City, Omaha, St. Louis (see also p. 72). The industry includes a large number of subsidiary manufactures based on meat by-products, such as soap from fats, leather from hides, combs and buttons from bone and horn, upholstering from hair. The fruit canning industries developed in the 'truck farming' areas, mainly in California, where the long distance to the chief markets in the East made preservation necessary. Sugar refineries are chiefly found along the Gulf coast, most raw sugar being imported from the West Indies.

7.10. Trade

7.10.1. Domestic Trade

Domestic Trade is favoured by an excellent transport system and by the large uniform market area formed by a prosperous population.

While intrastate commerce is the domain of the individual states, the Constitution provides that foreign trade and interstate commerce be regulated by Congress. The fact that today practically all domestic trade moves across state boundaries, and the constant redefinition of the term interstate commerce (e. g. to include radio and television) have led to almost complete federal regulation of domestic commerce through the Interstate Commerce Commission.

7.10.2. Foreign Trade

In spite of its very large volume of trade, the U.S.A. still remains with regard to its domestic economy mainly self-sufficient. It is therefore not so strongly affected by problems of international trade as other countries. Despite the unprecedented domestic population growth, export of agricultural products has remained high, because of the expansion of production through scientific land management and mechanization. Chief agricultural exports (in order of dollar value) are soybeans, wheat, corn and tobacco. However, the value of farm exports is far less than that of the manufactured goods exported, such as machinery and transport equipment, chemicals and computers.

7.10.2.1. Trade with Western Europe: After the two World Wars, the war-shattered European continent furnished a ready market for American goods. Immense loans extended to Western European countries under the Marshall Plan pursued the double aim of making them solvent trading partners and preventing them from becoming targets for Communist infiltration. By the sixties, the European countries had expanded their own economies to a point where they were forced to place controls on the inflow of American goods. The 'pullet war' with West Germany in 1963 made it clear that the European market was contracting, the more so as the U.S.A. protected its own economy by tariffs on imports that would have helped European countries to earn the dollars needed for purchases from the U.S.A. When the European countries began to turn to new markets and to integrate their own economies in bigger communities – the European Economic Community and the European Free Trade Area – the U.S.A. was threatened with being shut off from European markets. Although the Kennedy Round (p. 38) had reduced tariffs, a clandestine trade war with Europe revived when Nixon reintroduced tariffs and when expenditure on the Vietnam War had drained U.S. financial resources to a point where it began to constitute a severe threat to world financial stability.

7.10.2.2. International monetary crisis: The international monetary system had been established at the end of World War II, when America emerged as an economic super-power in a war-shattered world. The Conference of Bretton Woods, 1944, established the dollar as the world currency together with gold, by making the dollar the only national currency that other countries were obliged to accept as payment for foreign transactions. The dollar, fixed at an exchange rate of $35 per ounce of gold, was recognized as a reserve currency, and was the basis of the 'Eurodollar Pool' of the European coutries' central banks. Although the American balance of payments in 1969 had reached a deficit of $10 billion, with inflation still growing, European banks were still obliged to buy the dollar at an exchange rate well above its actual value. This caused American firms to make investments abroad rather than in their own country. The flow of dollars into European countries, especially those with hard currencies (Switzerland and West Germany) resulted in a monetary crisis in May 1971. Since the devaluation of the D-mark in 1969 had not led to full parity, most of the countries concerned resorted to floating exchange rates. The fact that the U.S.A., which was the cause of the crisis, continued to demand considerable trade concessions from its European partners, while propping up its own economy by protectionist measures, aroused world-wide ill-feeling. Finally Nixon, who did not care to risk a general trade war in the year of the presidential election, agreed after long negotiations with the expanded Common Market and Japan to a realignment of parities. The dollar was devalued against other currencies by increasing the official price of gold from $35 to $38 an ounce. In February 1973, a new dollar crisis led to a further devaluation of the dollar by 10 per cent.

7.10.2.3. Trade with Canada: America's largest trading partner is Canada. The U.S.A. buys 68 per cent of Canada's exports and provides 75 per cent of its imports. Moreover, Canada accounts for 30 per cent of U.S. investments abroad. Recently an upsurge of nationalism in Canada has begun to speak out against U.S. economic domination and its influence on Canadian life and culture, and has called for a curbing of U.S. investments and imports. In 1971, Canada extended its territorial waters in the Arctic Circle from three to twelve miles, which virtually shut the narrow Northwest Passage to foreign shipping. The U.S.A., whose potential transport routes for oil from the newly discovered arctic oil fields would thus be blocked, responded by reducing oil imports from Canada.

7.10.2.4. Trade with Japan: America's second largest trading partner is Japan. The international blockade of its continental neighbour, Red China, and the security treaty of 1960 with the U.S.A. had made Japan economically very dependent on the U.S.A. Low-cost Japanese goods produced by a highly skilled, disciplined work force at low wages began to invade the U.S.A. soon after the Second World War. The U.S.A. now buys one third of Japanese exports. Ships, cars, high quality equipment and cameras from Japan provided formidable competition to American domestic industry. When, from 1965, the former U.S. trade surplus with Japan began to turn into a rapidly growing deficit, the U.S. government stepped up the enforcement of its anti-dumping laws. This has induced Japan to relax its import quotas and to permit the selling and warehousing of U.S. products in Japan by U.S. firms.

7.10.2.5. U.S. trade with developing countries has given rise to the terms 'dollar imperialism' and 'neo-colonialism' to indicate the role of trade as a vehicle for U.S. domination of other countries. Starting in the 19th century, U.S. companies began investing heavily in countries supplying primary products, exploiting mines and controlling plantations furnishing tropical products not grown in the U.S.A. The United Fruit Company, owning South American banana plantations, and the Kennecott Company, which controlled Chilean copper mines, are conspicuous examples. The U.S. government protected these private American interests by diplomatic, commercial and military means. In 1898, the Spanish-American War secured the U.S.A. control of the sugar-producing islands of Cuba and the Philippines.

In South America, where this process of political interference became a major issue, socialist reforms aiming at the nationalization of American-controlled mines and companies were repeatedly prevented by military intervention. The *Sugar Act* of 1962 and the *Hickenlooper Amendment* to the *Foreign Assistance Act* provided that, unless a corporation whose foreign interests are nationalized, is compensated, the U.S. government is legally required to cut off economic aid to the country concerned, and to deny it its allocated share of the sugar market. Under these laws, the U.S.A. declared a blockade of Cuban sugar, which was later extended to all imports from the Communist-ruled island. When Chile's president Allende nationalized the copper mines of the Kennecott Corporation in 1971 and announced a moratorium on the repayment of debts, the U.S.A. exerted its influence on the World Bank to stop further loans to Chile. In 1974 it was revealed that I.T.T. and C.I.A. activities had largely contributed to the final overthrow of Allende's government in 1973.

Another major problem is the fact that credits which the U.S.A. extends to developing countries must be used to purchase U.S. goods. This has given rise to the slogan 'trade not aid'. A more constructive policy designed to improve the economic conditions of the trading partners (which would perhaps really conduce to the U.S. aim of containing Communism) has so far been prevented by the corporate interests controlling the State Department and the White House. Thus the indebtedness of Latin America has risen from $10 billion in 1960 to $20 billion in 1970, while interest on capital loans has risen from 25 to 36 per cent.

All this opens the way not only for Latin American revolutionary elements but also for Communist influence from abroad. When the International Petroleum Company, a subsidiary of Standard Oil, demanded compensation for the nationalization of its interests in Peru in 1968, the Peruan government established diplomatic relations with Soviet Russia and pleaded before the O.A.S. for the resumption of relations with Cuba. After the U.S.A. raised a so-called 'invisible blockade' against Chile, the Soviet Union replaced the U.S.A. as Chile's main creditor.

7.10.2.6. Trade with Communist nations: Immediately after World War II the U.S.A. established a virtual embargo on trade with Communist countries. However, the growing rift within the Communist bloc as well as the integration and increasing saturation of the European market have led the U.S.A. to establish trade relations with the U.S.S.R. and, since the admission of Red China to membership in the U.N., with Peking. Since 1970 a great number of goods ranging from chemicals to trucks have been removed from the list of strategic items that may not be exported to the Soviet Union, and China has placed orders for American jets. Thus trade relations even with America's ideological 'enemies' are now undergoing a process of normalization.

7.11. Communications

Mobility has always played a key role in America's history. Distances between settlements have always been great, and the continuous westward migration made them ever greater. Considerations of national unity as well as of economic progress have led Americans to place an extremely high value on communication and transportation systems. It is therefore not surprising that today the U.S.A. leads the world in these fields.

7.11.1. Waterways

Waterways were the first routes into the interior. The Mississippi was for a long time the only outlet for the produce of the Midwest, but the Erie Canal, completed in 1825, finally provided a direct link between the Atlantic and the Great Lakes and therefore played a historic role in unifying the country. The present system of inland waterways is very extensive, since the big Mississippi tributaries have largely been made navigable: the Tennessee as far as Knoxville, the Ohio beyond Pittsburgh, the Missouri as far as Sioux City, the Mississippi itself as far as Minneapolis. The Intracoastal Waterway along the Gulf coast links Texas with Florida and continues up the east coast to New York. There it joins the Hudson-Mohawk route to the Great Lakes provided by the New York State Barge Canal, the former Erie Canal.
The Great Lakes are the world's longest inland navigation system (2,300 miles), and one of the most important waterways for the shipment of grain, iron ore and coal. The considerable difference in the level of the Lakes is overcome by the Soo Canal (originally Sault Ste. Marie Canal) along the St. Mary's River between Lake Huron and Lake Superior – the continent' busiest waterway – and the Welland Ship Canal bypassing the Niagara Falls on the Canadian side. The Great Lakes are linked with the Gulf of Mexico by small canals connecting them with the Mississippi and Ohio.
The St. Lawrence route from the Atlantic to the Great Lakes became fully available for ocean-going ships only in 1959 when the St. Lawrence Seaway from Montreal

to Lake Ontario was opened, making it possible for large ocean-going ships to penetrate into the very heart of the continent. However, it is closed for five months of the winter.

7.11.2. Railways

In the middle of the 19th century, railways rapidly replaced waterways. Privately owned railway companies became the main agents for settling the West. They laid out villages and towns, conducted recruiting campaigns in Europe for settlers and took them to their destinations. They provided them with food, equipment and corrugated iron for houses in the treeless prairies. The companies eventually built the great transcontinental lines linking the isolated Far West with the East. They became for some time the most powerful representatives of big business in the country, enjoying many special privileges from Congress because of their role in America's 'Manifest Destiny'. Today, the railway system has considerably declined, owing to the development of road traffic. Many railway companies have merged, others have had to close down entirely. In 1969, one of America's largest railway corporations, the Penn Central, went bankrupt. In 1970, an Act of Congress established the independent federally supported National Railroad Corporation, Amtrak, to handle passenger transport, which runs at a deficit. Only inter-city lines of the densely populated Northeast run at a profit.

7.11.3. Road Transport

Ever since the presidency of Washington, the American government has taken an active interest in the construction of roads. With the development of automobile transport, the U.S.A. pioneered in the construction of multi-lane highways, with the federal government responsible for the principal routes. The enormous development of motor traffic, however, – one car to every two people – has made even this system inadequate. The building of the National System of Interstate and Defence Highways, which started in 1956, and is now almost completed, provides a nation-wide network of limited-access highways without traffic lights or stop signs. The federal government pays about 90 per cent of construction costs, the states pay the balance and the cost of maintenance. In recent years, even freight traffic has shifted more and more from railways to lorries. Automobile traffic today accounts for 75 per cent of air pollution in cities.

7.11.4. Aviation

At the beginning of the 20th century, America pioneered in the development of air travel with the inventions of the Wright brothers. In a country with large distances and great natural barriers, aviation soon began to play a major part in transport. Planes and helicopters have come to be used on large farms for sowing seeds and spraying crops.

Airlines, like railways, are in the hands of private enterprise. They are, however, strictly controlled by the Federal Aviation Authority and heavily reliant on the federal government for research and development. The biggest airlines are Pan Am (Pan American Airways) and TWA (Transworld Airlines). The supply of funds for an American supersonic transport system (S.S.T.) was stopped by a decision of Congress in 1971.

7.11.5. Space Travel

The foundation of modern space travel was laid when in 1926 the American Robert Goddard launched the world's first liquid fuel rocket. After World War II, the U.S.A. experimented with German V-2 rockets, chiefly under the direction of the German rocket expert Wernher von Braun. In 1957, the Soviet Union launched the world's first artificial satellite, Sputnik I, three months later, in January 1958, the U.S.A. followed suit with Explorer I. The ensuing race for supremacy in space travel has since been conducted on the American side by N.A.S.A. (National Aeronautics and Space Administration), which carries out the U.S. Space Programme in co-operation with the Air Force, private industry and universities. Manned space flight, which began in 1961 when the American astronaut A. B. Shephard was rocketed into space and the Russian Major Gagarin first orbited the earth, reached a first climax in 1969 when Apollo 11 landed on the moon (see also pp. 38, 40, 45, 92). With the sixth moon landing in Dezember 1972, the Apollo Programme was complete. In January 1974, the sky-lab – the first orbiting space laboratory – was put into operation.

N.A.S.A.'s chief space flight centres are the manned spacecraft centres in Houston, Tex. and at Cape Kennedy, Fla., the Goddard Space Flight Center in Greenbelt, Md., and the Jet Propulsion Laboratory in Pasadena, Cal.

8. Population Structure

According to the 1970 census, the U.S.A. has 203 million inhabitants (i. e. almost ten times the population of Canada, which is larger). Density varies between 953 per square mile in New Jersey and 0.5 in Alaska, the average being 57.5 (West Germany 642).

Recent population trends show a marked movement from rural to urban areas, which already contain 73 per cent of the total population. Most striking is the movement west and south, which has trebled the populations of states like California, Arizona and Florida since 1940. On the other hand Northern cities have been swelled by former Negro farmhands leaving the 'Old South'.

The social pattern inside individual American cities is also changing. The continuing trend of urban dwellers to move from city centres to suburbs is the result of business expansion and air pollution as well as of general prosperity allowing middle-class families to acquire homes of their own.

The U.S.A. has been called the melting pot of nations. Beside the survivors of the native Indians and the descendants of imported Negro slaves, immigrants from virtually all European nations and the Orient have contributed to form the American nation.

8.1. Europeans

Whites constitute 88 per cent of America's present total population. The first settlers came from northern and western Europe – from Great Britain, Germany, Scandinavia and France. They were readily assimilated and soon became a uniform nation. Only in a few areas are distinct national groups still discernible, e. g. Scandinavians in Minnesota, Germans in Wisconsin and Michigan, and the Pennsylvania Dutch from the German Palatinate, who have preserved their national customs and even their language.

From 1890, cheap labour from southern and eastern Europe – Italy, Greece, Poland, the Baltic countries – began to stream towards America to work in industry and the mines. These new immigrants were less readily assimilated, as the various ethnic groups congregated in distinct areas of large industrial cities and continued to speak their own languages.

In the 1920s, new laws reduced immigration in general and laid down quotas favourable to immigrants from western Europe. After World War II, these restrictions were relaxed to admit displaced persons, i. e. natives of eastern European countries who had been under compulsory employment in the German war industry, and could not return to their Communist-controlled homelands.

In general, it is the great majority of Americans of European descent who form the middle class and control the politics and economy of the country. The upper class, which is exclusively white, consists largely of the descendants of the earlier wave of immigration, the white Anglo-Saxon Protestants (W.A.S.P.). However, to be white in America is by no means an assurance of an adequate living standard. A particular problem of the South for example are the 'poor whites', a shiftless, largely illiterate rural proletariat living in slums on appallingly low incomes.

8.2. Negroes

8.2.1.

Negroes in the U.S.A. number 22.7 million (1970), more than the total population of Canada. They constitute 11 per cent of the U.S. population and have a higher birth rate than whites. They are descendants of the Negro slaves imported until 1808 when the slave trade was prohibited by provision of the Constitution. However, slavery itself was abolished at that time only in the Northern states.

The sharp contrast between the social systems of North and South led to a bitter conflict in the Civil War (1861–65). After the victory of the North, the Negroes were given citizenship and the right to vote (p. 17).

In the Southern states, however, traditional prejudice prepetuated discrimination. Negroes continued to be barred from white schools, public offices and amenities and to be deterred from voting by state laws and private intimidation. As a reaction to the pro-Negro policy of Northern 'reconstructionists' in the South, whites formed the Ku Klux Klan, a secret society practising political assassination by sentencing Negroes to death at secret trials staged during the night. It was not uncommon for Negroes to be lynched on the spot by fanatical crowds. Until recently, Negroes in the South were barred from white schools, hotels, restaurants, movies, bathing beaches, and churches. Marriages between whites and Negroes were forbidden.

For all these reasons, Negroes began to migrate to the North where they found work in the rapidly growing industrial cities. Harlem, New York's black ghetto, has become the world's principal black metropolis.

Even in the North, however, Negroes face discrimination and live in restricted areas, since whites tend to leave living quarters to which Negro families move. Poverty has made Negro ghettos hotbeds of riots and crime.

8.2.2.

The discrimination against Negroes led to a strong civil rights movement. At the beginning of the 20th century, the eminent Negro author and editor, W. E. Du Bois, who later led the movement for the liberation of African colonies, fought for the black cause with many publications like *Souls of Black Folk*, 1903, and became the idol of the Negro intellectuals in the U.S.A. It was largely owing to his influence that in 1909 the National Association for the Advancement of Coloured People (N.A.A.C.P.) was founded to fight discrimination by social pressure and legal action. In 1942, an interracial group of divinity students in Chicago founded the Congress of Racial Equality (C.O.R.E.).

The civil rights movement entered into its decisive phase when, in 1954, a Supreme Court decision required schools of the public system to admit Negro children. This decision was opposed by powerful interests in the South and gave rise to Citizens' Councils, which, together with the revived Ku Klux Klan, grew into a vigorous anti-Negro movement, which was often backed by governors and senators.

The most strictly segregated states are South Carolina, Georgia, Alabama, Mississippi and Louisiana.

In the fifties and sixties, the civil rights movement, in which many well-meaning whites, especially students and clergy, took an active part, gained enormous impetus under the leadership of the Negro pastor, Dr. Martin Luther King, who conducted his struggle against discrimination on a basis of strict non-violence. As pastor of a Baptists church in Montgomery, Ala., he won his first victory in the historic bus boycott which he organized in Montgomery in 1955 when the authorities and the bus company were forced to abolish segregation in buses, and the Supreme Court declared the segregation laws of Alabama void. Dr. King established the Southern Christian Leadership Conference (S.C.L.C.), consisting chiefly of Negro Protestant ministers, to help improve the Negroes' conditions through peaceful mass demonstrations and marches. In August 1936, thousands of Negroes and whites marched to Washington to demonstrate under the motto: 'We are all God's children'. They were backed by the federal government under President Kennedy, who also protected demonstrators in Southern states against white mobs. In 1964, Dr. Martin Luther King won the Nobel Peace Prize. On April 4, 1968, he was murdered in Memphis, Ala., by an escaped criminal.

Dr. King's work has been continued by his friend, pastor Ralph David Abernathy, now president of the S.C.L.C., who, like him, believes in non-violence. In May 1968, he organized the march of the poor to Washington D.C. to compel Congress to speed up legislation against poverty.

Nevertheless King's assassination dealt a blow to the movement of non-violence, which split up into several groups, and also strengthened the influence of radicals.

8.2.3.

Already in the early sixties the Black Muslims (officically called the Nation of Islam), who asserted that Islam was the Negroes' original creed, had stimulated national pride and hatred of the whites. Their early leader, Malcolm X, a powerful agitator, challenged his adherents to decide the Negroes' cause with 'bullets rather than ballots'. He rejected integration and demanded the recognition of the Negro population as a separate nation, and the division of the U.S.A. into separate states for Negroes and whites. When, after a trip to Mecca, Malcolm indicated his willingness to co-operate with sincere white supporters of desegregation, he was shot dead in a rally in Harlem in 1965.

After his assassination, the radicals rallied behind new leaders, Stokeley Carmichael and Rap Brown. Carmichael had come to the fore as leader of the Students Non-Violent Coordinating Council (S.N.C.C.). Like C.O.R.E., S.N.C.C. had achieved its greatest successes through non-violent sit-ins and voter registration drives supported by white Americans. But the slow progress of desegregation resulted in a radical change in the policy of these organizations. In 1966, Carmichael coined the slogan of Black Power, which rejects integration and openly advocates violence. By 1966 there were riots in the black ghettos of many cities, partly put down by regular troops. In 1968, they recurred after the assassination of Dr. King. The number of black convicts in the country's prisons indicates to what extent repression and poverty in the ghettos lead to violence and crime.

8.2.4.

By 1966 the centre of racial conflict had shifted to California, where the B l a c k P a n t h e r s Party became the largest militant Negro group. Its founders, the ex-convict Huey Newton and Bobby Seale, demand complete black control of Negro areas, the arming of Negroes as a means of enforcing their recognition as a separate Afro-American nation, which is to be admitted to the U.N. The literary exponent of the movement is the ex-convict Eldridge Cleaver.

The permanent state of war existing between the Black Panthers and the police has caused many casualties. In 1970, the conflict came to a head when the so-called Soledad brothers, three black militants, who were serving sentences in Soledad Prison in northern California, were on trial on the charge of having murdered a guard in Soledad. In a one-man attempt to free his brother George Jackson, Jonathan Jackson seized members of the court as hostages in the court room. In the ensuing gun battle, the judge, two convicts and Jonathan Jackson were killed. George Jackson (who had spent seven years of his ten-year sentence in solitary confinement), was later killed in an attempt to escape from St. Quentin Prison.

In 1970, the young black philosophy teacher, Angela Davis, a former student of Professor Herbert Marcuse, was discharged by the University of California on account of her inflammatory Communist speeches. In 1972, she was tried on the counts of conspiracy, kidnapping and murder because she had purchased the guns involved in the court-room raid to free her friend George Jackson. Her trial, which was followed with passionate interest by her sympathizers, especially students, throughout the world, ended with her acquittal on all charges. Angela Davis, who has been called the Black Joan of Arc because of her integrity and courageous fight against repression, has become an idol of white as well as black socialists throughout the world.

Black militancy has caused a dangerous white backlash. Plans for the building of model towns to replace Negro slums were blocked, and President Johnson had to ask Congress to appropriate funds for the police rather than for the clearing of slums.

8.2.5.

In spite of everything, there have been marked improvements. In the sixties, a number of Civil Rights Acts were passed (pp. 36, 40). Lynchings have decreased to 1 per cent a year of their former level. In the last decade, blacks nearly doubled their incomes (although they still earn less than two thirds as much as whites). The opening of black-run shops and factories by ghetto community groups in several cities has promoted the cause of 'black capitalism'.

An increasing number of Negroes advance into leading positions as doctors, teachers and officials. Negroes sit in legislatures, and there are more than a hundred black mayors in the U.S.A. Ralph Bunche, the U.N. Mediator between Israel and the Arab countries, and the civil rights leader, Dr. Martin Luther King, both won the Nobel Peace Prize.

Individual Negroes have played a part in cultural life. Early in this century Booker T. Washington, who was born in a slave hut, rose to become an influential Negro educator and reformer. His autobiography *Up from Slavery*, 1901, was translated into eighteen languages. George Washington Carver gained distinction as a scientist, Mary Anderson as a concert singer. Louis Armstrong and Duke Ellington won fame as 'kings of jazz'. Gordon Parks and Melvin Van Peebles are successful independent film producers, who brought on a 'black movie boom'. New York has a militant black theatre and exhibitions of Afro-American art. There are a large number of black newspapers. Black Panther leaders are interviewed on television. Many schools and universities have initiated programmes in Black Studies. Pop culture cultivates black styles not only in music but also in fashion, which propagates the Afro-look under the motto: *Black is Beautiful*.

Several Negroes have gained literary distinction, Laughton Hughes as a poet,

James Baldwin and LeRoy Jones as novelists. In recent years, black literature has begun to deal with revolutionary themes. George Jackson's book *Soledad Brother*, a collection of letters from prison, and Eldridge Cleaver's *Soul on Ice* became world bestsellers. *The Autobiography of Malcolm X*, which describes the development of the most dynamic Negro leader from utter poverty, crime and imprisonment to leadership as a Muslim minister ending in final frustration, is one of the most remarkable documents of the Negro tragedy.

8.3. Indians

8.3.1.

Indians number 523,600, i. e. 0.25 per cent of the total U.S. population. About 350,000 live in reservations.

It is estimated that at the time of the arrival of the white man about 2.5 million Indians occupied the area covered today by the continental United States. Hunting tribes in the northern and eastern forests lived a nomadic life, while the Pueblo Indians in the Southwest, who grew crops by primitive irrigation methods, lived in permanent homes in adobe towns and cliff dwellings, which are the only traces of an ancient Indian civilization north of Mexico.

8.3.2.

Contact with the whites changed the Indians' material life, but did not help to integrate them into a new American nation.

When the white man brought the horse to America, agriculturists on the edge of the Plains abandoned their garden patches and became buffalo hunters. Sheep provided a new subsistence for Indians in the Southwest. Firearms changed hunting habits and brutalized warfare. Other devastating effects of contact with the whites were diseases and epidemics. The Pilgrim Fathers considered it as divine intervention that an epidemic brought by foreign sailors had decimated the population of eastern Massachusetts shortly before their arrival. The missionary impulse which in the Spanish colonies helped to protect the Indian from white greed and introduced him to Christian culture was absent in British America. Nor were the early British colonists primarily fur traders like the French in Canada who needed the Indian's skill as a scout. The English colonists were farmers who coveted the Indian's land, and whether treaties were negotiated or not – if the land was needed, it was taken. The Indians who were driven from their hunting grounds were not only a nuisance, they became a danger.

Thus, apart from a few instances in which friendly relations existed for a time, as in

Quaker Pennsylvania, the early history of the British colonies was an endless succession of raids and wars, in which colonial governments offered bounties for Indian scalps. These wars strained British resources to such a degree that, in 1763, the government issued a proclamation restricting the westward movement of British settlers, but the migration was resumed with all the greater vigour after the colonies had separated from Britain.

8.3.3.

The westward movement brought in its wake the ruthless displacement of Indian tribes, which was abetted by the Bureau of Indian Affairs established in 1824. President Jackson, who had been reared on the frontier and embodied its views on Indians, denounced the government's practice of negotiating treaties with tribes as though they were independent nations as 'an absurdity' and 'a farce'. Under his influence, Congress sanctioned the *Removal Bill* of 1830, which proposed to bring about the forced emigration of the Indians at a cost of $500,000.

As they were moved from place to place, often under armed guard, as diseases and unaccustomed climates took their toll, the tribes were decimated and were finally settled in reservations in the arid parts of the West, which were of no apparent use to the whites.

The merciless extinction of the buffalo herds during the settlement of the Great Plains had already doomed the buffalo Indians. Pressure was now brought to bear even on the Indian Territory west of Arkansas and Missouri. In Oklahoma, where some 25 tribes had been located, about 20,000 white settlers were, at the firing of a gun at noon on April 22,1889, allowed to flock over the frontier and stake out claims on Indian land (cf. Edna Ferber's novel *Cimarron*).

8.3.4.

Between 1850 and 1934, a new policy of cultural assimilation sponsored by philanthropic organizations tried to civilize the Indians by missionary and educational efforts and by introducing them to private property. None of these policies, however, proved a success. The Indians resented missionary activities by a people that had robbed and humiliated them. The young Indians who returned from off-reservation boarding schools to their families were regarded as outsiders. An Indian spokesman explained that they became bad runners, susceptible to cold and hunger, 'neither fit for hunters, warriors nor counsellors'. Day schools, where frustrated teachers often resorted to corporal punishment, enjoyed no greater popularity. In 1887, the *Dawes Severalty Act* provided for individual allotments to Indians on the assumption that these would not rouse the greed of whites to such an extent as enormous tribal lands claimed by no definite individual.

But severalty proved a failure. Whites immediately took advantage of the Indians' aversion to work in the fields by leasing the Indian allotments at ridiculously low rents. The 'oil Indians', who attracted much publicity in the twenties, were easy targets for salesmen and swindlers. Moreover, the lands in the Indian reservations not needed for allotments to members of the tribe were opened to settlement. As a consequence, more than half the land that had been tribal property was sold to whites. The desert in the Southwest, which was undesirable to the whites, remained reservation territory, where Indians were allowed to continue their accustomed way of life as sheep and cattle herders.

However, certain governmental efforts on behalf of the Indians did bring improvements.

8.3.5.

In 1924, Indians were granted citizenship. In the individual states, however, they did not receive voting rights until the forties. The Roosevelt Administration reverted to a policy of community ownership, spending vast amounts of money to repurchase land and provide for Indian agricultural and industrial projects. The development scheme for reservations devised by the Bureau of Indian Affairs included irrigation of dry land, reclamation of eroded soil and the construction of roads and new houses to replace the dirt and timber huts. Indians who wished to leave their reservation were helped to find employment and buy farms.

All this has had a significant effect on Indian morale and helped to further a Pan-Indian movement. The improvement of medical services is reflected in the steadily declining death rate after 1930. The Indians are now on the increase, numbering 523,600 as against 250,000 in 1900. Their life expectancy, however, is still only 44 years as against 70 among whites.

8.3.6.

A problem which has not yet been solved is the high rate of alcoholism and arrests for offences arising from excessive drinking. The authorities try to mitigate this state of affairs, which arises from inadequate leisure-time facilities and escapism, by encouraging Indians to revive their ancient handicrafts, such as pottery and blanket weaving, in order to help them achieve greater financial independence. Another handicap is the Indians' cultural diversity, reflected in more than a hundred different Indian languages.

Although the reservation is an anachronism in modern America, a feasible alternative is difficult to find in view of the fact that the Indian is far less susceptible to cultural adaptation than the Negro. Unemployment is still ten times as great as among the white population. On the other hand, 'reservation Indians', as semiwards of the federal government, are not subject to taxation.

8.3.7.

In a few places, Indians themselves have made efforts to promote their education. The first higher educational institution founded by Indians is Navajo Community College in the reservation of the Navajo Indians in Arizona.

Spurred on by the successes of the Black Power movement, by the discrimination under official Indian policy and, above all, the disparagement of the Indians in films and television, the various tribes in both the U.S.A. and Canada have organized themselves into a Red Power movement. They try to draw attention to their plight through symbolic acts, such as the occupation in 1973 of Wounded Knee, a historic trade post in South Dakota, where the last massacre of Indians by American cavalry took place in 1891. In 1972, Indians occupied the Bureau of Indian Affairs in Washington D.C. demanding more land, more self-government, and damages for wrongs done to them during the last 200 years.

8.4. Minor Ethnic Groups

8.4.1. Orientals

The Orientals, who constitute 0.35 per cent of the total population, settled chiefly on the Pacific coast about 1850 and were employed in mining and in building railways. C h i n e s e workers aroused the antagonism of Californian labour, because their lower living standard made them willing to work for lower wages, and were barred under the *Exclusion Acts* of 1882 and 1902. Immigration of J a p a n e s e labourers was prevented under an agreement concluded between Theodore Roosevelt and Japan in 1907. In World War II, the Japanese along the West coast were interned, as they were considered a threat to the security of the U.S.A. The Chinese are most numerous in San Francisco, where they inhabit a separate quarter, Chinatown, but they are common in the East as well, particularly as laundrymen and restaurant keepers. The F i l i p i n o s came to America after the U.S.A. took possession of the Philippines in 1898. Filipinos live today primarily in Hawaii and on the West coast. Orientals comprise over half the population of Hawaii, where they are totally integrated into the social fabric.

8.4.2. Puerto Ricans

The Puerto Ricans, whose mother tongue is Spanish, occupy a unique position in America. The Caribbean island of Puerto Rico was annexed at the end of the Spanish-American War. The population of the island has today reached nearly 3,000,000, but its relationship to the U.S.A. has never been fully clarified. In 1952, a group of armed members of the Puerto Rican independence movement opened fire from the visitors' gallery of the U.S. House of Representatives, wounding several Congressmen. Thus Congress was finally made aware of the need for action; but, unable to decide between independence and statehood, they settled for a middle course. Thus Puerto Rico is today neither a territory nor a state, but a semi-independent 'Commonwealth'. This special status allows the Puerto Ricans freedom of movement to the mainland. Largely in the hope of economic improvement, they have migrated in hundreds of thousands to major American cities. Following the traditional pattern of newly arrived ethnic groups, they have congregated in the poorest sections of the cities, often living under conditions similar to those in the worst Negro slums. By sheer force of numbers, they have become a major political factor in New York City. In recent years economic improvements in Puerto Rico have stemmed this influx, and now the number of Puerto Ricans returning to the islands is about equal to those leaving.

8.4.3. Chicanos

In the states along the Mexican border live Spanish-speaking Americans of Mexican parentage known as Chicanos. Like the Puerto Ricans, they came to the U.S.A. in the hope of economic betterment. They found employment principally on the fertile irrigated farms of the region, where they followed the crops and the harvest season. As migrant workers they became the most exploited part of all America's labour force. Their constant movement from place to place has virtually deprived them of the vote and their children of an adequate education. Recent efforts to unionize have brought them the beginnings of a political organization. When the employers refused to deal with the unions, they found themselves confronted with boycotts of their products. These student-organized boycotts had the secondary effect of bringing the plight of migrant workers to the attention of the American press.

8.4.4. Eskimos

In the remotest regions of Alaska live 50,000 Eskimos, a people of Mongolian ancestry. They are a peace-loving people, unable to prevent the white man from taking their best land, unable to resist his diseases and his alcohol. They live by fishing under the most primitive conditions. Recently, the discovery of the vast oil reserves of the North Slope, which lie largely under land owned by Eskimos, has brought them at least a hope of being able to participate in the American dream.

9. American Society

9.1. The American Dream of a Classless Society

One of the chief factors which have formed American society is the belief in the equality of all human beings characteristic of the Age of Reason, the period when the U.S.A. was formed. This idea is the philosophical root of the American dream of a classless society where the common man is free to build his life in accordance with his natural abilities. 'Life, liberty and the pursuit of happiness' are pointed out by the Declaration of Independence as fundamental, inalienable rights, whose protection constitutes the only justification of governmental authority. These beliefs have encouraged a confidence in progress and perfectibility which applies to the civilization created by man as well as to man himself.

Although the classless society has so far been realized only to a very limited extent, it is an interesting fact that among the highly industrialized nations of the world, America is the only country which has no socialist party of any importance which represents the interests of the working class. Even trade unionism was not a significant factor until the Great Depression, which destroyed the traditional belief that in the U.S.A. any man can eventually earn enough money to become an independent businessman or even an employer himself.

The fact that, at the time when the U.S.A. was founded, fifty per cent of the population in the South were legally considered as chattels did not disturb the American dream in an age in which slavery was an accepted social pattern. Growing awareness of the debt 'the classless society' owed to its members was the main cause of a civil war which resulted in the abolition of slavery but did not solve the problem of racial discrimination.

9.2. Pluralism and Distrust of Authority

Another important characteristic of American society is its pluralism, the general assumption being that the free competition of a large number of interests makes for efficiency, and thus, ultimately, for progress. The lobby of rival pressure groups (e. g. ethnic minorities, social, industrial and agrarian interests) forms a legalized part of political life, which public opinion tends to accept more readily than it accepts governmental authority.

The distrust of authority in political life, a legacy from the colonial period, has, in the course of time been mitigated by the average citizen's belief in the sacredness of political institutions. It has, however, remained a motif in other spheres, e. g. in American child rearing. The American father often exercises guidance only by contenting himself with playing the part of a big brother to his son and helping him to develop resolution and an independent spirit in the natural rivalry of children of his own age. This may have contributed to giving the American that greater ease in his behaviour towards persons of superior standing which has often been noted.

The leniency of American parents tends to encourage a freedom of behaviour in their children which sometimes develops into rowdyism. This, again, is in keeping with the inveterate American belief in individual strength which is glorified in books and films. It appeared in the industrial cut-throat competition of the early 'captains of industry' as well as in the criminal methods used by some trade unions to enforce membership, and in the practices of the gangs which plague America's big cities.

A new distrust of authority appears in the young people's lack of veneration for anything representing age and tradition. This attitude is fostered by their disillusionment with what to them seem the cheap slogans of a hypocritical establishment (cf. the humorous maxim: "Don't trust anybody over thirty!").

9.3. The Influence of Religion

The influence of religion on American life has always been strong. A stimulus provided from the earliest days of colonization was the Puritan settlers' belief that they were God's chosen people, called to take possession of their promised land. The Calvinist doctrine of predestination became a basis of the American work ethic. The belief that success was a visible sign of God's grace, which man cannot acquire by good works, inspired the wish to achieve success through hard work.

The evangelical Protestantism of the 19th century added the principle of charity, which makes it as obligatory to dispose of wealth as the belief in success makes it desirable to acquire it. In no country of the world has property ruthlessly acquired been so lavishly distributed in charities and public endowments as in the U.S.A. This is particularly obvious in the world-wide support of scientific, educational and humanitarian activities by the Rockefeller, Carnegie and Ford foundations.

The effectiveness of private charity may have been one of the factors preventing socialist thought from gaining influence in American society, all the more so as trade unions have often proved just another embodiment of big business. The conception of social welfare as an obligation of the government came later in the U.S.A. than in most other countries. The American attitude towards Communism has been determined by social factors and Christian rejection of atheist ideologies as much as by aversion to Stalinist tyranny.

9.4. Public Spirit and Gregariousness

The tradition of participatory democracy has encouraged interest in public issues, which are promoted by associations and clubs of all kinds. Associations for political and humanitarian activities have had a far greater influence on public life than in most other countries except Britain. The abolitionist movement in the 19th century, the civil rights movement, the opposition of a large part of the population to the Vietnam War, Ralph Nader's team of young idealists fighting corruption have significantly influenced national policies.

Among the groups encouraging a vigorous community life, perhaps the most important are the religious congregations, to which 60 per cent of the population belongs. Their social activities range from tea parties, music and drama to charities and public campaigns. The Young Men's and Young Women's Christian Associations (Y.M.C.A. and Y.W.C.A.) mainly take care of young people in large cities. A number of bigger social organizations are engaged in charitable activities. The Lions Club carries on a programme of aid to the blind, the Masons – like the Elks, a secret fraternal organization – have hospitals and homes for orphan children and the aged. The Rotary Club, whose members are generally chosen from those holding leading positions in their communities, has grown into an international organization. Its membership is consciously chosen to represent as wide a variety of professions and interests as possible.

The general gregariousness continues at weekends and during holidays on overcrowded camping sites, which reproduce the classless society. The camping sites are symptomatic of another feature of American society: the mobility of a nation forever on the move, which may be observed in working as well as in dwelling habits. It appeared in the 19th century in rural areas where farmers often abandoned their land several times when the soil was exhausted.

A feature which strikes Europeans as one of the essentials of American society is its uniformity, which was favoured by the ideal of the classless society and early mass production. To possess the same things as other people, to 'keep up with the Joneses' has become an obsession. It is the tragedy of the Negroes that, despite a pronounced tendency towards adaptation to the white man's habits, they have been mercilessly discriminated against because they have not been physically assimilated. The same holds true to a lesser extent for the Chinese and Japanese, the Mexican Americans and Puerto Ricans. This discrimination against the less easily assimilated elements appears in their virtual exclusion from the whites' residential areas, which constitute one of America's main status symbols.

9.5. Women

It has been pointed out that women in American society have a status higher than in any other country. The roots of this development lie in the pioneer era when the scarcity of women made them a contested prize among rivalling males. Modern trends have helped to increase the importance of women in the family as well as in public life. The great demand from America's highly developed industry for labour encourages women of all ages to seek employment. Many married women go back to work when their children have grown up. Through legislation favouring equal opportunities and under pressure from the Women's Liberation Movement, women are increasingly admitted to higher positions in the professions as well as in political institutions. They have always been a majority in the teaching profession, thus wielding an important influence in education.

Lately, women have gained considerable importance in economic life, not only because they are (much more than in Europe) aware of their economic power as the decisive consumers of the nation, but also because they own about half the nation's houses and (especially as widows and heirs to big fortunes) half the stock of the great corporations.

The sex revolution of the sixties has accelerated the emancipation of women in private life too. It has made women the main topic of magazines and show business. The Puritan ideal of chastity has been widely superseded by greater freedom in sex life. Despite this development, however, the ultimate aim of most American women is the economic and social security of married life (reaching for the man's cheque book, as the critics would say); the great number of early marriages testify to this. Even in this sphere, however, the woman often dominates in the personal relationship between man and wife as well as in the children's education, where the rejection of authority as the basis of parental influence has reduced the father's importance in favour of the mother's.

Interest in public issues is a distinguishing mark particularly of the older generation of women. In innumerable clubs, these women, who are often ridiculed, pursue their social and cultural aims with the greatest dedication, and have, through their struggle against corrupt practices in local government, become a potent force in American life. Thus the League of Women Voters, for instance, has become influential in American politics. The National Organization for Women (N.O.W.) has lately conducted a campaign against television programmes which they feel degrade women in sexist scenes. The radical Women's Liberation Movement wants to do away with a society dominated by men.

In 1973, the emancipation of women in the sexual sphere was advanced by a momentous Supreme Court decision, which declared abortion laws to be in conflict with the Bill of Rights.

Comment on the American woman in general ranges from praise of her as the most modern and independent woman in the world, endowed with exceptional initiative, to her depreciation as the most self-centred, dissatisfied and restless of creatures, less feminine and individual than women in other countries.

9.6. Sex Revolution

What is generally termed the sex revolution came later in the U.S.A. than is generally assumed by Europeans. In the fifties, the Kinsey Reports of the Institute for Sexual Research at the University of Indiana first drew sexual behaviour from the twilight of mystery into the open field of public investigation. In the sixties the development of birth control methods helped to remove sexual taboos from the contact of young people, doing away with the last remnants of Puritan morality. Today, there is nothing that plays a greater part in discussions, publications and films than sex. Teenage flirtation had long been an institutionalized form of early sexual behaviour in the American practice of dating. A boy invited a girl to some public entertainment, which was usually connected with the consumption of a meal or a pizza, and ended when the boy took the girl home in the car borrowed from his parents. This usually led to sexual play, which was not supposed to go beyond 'petting' and 'necking', the assumption being that such dates were not to lead to permanent love affairs. For dating was also considered a test of social success and popularity, the girl's ambition being to get as many invitations as possible, the boy's aim to get a date with the most popular girl. This behaviour could of course develop into the more exclusive relationship of 'going steady'.

The desire for emotional security has, however, since the sixties, encouraged a new pattern of 'going steady', which approves of more intimate relations. Thus it has become common for young people to live together away from their parents soon after leaving school.

These practices have, in spite of the invention of the birth-control pill, resulted in a considerable increase in the number both of illegitimate births and of premature marriages, as abortion is still penalized in most states. Such premature marriages and the general trend to mistake sex for love keep the divorce rate higher than in other countries. Particularly in well-to-do circles, where the temptation to sacrifice the emotional security of children for a life of dissipation and pleasure is greater than among the lower classes, the neglect of children tends to create the very neuroses which American education is so anxious to spare them, and encourages juvenile delinquency.

Today free love, seen as a natural activity conducive to the physical and psychological health of both sexes is openly engaged in by many young people. Hippies added the new pattern of group sex, in which full promiscuity blends with religious dreams of universal peace and brotherhood.

9.7. Decline of Individualism

In contrast to the free behaviour of the young, the majority of the people who have been integrated into the 'establishment' find their lives being more and more manipulated by the impersonal forces of big business and 'big government'. Since the thirties, the gigantic economic problems of the country, the need for social welfare, and the struggle against corruption and crime have given the central government the very power the American Constitution had sought to prevent with its system of checks and balances. Government agencies connected with national defence and security employ hundreds of thousands of people, who find even their private lives controlled by security regulations. In his book *The Organization Man*, 1956, William H. Whyte calls attention to the growing number of scientists, lawyers and doctors employed in the large impersonal organizations of the government or big business, which exert a greater control over their lives and social patterns than the traditional ties of social class, neighbourhood or church.

9.8. Youth Movement

The American youth movement is essentially a revolt against the subjection of the individual to the impersonal forces of the establishment. It began as a students' revolt on the campuses of the big universities, whose aims were voiced by the Students for a Democratic Society. The 'New Left' sympathized with other anti-establishment groups like the Black Panthers and the Revolutionary Action Movement.

The majority of the young people, however, are not politically engaged. True to the American myth of total individual independence, they question the whole principle of a society tied to material values and do not feel social responsibility in the traditional sense. Shunning private property as detrimental to their freedom of movement, many leave or never take up steady jobs and often travel for years all over the world with nothing but a rucksack and a sleeping bag. Others gather in communes (largely in Western states) and engage in 'organic agriculture', i. e. avoiding the use of pesticides and chemical fertilizers. They do not worry about their future position in a society of abundance which can support members who do not make direct contributions to its economic progress. The accompanying lack of responsibility of purpose may account for the liberal use of drugs by some of these groups.

The Hippies, who received extensive news coverage during recent years, chiefly because of their sexual promiscuity, were only a part of this movement. Although politically largely inactive, they joined the protest against the Vietnam War with their slogan 'Make love, not war!'.

The growing alarm at the anarchical tendencies of many of these groups caused rigorous action on the part of the government and the law-enforcing agencies, which heralded the decline of militant student power and resulted in deep resignation among the young generation. The recent recession has added economic aspects to the general disillusionment. Students, intent on passing exams in order not to enlarge the rolls of the unemployed, are no longer interested in revolts. The gay Hippie movement has dissolved into scattered groups of begging 'street people'; their spokesman Timothy Leary, who had promised liberation through drugs, is imprisoned.
Even Black Panther militancy has declined.

9.9. A Decadent Society?

The facts that the U.S.A., which fought crusades against oppression, was for more than a decade engaged in a merciless war, that sexual promiscuity is beginning to break up public morality, that a large number of young people try to escape from reality with the help of drugs, which send ever increasing numbers into sanatoria, have jarred the American dream. Today, many Americans who believe that their country was called to world leadership are bewildered to find that much of the world looks upon America as a society doomed to decay and as a hotbed of violence. Even those among the younger generation who protest against brutality and corruption seem no longer able to contribute to society values that point towards a healthier and more humane future.
However, despite the present world-wide anti-Americanism, the American style of life, American principles of education, American publicity, the cult of youth, American jazz have permanently asserted their influence in Western countries.
Even the unhealthy sides of American life, the pursuit of money and pleasure, alcoholism and drug addiction, are being copied by young people who adore Mao and Che Guevara, and openly profess their contempt for the U.S.A.
The problem of American society seems to be that its very ideals tend to produce effects contrary to what was originally aimed at. Individualism tends to degenerate into brutal egotism, freedom into lack of discipline, mobility into rootlessness, lack of sophistication into what Europeans consider bad taste, democracy into uniformity and mediocrity.
Nevertheless critics of America should remain aware of the fact that millions of Americans, above all in the country and the small towns, lead a life governed by traditional standards of self-discipline, constituting a moderating force and a reserve of national strength. Even this way of life, however, now seems threatened by the modern trend towards mass urbanization.

10. The American Character

It is extremely difficult to define a national character, but in view of many widely held preconceptions, it may be useful to elaborate on certain traits arising out of the history of America.

The American character has its roots in two basic factors: the pioneer spirit of the early settlers, most of whom had left Europe to escape from poverty and oppression, and the belief in progress and perfection inherited from the Age of Reason during which the United States took shape. American energy and capacity for work may also be traced to the Puritan work ethic as a result of the belief in success as a visible sign of God's grace. Puritan energy and pioneer adventure have worked for a spirit of hardiness and youthful enterprise, sometimes degenerating into ruthlessness. This may be seen in the fights against the Indians as well as in a reckless scramble for economic gain – first in the exploitation of the nation's own resources, later in the underdeveloped countries of Latin America.

The belief in progress and perfection is the root of what has today become the most controversial side of the national character, American idealism. It is identical with the 'American Dream', the conviction that man is essentially good and has the noble task of creating a better world. It appears in its most naive form in the manly spirit of sacrifice with which the hero of the Western frees the community from the lawlessness of the villain, and the generosity with which he treats him after he has forced him to surrender. It may be found in the enthusiasm with which Americans in the first half of this century went to war convinced that they were fighting crusades for freedom against oppression. It appears in the generosity with which the very 'land of the dollar grabbers' rushes to the rescue of countries stricken by earthquakes, war or famine with fleets of supplies and medical help. After World War II, the most effective aid to the population of war-shattered countries came not only from American-supported official organizations, but also from C.A.R.E. parcels paid for by American individuals to relieve the hunger of their former enemies. The reckless scramble for gain is offset by an easy-going generosity, which prompts the American to dispose of property as readily as he acquires it, a liberality of spirit whose law is live and let live.

One of the roots of this carelessness about possessions is the abundant wealth of the nation; another aspect is the continuing American desire to be on the move in order to take advantage of ever new possibilities.

American restlessness, blending with an inveterate belief in progress and the practical ingenuity to achieve it, has provided the chief stimulus to technical advance and economic development. American ascendancy over other nations in nearly everything pertaining to material life is founded largely in the American genius for improving and perfecting things which in other civilizations have been accepted as final solutions for centuries. It seems ironic that the same nation which, through its invention of mass production, has made the benefits of material civilization, formerly enjoyed by a privileged minority, available to everybody has also provided the world with the perfection of destructive power in its nuclear and chemical weapons. Their general preoccupation with material things, going hand in hand with a lack of spiritual penetration, has subjected the Americans to much criticism. European students and visitors from Europe tend to be struck by the superficiality of talk and interests, and the young generation in America itself begins to revolt against the materialism of their elders, against the fact that a nation of pioneers has become a complacent society of manageable consumers and television viewers.

A lack of cultured sophistication has by no means always been an American characteristic. The Puritans of New England cherished an austere religious and intellectual culture, and the Southern aristocracy cultivated the joys of a gracious way of life. Puritan intellectualism might still be traced in a capacity for logical systematization and a consequent disinclination to compromise which distinguishes Americans from their Anglo-Saxon brothers across the Atlantic, though both nations share a fundamentally pragmatic approach to life. The fact that the vast U.S.A. is ruled according to a clear-cut document of ten pages supplemented by some twenty amendments, while the so-called British Constitution is nothing but a maze of individual laws and conventions, is symptomatic.

However, it was not the sophisticated heirs to the culture of the old continent, but the adventurous settlers pushing farther west who became the dominant force in shaping the character of modern America. The plodding, hard reality of life in the Western settlements has contributed to the American character as much as the myth of the pioneer hero, who was as rough and reckless as he was liberal-minded, open-hearted and hospitable. Both influences gave the new type of American his buoyant optimism and energy as well as his inclination towards unquestioning contentment with personal and national achievements.

The democratic school in which the nation was reared has added other strains to its character: a passionate community spirit – especially in smaller towns –, a generous acceptance of criticism in public life, the readiness to investigate and punish wrong (e. g. trials of war crimes committed by servicemen in Vietnam and Watergate) and a tolerance of other people's views, which has its roots also in the coexistence of a vast number of religious creeds brought over by the immigrants.

A gregarious spirit appears in the unbounded hospitaliy of the American as well as in his habit of joining clubs and engaging in community activities of all kinds. The fact that in many American suburbs there are virtually no fences between people's yards is again symptomatic. The American cocktail party may be seen as a symbol of the American pleasure in meeting other people, even with no end but superficial talk in view.

It was only after the two World Wars that many of the characteristics developed in the era of Manifest Destiny changed. The 'lost generation' after World War I abandoned the optimism of the prewar era and developed a new realization of the tragedies of life, which found its expression in the great novels of the twenties and thirties. After World War II, the growing influence of American educational theory and psycho-analysis and the spectacular achievements of American science and technology created a new respect for intellectual activity, which gave America a lead in education, letters and science, and produced a new, more subtle self-respect. John F. Kennedy introduced a new intellectualism into politics. The anti-establishment groups rebel against American materialism and militarism, and, by engaging themselves in the civil rights movement on behalf of the Negroes, work for a more humanitarian outlook on life.

It remains to be seen whether the general bewilderment in America today is a symptom of approaching maturity, or whether sexual promiscuity and the high rate of drug addiction and crime are signs of an approaching decline.

11. Government

The U.S.A. is a federal republic consisting of fifty states having their own governmental, judicial and educational systems.

The American flag has fifty stars, representing the fifty states, and thirteen stripes indicating the thirteen colonies which became the original states of the Union.

The U.S.A. has territorial dependencies ruled from Washington: Puerto Rico and the Virgin Islands in the Caribbean, Guam and Samoa in the Pacific. The District of Columbia (D.C.), in which the national capital, Washington, lies, is also ruled as a territory by the federal government, although it has recently gained a measure of self-government.

11.1. The American Constitution

The American Constitution, which is, unlike the British, a written document, is the oldest constitution still in force, and America's greatest contribution to modern political thought.

The first plan of a national government, the Articles of Confederation, which had been drawn up during the War of Independence, had created a loose union of states, giving only limited powers to the central government. It did not provide for a national executive or judiciary, and the legislative assembly it established had only limited law-making powers and no taxation rights.

In 1787, a convention of 55 delegates, including George Washington and Benjamin Franklin, was called to Philadelphia to revise the Articles of Confederation. Instead they produced a document outlining a far more powerful central government for the thirteen states.

The three main controversies raised by the diverging interests of the thirteen states were solved by three compromises. The Great Compromise met the demands of the small as well as the large states with regard to representation in the legislative assembly by giving Congress two Houses. The House of Representatives was to be elected by popular vote according to the population of the various states. The Senate, to which two senators were to be elected by the legislature of each state, was to represent the interests of the states. The bicameral system prevailed over Jefferson's and Franklin's concept of a 'simple democracy' representing the common will, because it was also considered as a safeguard against rash legislation by one popular assembly reflecting fickle public opinion.

The Three-Fifths Clause settled the controversy between North and South as to whether the Southern slaves were to count as population for the purposes of representation in the House of Representatives. It allowed three fifths of a state's slaves to be counted as population for the purpose of representation.

Finally the commercial interests of the agricultural South and the industrial North were balanced by giving Congress the power to regulate not only foreign trade but also interstate commerce.

In the course of time the Constitution has been supplemented by a number of amendments, most of which were designed to guarantee the rights of the individual or of underprivileged groups. The first ten amendments, known as the Bill of Rights (p. 131), guarantee freedom of speech and religion, and protection against executive action without due process of law.

Amendments 13, 14, 15 gave Negroes the rights of citizenship, including the vote. The fact that Southern states continued to keep Negroes from the polls eventually made the federal government and the Supreme Court the main agents for assuring Negroes equality of voting rights. Female suffrage, first introduced in the state of Wyoming in 1869, was made nation-wide under Amendment 19, 1920.

Amendment 16, 1913, which empowered the federal government to tax incomes directly, was to increase the federal revenues immensely.

Amendment 17, 1913, provided that senators were to be elected by direct popular vote. Amendment 22, 1951, prohibited any President from serving more than two terms.

Today, the Constitution, including the amendments, is a document of about fifteen printed pages, which meets the complex requirements of a highly sophisticated society in which the legislature faces more than 10,000 bills and resolutions in a two-year session. This simplicity, conciseness and adaptability may explain the frequently mentioned 'reverence' which Americans feel for their constitution.

11.2. Federal Government

11.2.1. Branches of Government

Executive power consists of the President, the Vice-President and Cabinet. The President (minimum age 35) and the Vice-President are elected for four years by popular vote through an electoral college. The President is the Chief Executive and the Commander-in-Chief of the Armed Forces. He is limited to two terms of office.

The Cabinet (not provided for in the Constitution) consists of Secretaries (heads of departments), who are chosen by the President independently of the Congressional majority. Their appointment is subject to the approval of the Senate.

Legislative power is represented by the Congress.

The House of Representatives is the lower House with a membership currently fixed at 435. Representatives (minimum age 25) are elected for two years according to population to represent the country as a whole.

The Senate is the upper House, consisting of two senators from each state (i. e. 100 in all). A minimum age of 30 and a six-year term of office with re-election of only one third of the senators every two years were intended to guarantee stability of policy.

Judicial power is entrusted to a system of federal courts. The Supreme Court is the highest court of appeal with the power to annul laws as unconstitutional.

11.2.2. Checks and Balances

As a result of experiences in the colonial period, when laws made by colonial legislatures had often been overruled by the authorities in England, the American Constitution has established a balance of power which prevents the various branches of government or the central government itself from becoming too strong.

The simple fact that the U.S.A. is a federal republic allows the national government to exercise only such powers as were delegated to it in the Constitution.

A rigid system of checks and balances controls the various branches of government. Cabinet members have no seats or votes in Congress, and the President himself is allowed only to deliver 'messages' to Congress. The President's appointments and treaties must be approved by the Senate. In contrast to Britain, where the latest enactment of Parliament supersedes any provision of earlier statutory law, congressional legislation may be annulled by the Supreme Court (which happened frequently in the thirties when the cry for a strong government during the Great Depression gave the President unprecedented influence over Congress, thus creating a threat of dictatorship).

11.2.3. The President

The U.S.A. is a presidential democracy. The President is official head of the Union and active leader of the government, whereas in most other democracies the two offices are divided between a monarch or president and the prime minister. American presidents are thus more powerful than chief executives in countries with parliamentary democracies. Moreover, America's position as one of the world's 'super-powers' has made its president one of the central figures in world politics.

As the President's term of office is fixed independently of congressional elections, he is not dependent on the majority party in Congress. In contrast to most European democracies, he and the Cabinet members he chooses remain in office when a congressional election brings a new party to power.

Nevertheless his election is determined by the parties. The original provision of the Constitution was to permit the states every four years to choose 'electors', who should then select the President. The development of political parties has changed this process beyond all recognition. Candidates for President and Vice-President are now nominated in a complicated process of party caucuses and primaries (preliminary elections in the various states) extending over many months.

Once elected, the President has immense power and influence. He is charged with the execution of the laws and with informing Congress as to the state of the Union. He can also recommend and veto legislation. He is Commander-in-Chief of the Armed Forces. He can pardon offenders against federal laws. He appoints officials and concludes treaties subject to the consent of the Senate. As leader of the party that elected him, he holds the power associated with a popular mandate. The gigantic economic and social problems since the Great Depression have given the presidents the power of continuous intervention in the economic and social life of the country, exercised through departments and agencies directly administered by the President in what is known as the Office of the President.

The succession of international crises since World War II has further expanded presidential power. Roosevelt had been the chief organizer of the New Deal and the Allied war effort against Germany and Japan; Truman sought to unite the Western powers after the war with his Truman Doctrine. Johnson and Nixon conducted a prolonged war in Vietnam without a declaration of war. The way in which Nixon passed over Congress also in other major decisions, later aroused nation-wide criticism, which came to a head in the Watergate affair.

11.2.4. Congress

Although the two Houses of Congress are almost completely equal in legislative powers, the Senate, whose approval is required for the conclusion of treaties and presidential appointments, commands a greater prestige; it has far more influence than the upper House in Britain. In recent times, the work of its committees (e. g. for international affairs or the investigation of crime) has attracted world-wide attention.

Bills may be introduced in either House. They are at once referred to the appropriate committee of the House in which they have been introduced. When the bill has passed the committe stage, it is debated and voted on in both Houses. If a bill has been passed, it must be signed by the President. If he fails to do so, it becomes a law without his signature. If the President vetoes the measure, it is returned to Congress, which may then pass it over the President's veto by a two-thirds majority in each House. Rarely are vetoed bills subsequently passed by Congress.

The growing power of American presidents in recent decades tended to diminish the authority of Congress. It was only through the Watergate Affair, which raised the question whether the President would have to be impeached (p. 48), that Congress regained some of its original authority. Watergate proved to be one of the severest trials of America's constitutional form of government.

11.2.5. The Lobby

Private interests often form economic, social, religious or racial pressure groups, which seek to influence members of Congress in the lobbies of the legislature. The uncontrolled influence of these 'lobbies' caused various states to introduce measures to regulate their activities. In 1946, Congress enacted the *Federal Lobbying Act* requiring lobbyists to register with the Clerk of the House and the Secretary of the Senate.

The American public, far from holding the view sometimes expressed in European countries that lobbying is but a form of institutionalized corruption, considers these private pressure groups as virtually parts of the machinery of government. A 1964 report of the Senate Foreign Relations Committee states that 'lobbying has always played a necessary part in our democratic form of representative government. In effect it is the institutionalization of the people's constitutional right to petition their government'.

11.2.6. Federal Administration

Federal Administration is carried out by the various departments of the executive branch (the equivalents of ministries), which are headed by a Secretary and staffed with officials recruited from the Classified Civil Service on the basis of competitive examinations.

11.2.6.1. Departments are not mentioned in the Constitution. They developed gradually as the business of government expanded and had to be organized in responsible, competent agencies. The first to appear were the Departments of State and of War and the Treasury. Then came the departments of Justice, of the Interior and of Agriculture. The problems of the 20th century gave rise to the departments of Labour and Defence (uniting Army, Navy and Air Force), the Department of Housing and Urban Development, and the Department of Health, Education and Welfare.

Today, most departments have a number of different, often loosely related responsibilities.

The State Department for foreign policy is also in charge of cultural exchange, disarmament, and international technical and economic aid.

The Department of the Interior is responsible for U.S. territories, Indian affairs, water and power resources, fisheries and wildlife, national parks, public lands, oil and mineral resources. The Department of Justice deals with prosecutions, including anti-trust and civil rights (Negroes), prisons, immigration and naturalization.

11.2.6.2. Since the New Deal, agencies not formally designated as departments have gained and even exceeded the importance of many departments. These include the Federal Reserve System, the National Labour Relations Board, and the National Aeronautics and Space Administration. The heads of some of these now sit in the Cabinet on the invitation of the President. Some are gathered in the Office of the President, which also includes the National Security Council and its organ, the Central Intelligence Agency (C.I.A.) for political activities in foreign countries. There are also a number of important commissions (e. g. Atomic Energy, Interstate Commerce, Civil Rights, Subversive Activities), and corporations owned by the federal government, e. g. the Tennesse Valley Authority, the Panama Canal Company, the St. Lawrence Seaway Development Corporation.

As the government was drawn into more and more fields of national life, its work consistently moved from mere administration into the spheres of planning and research, leading to a close co-operation with universities and scientific institutes. N.A.S.A. (National Aeronautics and Space Administration) may be mentioned as probably the most spectacular example of this development.

The Cabinet, which consists of the heads of the departments and a few of the principal agencies, has never played as important a role as the British. Moreover, it has grown less effective as the government machinery grew too big to maintain collective consideration of major policies.

11.2.6.3. Secretaries of government departments are political appointments made by the President, who is free and, for that matter, even expected to choose men of his party in accord with his policies. The same is true of the under-secretaries and assistant secretaries and the chairmen of the independent commissions.

All other positions are filled by the Classified Civil Service, on the basis of merit (competitive examinations), and classified according to the work performed. The Classified Civil Service covers about one million employees, most of whom have permanent tenure.

However, 'officialdom' does not play the same part as in Europe. The American government makes much greater use of employees without permanent tenure. A streak of restlessness in the American character and the relatively greater prestige attached to a business career may account for this fact. Men move back and forth between business and government as personal advantage may dictate. Moreover, salaries are usually higher in industry.

11.3. State Governments

'The more perfect union' which the American Constitution sought to bring about could come into force only after ratification by the thirteen states. These were therefore granted the highest degree of autonomy consistent with an effective central government. When the West was settled in the 19th century, the new territories, which were first ruled from Washington, acquired statehood with equal rights when they had reached a population of 60,000.

Today, the U.S.A. consists of 50 states with their own constitutions, which hold the powers not specifically reserved by or delegated to the federal government. However, where a state law conflicts with a law of Congress, the federal law has precedence.

The governments set up under the state constitutions are not unlike the federal government. All the states except Nebraska have bicameral legislatures, most of which have biennial elections. All provide for a governor elected by the people, in most cases for a term of four years. In the majority of cases the voters also elect several state officials. In recent decades, however, there has been a tendency in many states to strengthen the power of the governor, to lengthen his term of office and to vest in him the exclusive right of appointing department heads.

The main responsibilities of state governments are education, public health, welfare, business, farming, roads and highways. A number of these functions, such as education and welfare, are shared with local governments. States may enter into compacts with each other, e. g. on water rights or industrial development, if they are approved by Congress. State militias (known as the National Guard) are integrated into the national defence system. Throughout American history there has been a tendency to concentrate more and more power in the hands of the federal government. Especially since the Great Depression, the national government has increased its influence through an extensive system of grants-in-aid to the states for their various social services. Its power to regulate interstate commerce has been widened at the expense of state commercial legislation. Moreover, organized labour has tended to make even labour questions a matter of federal legislation.

11.4. Local Government

Most of the fifty states have granted a considerable measure of autonomy to their local units, which often leads to overlapping and conflicting jurisdiction. All but three states are divided into counties, whose populations range from a few hundred in rural and mountainous areas to 7 million in Los Angeles.

11.4.1.

County governments consist of boards or councils with officials either popularly elected or chosen by the board. Counties are again subdivided into incorporated cities, boroughs and villages. In New England, the 'town' is the chief unit of rural local government, consisting of a village and a considerable amount of surrounding territory. Its governing authority is the town meeting, at which all eligible voters who care to attend meet to adopt ordinances and vote upon taxes and expenditures and to elect officials and school boards. These New England town meetings have become the original pattern of vigorous direct democracy in America. In the Midwest, 'townships' – originally legal districts fixed by surveyors for the purpose of subdividing and selling land – are the characteristic form of government for rural areas, in which small built-up communities organize further as villages or boroughs. These have their own locally elected board with a mayor or chairman.

11.4.2.

American cities have a much greater measure of self-government than their equivalents in Britain, the British boroughs. They are either governed by a charter usually framed by the state legislature or given discretion to draft their own municipal governments. Cities may be ruled by a mayor (ca. 42 %), a commission (ca. 13 %), or a city manager (ca. 45 %).

The government by a mayor is most similar to the system of national and state government. The mayor, who is elected independently of the council, usually appoints the heads of the departments. The council passes ordinances, adopts the budget and confirms the mayor's appointments. The division of powers between mayor and council varies, but the modern trend is, as in the national government, towards greater power for the chief executive. Correspondingly the commission type of government, which divides the functions of government between three to seven elected commissioners with collective responsibility has declined, as it lacks co-ordination of the various departments and hence centralized leadership.

The type of municipal government which is now most popularly adopted and has, like many other examples of American efficiency, attracted world-wide attention is the city manager rule. It provides for a council, which is the official law-making body and chooses the manager, who in his turn appoints the heads of the departments, presents the budget and makes policy recommendations to the council. City managers are not chosen on a political, partisan basis, but are career administrators; this has become a regular profession with its own organizations, publications and training. Cities under city managers are therefore usually run more efficiently and economically than cities with a mayoral government. Dynamic city managers have in some cases assumed more power than originally intended by this form of government. City management naturally implies the danger of a decline in civic spirit and interest. However, its emergence is also indicative of an altered conception of the city itself. Cities tend no longer to be seen as political units, but rather as highly complex technical organisms much like large corporations and thus best run by experts.

In most of the smaller communities, however, the long tradition of real self-government, which has been one of America's great achievements, furthering the values of differentiation and political education, has remained substantially unimpaired, and still makes for a marked sense of responsibility in national affairs as well.

11.5. Parties

The American Constitution makes no mention of parties, yet, from the beginning of U.S. history, parties have served to consolidate various opinions and interests into stable groupings striving to dominate the policies of the government. In the course of time, parties have become the chief agents in organizing the election of candidates for legislatures and the major political offices (e. g. presidents, governors, mayors).

The U.S.A., like Britain, may be considered as having a two-party system, although there have sometimes been 'third parties'. In the 19th century, the National Greenback Party and the Populist Movement stood for greater social justice and political influence for the common man (p. 20). In the 20th century, the Progressive Party endorsed these ideas in platforms demanding industrial and electoral reforms. In 1968, George Wallace's American Independent Party, which represented mainly the interests of the Southern whites, gained 10 million votes.

The great majority of the people, however, support the programme of one of the two great parties, Republicans and Democrats.

In early U.S. history, the Democratic Republicans respresented the interests of the individual states and the common man, while the Federalists favoured business interests and centralization. Owing to the pronouncedly democratic tendencies of the Democratic Republican Party under President Jackson, the party's name was changed to 'Democratic', while the Federalist Party disappeared. On the other hand, opposition of the educated classes to Jackson's tyrannical policy gave rise to a Whig Party with liberal tendencies. Between 1850 and 1860 the banking and industrial interests of the North, which came into conflict with the farming interests of the South and West, gave rise to a new Republican Party, the main agent in the Civil War on the Northern side. Since that time the Republican Party has stood in the South as the symbol of the repressive policy of 'reconstruction'. The working classes saw in it the exponent of big business. Thus both labour and

129

the farmers of the South joined forces in the Democratic Party. During the Kennedy and first Johnson administrations, however, the firm stand of the Democratic Party for integration of the Negro population alienated the reactionary forces in the South. Its liberal policy was held responsible for the encouragement of violence and immorality in an increasingly 'permissive society', and caused the conservative 'silent majority' to turn Republican. This decided the country's vote in the presidential elections of 1968 and 1972 in favour of Nixon.

12. Law

Law in the U.S.A. is based on legal principles inherited from English Common Law, which were re-embodied in the *Bill of Rights*, the first ten amendments to the American Constitution. These include freedom of speech and religion, the right of assembly and petition, security against unreasonable search and seizure, against excessive fines and cruel punishments. They guarantee the right of accused persons to a speedy and public trial by an impartial jury with all the safeguards against unfair procedure inherited from English Common Law.

The U.S.A. has no uniform legal code because each state has an independent legal system. State jurisdiction, however, is supplemented by a system of federal courts provided in the Constitution, which deal with all cases concerning the U.S.A. as a whole (e. g. cases arising under federal laws and treaties), with controversies between citizens of different states, and cases to which the U.S.A. or a state is a party. There are also cases of concurrent jurisdiction that can be decided in either a federal or a state court. As in England, statutes enacted by the legislatures override judge-made common law relying on precedent.

Equity, a legal inheritance from England, which grew out of petitions to the king to redress wrongs for which the law provided no remedy, is still used in cases where the common law does not apply. Equity procedures are less formal than regular court procedures, and no juries are used. Equity is designed to provide effective justice where damages after trial may come too late. Thus courts may issue injunctions to perform or restrain from an act, and violation of these injunctions constitutes contempt of court punishable by fine or imprisonment.

The diversity of the legal system in the U.S.A. has the advantage of flexibility, but lack of uniformity has in many respects also proved a disadvantage. Thus persons convicted of murder, who might have been sentenced to imprisonment and ultimately pardoned in another state, may be sentenced to death in a state with capital punishment. Marriage laws in Nevada make it possible to get an easy divorce after a few weeks' sojourn in the state.

12.1. Judicial Institutions

12.1.1. Department of Justice

Like Britain, the U.S.A. had originally no Department of Justice, section 1 of Article III of the Constitution providing that 'the judicial power of the United

States shall be vested in one Supreme Court and such inferior courts as the Congress may from time to time ordain to establish'. Owing to the great volume of legal work after the Civil War, however, Congress established a Department of Justice in 1870, in which the government's legal business was to be concentrated. Its best-known division is the Federal Bureau of Investigation (F.B.I.), which investigates serious crimes, rather like Scotland Yard in Britain.

12.1.2. Courts

In the states, the lowest courts are those held by justices of the peace (in rural areas) or by magistrates (in urban communities), who have no legal training and handle civil cases and minor offences in summary proceedings without a jury. In larger cities, special municipal courts consisting of numerous professional judges have a wider jurisdiction. At the higher level, county (circuit) courts conducted by judges on circuit in the various counties try more important civil and criminal cases from minor courts. From county courts it is possible to appeal to higher state courts of appellate jurisdiction, the State Supreme Court being the court of the last resort in the state.

In the federal system, the lowest courts are called district courts, having original jurisdiction in both civil and criminal cases. From district courts appeals can go to circuit courts of appeal. Cases decided by federal and the highest state courts may be taken on appeal to the United States Supreme Court, which may rule on the constitutionality of state or federal laws. Through the exercise of this power of judicial review, which is based on the assumption that the judiciary is to act as guardian of the Constitution, the Supreme Court has played a major part in the development of public policy throughout American history. Several hundred state laws and many laws of Congress have been declared unconstitutional by the Supreme Court. As the Supreme Court is composed of nine judges, and decisions are made by majority vote, much criticism has been aroused as to the validity of 5 to 4 votes, which have decided many important cases by what is referred to as a one-man decision. The immense political power the Supreme Court wields as judge of the validity of laws has made the appointment of Supreme Court judges a highly political issue, since American presidents tend to appoint men of their own political persuasion when a vacancy occurs.

12.1.3. Jury

The jury, consisting of persons without legal training, was inherited from English Common Law. The petty or trial jury is directly concerned with determining the guilt or innocence of persons accused of an offence (while the judge decides questions of law). It usually consists of twelve persons, and their unanimous agreement is traditionally required for a verdict in criminal cases.

The grand jury is concerned with the initiation of proceedings against persons suspected of crimes. Whereas Britain has abolished the grand jury, in the U.S.A. the problem of organized crime since the 1930s has made it desirable to maintain public indictment as long as private prosecutors are liable to be murdered by members of criminal organizations.

12.1.4. Offices Connected with the Law

The head of the Department of Justice is the *Attorney-General,* who is a member of the Cabinet and the chief law-enforcement official in the U.S.A. He serves as legal adviser to the President and all executive agencies.
Another officer of the Department is the *Solicitor-General,* who represents the United States before the courts. Moreover, the Department has a *district attorney* and a *marshal* in each of the 84 judicial districts of the national system.
The most popularly known office connected with the enforcement of law is that of *sheriff,* which dates back to ninth-century England. The sheriff is the head of the county police force. He makes arrests, keeps accused persons in custody, enforces orders, maintains the jails, collects taxes and performs other functions varying from state to state.
The U.S.A. has no national police system, nor has it like England an unarmed police force relying on the sympathy and support of the public. Certain local police forces have recently come into disrepute because of their ruthless actions in racial and student riots.
In the sphere of jurisdiction, the highest office is that of *Chief Justice* of the United States or of a state. The Chief Justice of the Supreme Court, who is appointed for life by the President with the consent of the Senate, performs also a variety of administrative functions as head of the federal court system. In the states, chief justices are chosen in a variety of ways (election, appointment, seniority).
While federal judges at all levels of jurisdiction are appointed by the President and the Senate, most state judges are lawyers chosen by popular vote and usually after partisan nomination. This has aroused much criticism because it often results in the choice of persons not sufficiently qualified for the highly technical work required of the judiciary. Nevertheless the system has become so firmly entrenched that there seems little prospect of an early return to either election by the legislature or appointment by the executive, which was common in the early history of the country. The term of office of judges ranges all the way from two years to life. The term of judges of county courts is rarely longer than four years, while in the highest state courts six years is most common.
Another office which has been under attack in recent years is that of *justice of the peace* on the ground that justices of the peace are usually not trained in the law and that the fee system leads to corruption and biased judgement.

Public prosecutions are conducted by *district attorneys,* who wield great power in local government. Whether prosecutions are brought rests largely in their discretion and in the evidence they present to the grand jury.

12.2. Sentencing

While misdemeanours (minor offences) are punishable only by fines, crimes are punished by imprisonment. Persons convicted of felonies (serious crimes) like murder, robbery, rape, kidnapping and treason may be sentenced to death.

Capital punishment has long been debated on moral and legal grounds. Though only 14 states have abolished it, the number of executions has decreased considerably chiefly because of reluctance on the part of judges to assign the death penalty. In other cases, death sentences pronounced by the courts have been simply suspended. The last execution took place in 1967. In the fifties, world-wide criticism was aroused by the case of Caryl Chessman, who was sentenced to death in California for crimes not punishable by death in other states, and whose execution was postponed for eleven years as a result of the ample posibilities of appeal in the U.S.A.

Lynchings of Negroes by Southern fanatics according to practices inherited from the Ku Klux Klan have ceased with the spread of racial toleration propagated by the civil rights movement. On the other hand, it is still true that whites are seldom convicted of crimes against Negroes in the Southern states.

12.3. Crisis of American Justice

In the 1930s, the U.S.A. was haunted by organized crime, whose detection was largely frustrated by the fact that suspects and witnesses refused to give evidence for fear of Mafia vengeance. Frequently gangster bosses like Al Capone could be sentenced only on minor charges, such as tax evasions. During the fifties, findings of the F.B.I. and the Kefauver Committee helped to alleviate the problem, but in the sixties a new wave of violence caused by political and racial fanatism and social injustices began to sweep the country. It was responsible for the death of three eminent public figures (John F. Kennedy, Robert Kennedy and Dr. Martin Luther King) and reached its climax in the race riots which occurred in U.S. cities in 1968. In most big cities, gang warfare reached new proportions.

All this led to an overall increase in criminality by 176 per cent between 1960 and 1970, which has crowded the dockets of the courts, slowing down and even frustrating justice. The ratio between perpetrated crimes and conviction is 12:1. As many as 90 per cent of the crimes in black ghettos, which have the highest rate of crime, are not reported for lack of confidence in the justice of the white establishment. Drug addiction has greatly contributed to the increase in crime. When in 1970/71 members of the Manson commune stood trial for having committed nine cold-blooded murders, one of the chief defendants confessed that she had been constantly under the influence of LSD (p. 45).

The increase in criminality, to which during the Vietnam War refusals to be drafted were added, has led to increasingly strong measures from the government. After the assassination of Dr. Martin Luther King, the national guard began to put down riots. In Washington, the No-Knock policy has been introduced, authorizing the police to search private homes without warning.

The authority of the courts has been placed in jeopardy by the fact that the recent trials of Negroes, who were supported by a strong wave of sympathy on the part of the general public, have helped to make contempt of court, originally punished as a serious offence, a common phenomenon. In the trial of the Soledad brothers (p. 104) a judge was killed in a court room riot. The police feel frustrated by the fact that criminals they arrest at danger of their lives are released by the judges until their trial.

Two court proceedings have recently attracted world-wide attention. The My Lai trial (p. 45) demonstrated the conflict between the American readiness to censure cruelty even though perpetrated by members of the American forces, and the inclination to condone violence committed in a merciless war. This became evident when Calley's sentence met with an intense emotional reaction from the general public. (The sentimental 'Calley Song' sold 4 million records). In the Angela Davis trial, which has been called 'one of the severest tests yet faced by the embattled U.S. judicial system', the jurors' verdict of 'not guilty' was generally hailed as a token of unbiased justice preventing the growth of racial radicalism.

13. Education

13.1. Special Features

Education in the U.S.A. is decentralized, schools being maintained by thousands of locally elected school boards, which pride themselves on their local autonomy. The U.S. Office of Education, which is a part of the Department of Health, Education and Welfare, has only advisory functions. Although individual local school systems vary greatly in quality, voluntary co-operation has made education policy throughout the U.S.A. fairly uniform.

A characteristically American feature is the egalitarian tendency of making children of all social levels attend comprehensive schools together as long as possible. It is only during the last decades that the growing demand for specialization to meet the requirements of modern science and technology has, in many areas, led to the lowering of the age for beginning secondary education with its relative selectivity and specialization, from 14 to 12.

On the level of higher education, a special feature is the large number of separate colleges for undergraduate studies, based on the pronounced division of university education into undergraduate (first 4 years) and (post) graduate level.

Principles of education are less authoritarian in the U.S.A. than in most European countries. This applies to schools as well as to family life (p. 114).

The democratic American tradition and the fact that schools have always played a major part in the process of naturalizing alien immigrants have had important results. American schools are interested in forming responsible citizens rather than scholars, in personal development rather than intellectual training. This is in keeping with the principles of the American philosopher and educationalist John Dewey (p. 152), whose disciples staff the university departments, teachers colleges and schools. It was not until 1957 when the launching of Sputnik I demonstrated the efficiency of rigorous formal training that these principles began to be seriously questioned. However, the U.S.A. has pioneered in the field of pre-primary education because the findings of American psychologists have supported the thesis that a child's interests and abilities are largely formed at an early age. Thus many three-to-five-year olds are enrolled in some kind of pre-school educational programme.

13.2. Educational System

13.2.1. Elementary Schools

The elementary schools, which are called grammar or grade schools, were originally for children aged from 6 to 14, now more often from 6 to 12. They are usually public and co-educational, though there are also private schools (mostly Roman Catholic), often for boys or girls only.

Institutions for children below school age are nursery schools (age: 2 to 3) and kindergartens (usually for children between 4 and 5), many of which with pre-school programmes.

13.2.2. Secondary Education

Secondary education is provided in co-educational high schools. While the traditional high school contained 4 years (age 14–17), secondary education now usually comprises 6 years in two divisions: junior high school (12–14) and (senior) high school (15–17). Vocational programmes are usually part of the public high school curriculum, although in larger cities they may be organized as separate schools. Advanced vocational schools for specialized studies can be entered after high school. 75 per cent of all American pupils graduate from high school.

13.2.3. Higher Education

Higher education may be full-time or part-time. Colleges of liberal arts (humanities, social studies, natural sciences), and professional colleges (engineering, education, business) are attended usually from 18–21. They offer programmes mainly on the undergraduate level (4 years) completed by the Bachelor's Degree.

Junior colleges (18–19) provide either the first 2 years of an undergraduate curriculum or terminal vocational training. They are usually municipal institutions attended largely by students who want to live at home in order to avoid the fees of a boarding establishment. They also offer adult evening courses, serving as cultural centres for whatever educational services the community may demand.

Universities include undergraduate as well as graduate departments and 'professional schools' in such fields as education, medicine, law, theology and the sciences. Graduate studies after the Bachelor's Degree are completed by the Master's Degree after about 2 years and/or the Doctor's Degree which requires about 3 years more.

In most American cities there are several universities, some famous for specialized studies, e. g. in Boston: Boston University, Harvard University (in Cambridge across the Charles River), the Massachusetts Institute of Technology and the Harvard Business School.

13.3. Colleges and Universities

The U.S.A. has about 2,200 institutions of higher education ranging from small vocational and liberal arts colleges to giant state universities, such as the University of Minnesota with 40,000 students on one campus, or the University of California with 80,000 students distributed over seven university campuses. The total enrolment has doubled since 1960 to reach 7.5 million.

13.3.1. Liberal Arts Colleges

The Liberal Arts Colleges are most commonly small residential institutions averaging between 500 and 600 students, often located in small towns. The idea of a college which offers a general education and also attends to the development of student character was imported in colonial times from England. Although these colleges still enjoy great popularity as the ideal atmosphere in which students (often either men or women only) can live a life entirely devoted to their interests in close contact with their faculty, the costs ($1200–3000 per year) are prohibitive for families in the lower income groups.

13.3.2. State Universities

The State Universities are public institutions, most of which were founded on federal land donated to the individual states under the *Morrill Act, 1862*. There are altogether 72 such land-grant universities, 17 of which for Negro students. The largest of these institutions is the University of California, which also ranks first among American universities in the number of Nobel Prize winners on its faculty. Its 'mother campus' is at Berkeley, San Francisco.

Intended under the *Morrill Act* to specialize in 'such branches of learning as are related to agriculture and the mechanic arts', many state universties have become important research centres for regional studies. Those that specialize in agriculture contain experimental stations of the U.S. Department of Agriculture. Developments such as hybrid corn and high-yield rice have been among the results of their work. Other universities have schools of medicine, which help in developing new techniques for the control of animal diseases as a way to increase food production. Many state universities have long outgrown their original functions as agricultural and technical institutions and now make important contributions also to the humanities and social sciences. An essential element of the services of state universities is the extension of knowledge off campus through elaborate agricultural, engineering and teacher education programmes. They have taken a lead in making contracts to provide education for underdeveloped countries.

138

13.3.3. Private Universities

The Private Universities include older foundations like Yale (New Haven, Conn.) or Harvard, which in spite of the rise of other universities of equally high academic standards, has retained its reputation as the best American university. More recent universities, which were usually endowed by great industrialists, include Johns Hopkins University, Baltimore, and the University of Chicago, which Rockefeller endowed with $32 million. These foundations marked the beginning of a close co-operation between industry and academic research, which resulted in the development of new materials and pharmaceutics and the improvement of methods of business management. This partnership, which is also reflected in the importance of giant endowments, such as the Rockefeller, Carnegie and Ford foundations for the promotion of education in the U.S.A. and other countries, has given rise to great industrial and technological research centres at universities, such as the Massachusetts Institute of Technology in the East, the University of Michigan in the Middle West, or the California Institute of Technology. Indeed, the establishment of industries which depend on research is today largely determined by the location of such research centres.

Since the war, the federal government has become the chief source of research funds, today financing 70 per cent of all major research work. This increase in federal influence is widely resented by the universities as a danger to the freedom of research.

13.4. Recent School Reforms

Though nearly all states require school attendance until the age of 16, there is still a significant amount of illiteracy in many states, particularly in those with a large Negro and alien population. Moreover, the shock caused by the launching of Sputnik I in 1957, which demonstrated to the nation the Russian superiority in space technology, prompted the demand for improved educational standards, which could only be implemented by a more efficient national policy of education. Under the *Economic Opportunity Act*, 1964, which for the first time planned educational investment in terms of the needs of economic growth, 65 per cent of the federal grants for the War Against Poverty are expended on educational programmes to help disadvantaged and culturally deprived children. The *Project Head Start* prepared pre-school children in slum areas for joint elementary education with children of the middle classes. After World War II, the 'G.I. Bill of Rights' had opened to millions of veterans the right to study with a federal scholarship. Similar aid is now given to needy college students, especially Negroes. Today the proportion of students coming from the working classes is about 4 times as large as in Western European countries.

Many of the reforms in the methods of teaching now introduced in most modern countries were initiated in the U.S.A. One of the most important of these innovations is programmed learning. Starting from the theories of the Harvard psychologist Dr. J. S. Bruner, educationalists like B. F. Skinner and W. F. Crowder have pioneered in this field and developed the two main types of programmed instruction. Intelligence and achievement tests independent of the kind of schooling which the pupils have had have supplemented and partly replaced conventional examinations based on the subject matter of curricula. The innovation of ability grouping has had an influence on school architecture. The classroom pattern is increasingly being replaced by a more flexible arrangement of rooms which may be subdivided or expanded according to the size of the group being taught.

13.5. Education of Negroes

Until 1954, the generally established principle of 'separate but equal facilities' largely barred Negroes from white schools, especially in the South. In 1954, a Supreme Court ruling required the integration of Negroes into the public school system. This led to many conflicts in the Southern states, where it became the general habit to admit a few Negro children to a school merely as a token. In recent years, court orders for 'busing' as a means for achieving integration (p. 46) have often led to racial confrontations among students in the schools.

Most Negro children still go to segregated schools, which, for lack of funds and qualified staff, prepare pupils inadequately for higher education. Most of these children leave school early, partly for lack of money, partly from the belief that education will not help them to get employment. Of the still relatively small number of Negro students who enrol at colleges, most students in the South go to Negro colleges, which, however, have a drop-out rate about three times higher than other institutions, because their students come from segregated schools with very low standards. Undergraduate enrolment in white institutions was until recently only a fraction of one per cent, not only because Negroes coming from segregated schools could seldom compete with better prepared white applicants but also because they tended to avoid social discrimination in an overwhelmingly white milieu. Moreover, private colleges are financially beyond the reach of families whose incomes are usually low. In recent years, many large white universities have initiated programmes to enrol disadvantaged students, who normally fail to achieve entrance standards.

13.6. Student Revolts

As in many other countries in which the student population has more than doubled during the last ten years, the student explosion has created 'student power', which made itself felt in the sixties in hundreds of institutions of higher education. Discontent with curricula and lack of participation in college administration blended with political protests against racial inequality, the Vietnam War and general conscription. In 1964, thousands of white students flocked to the South to Mississippi to enrol Negro voters. The brutal reality of racial conflict in the South meant to them a jarring of the American dream. In 1965, Vietnam committees of three Western universities set 80,000 people in motion to demonstrate against the war in Vietnam.

The student revolts, which began at the Berkeley campus of the University of California in 1964, reached their climax when, in 1968, the buildings of Columbia University, New York, were stormed and occupied, offices raided and high functionaries held hostage. The reaction caused by these acts of violence checked the student revolution under Nixon's presidency. In 1970, when four students from Kent State University, Ohio, were shot dead by the National Guard, many students began to give up hope of realizing their ideals and became apathetic.

14. Religion

14.1. Historical Background

The British colonies were founded primarily by Anglican settlers in the South and by Puritans in New England. The predominant Puritan group was the Congregationalists, who established Bible commonwealths in which strict rules governed the church members' private lives and permitted no dissent. Settlers who did not conform were banished, and some established new colonies allowing greater freedom with regard to doctrine and church attendance. Full religious tolerance was established only in Rhode Island and in the Quaker colony of Pennsylvania, whose founder, William Penn, admitted any settlers believing in God as 'creator, upholder and saviour of the world'.

By the 18th century, the New World had become a refuge for persecuted sects. When the United States was founded, the American Constitution provided for the separation of Church and State in order to guarantee religious freedom and to avoid the concentration of undue power in the hands of a state-supported Church (Amendment 1: 'Congress shall make no law respecting an establishment of religion or prohibiting the free exercise thereof').

The vast migration to the Mississippi Valley at the beginning of the 19th century brought new religious groups, especially Lutherans from Germany and Scandinavia.

When it became known that many outlying settlements were without any religious organization, that many settlers had never seen a Bible, local groups in the East linked up into interdenominational missionary organizations, such as the American Bible Society and the American Sunday School Union. In 1826, the American Home Missionary Society was formed on the understanding that 'a more extended effort for the promotion of Home Missions is equally indispensable to the moral advancement and the political stability of the United States'.

The Young Men's Christian Association has remained an effective instrument for counteracting the weakening of religious and moral ties of people lost in the anonymous atmosphere of big cities.

The most powerful agents of evangelism were the Methodists and Baptists. Like many radical Adventist bodies, they introduced a strongly popular and emotional element into 19th century religion.

A new wave of immigration from eastern and southern Europe during the latter half of the 19th century brought large numbers of Roman Catholics to the country, while the immigration of Jews established a strong Jewish community (today 5.5 million members), chiefly in the larger cities.

All the new groups challenged the dominance of traditional Protestant groups, whose religious fervour weakened as religion began to be more and more identified with social work and cultural achievement rather than worship. Moreover, when small communities were unable to afford several churches, doctrinal considerations had to give way to the necessity of establishing one non-denominational church for the whole community. The process of gradual integration culminated in 1950 when the various interdenominational agencies which had been formed to co-ordinate the work of Protestant churches were united to form the National Council of Churches. Even non-Protestant bodies, e. g. Armenian and Greek Orthodox, became members of the Council.

14.2. Denominations

14.2.1. Denominations of European Origin

Roman Catholics, who, at the time of the first census in 1790, constituted 1 per cent of the population, have become the largest single religious body in the country, with a membership of 48 million. Their strength is centred in the cities. As in other countries, the Catholic Church maintains its own school system and takes a prominent part in social activities, especially through a large number of youth organizations.

P r o t e s t a n t i s m , with some 70 million members, is the dominant creed in the United States. In contrast to the Roman Catholics, however, the Protestants are split up into a number of churches. The largest denomination is formed by the various Baptist groups with a total membership of 26 million.

Baptists, who believe in the necessity of adult baptism, established themselves on the frontier of the South. It was from the southern Piedmont Belt that self-supporting farmer-preachers moved over the mountains with the initial wave of westward migration, forming churches which did not wait for missionary societies, but 'raised up' preachers out of their own number to evangelize in neighbouring communities. With their opposition to a centralized church organization, the Baptists are the most fervent representatives of religious individualism. In their missionary efforts, they were as active as the English Baptists. The civil rights struggle in the South was mainly fought by black Baptist ministers like Martin Luther King and Ralph Abernathy.

Methodists (11 million), who believe in the conversion experience as the beginning point of a Christian life, became the most powerful force in the revivalist movement of the 19th century. The Methodist circuit riders would address camp meetings for hours with such fervour as to rouse actual ecstasies and convulsions among the uneducated population of the frontier. Moreover, the Methodist belief in free will and the possibility of Christian action appealed to the American character more than Calvinist predestination.

Lutherans, who take the third place among Protestant bodies with a membership of 9 million, hold their strongest position in the German and Scandinavian-settled Middle West.

Episcopalions (3.3 million) were in colonial times the members of the Anglican Church, but changed their name after America's separation from England. Their Anglican tradition of an episcopal administration and a well organized liturgical life based on the Prayer Book has made them one of the more conservative groups with their membership drawn from the more sophisticated upper classes.

Presbyterians with their hierarchical organization of church assemblies consisting of presbyters number about 4 million.

Congregationalists, who believe in the autonomy of the individual congregation, were in colonial times the strongest denomination. They were the English 'Separatists' who established the first Bible commonwealths in New England. Today their membership has dropped to 2 million because Congregationalist bodies tend to amalgamate with the Presbyterians in order to profit from their more effective organization.

Quakers, whose tolerance and humanitarian principles had secured their colony Pennsylvania a large number of immigrants and a prosperous development not disturbed by Indian hostility, suffered heavily as a result of the Revolution, when their principle of not taking part in war caused numerous defections. In spite of their small membership (69,000), they have remained widely influential as a minority group devoted to social reform and humanitarian service, particularly in times of war.

Unitarians, founded as an anti-Trinitarian sect denying the Godship of Christ, now form a small group of free-thinking intellectuals, who have played a part far out of proportion to their number (265,000) in the development of American thought. Transcendentalism (p. 149), with its reliance on the inspirations of the 'Over-Soul' rather than the revelations of the Bible, was strongly influenced by Unitarian liberalism of thought.

14.2.2. Religious Groups Founded in the United States

The *Church of Latter-Day Saints* or *Mormons* has 2,2 million members. Doctrines are based both on the Bible and on *The Book of Mormon,* which is believed to contain revelations of God to an Israelite tribe which had migrated to the New World and become the ancestors of the American Indians. Under the guidance of an angel, its founder, Joseph Smith, excavated tablets of gold, from which he translated *The Book of Mormon,* which records Christ's modern revelations on his visits to the New World after his ascension.

The sect was founded in New York State (1830), but its members, being persecuted on account of their practice of polygamy, moved west to Missouri and Illinois, where Smith was shot by hostile settlers. Under their new leader, Brigham Young, 80,000 Mormon pioneers trekked to Utah, where in 1847 they founded Salt Lake City. Since 1890, when polygamy was declared unconstitutional and punishable by confiscation of property, it has no longer been practised.

The Mormons' main activity is missionary work. They have no professional clergy, but all members are encouraged to perform some religious service.

Disciples of Christ originated in the revival period of the early 19th century. At first an informal movement including persons of many denominations, they developed into a typically American denomination of liberal character with largely autonomous congregations. Their membership is 1.4 million.

Seventh-Day Adventists are the best-known of the many Adventist bodies in the U.S.A., which believe in the imminent Second Coming of Christ. The sect was founded in 1863 and has like most revivalist groups a strongly emotional appeal. The Seventh-Day Adventists are very active in evangelistic preaching and maintain publishing establishments in many countries. They observe the Jewish Sabbath. Their membership is 433,000.

Jehovah's Witnesses, founded in 1884 by Charles D. Russell, are also known as the *International Bible Students Association.* They are Adventists and pacifists who do not recognize state authority when it conflicts with their religious principles (in Germany they were persecuted under Hitler). They publish *The Watch Tower.* Their membership is 360,000.

Christian Science was founded in Boston as the *Church of Jesus Christ, Scientist* in 1893 by Mary Baker Eddy, whose book *Science and Health with Key to the Scriptures* became the basic work of the faith. Christian Science starts from the premise that God, the Divine Mind, is the only reality, and that matter and evil are consequently unreal. Disease is a delusion of the human mind, which can be cured by praying for the spiritual understanding that all evil can be overcome as soon as man becomes conscious of his connection with God's all-pervading spirit, which is health. Hence Christian Science rejects medical treatment and maintains practitioners who pray for their patients. Clergy and church services are rejected, but meetings are held at which two lecturers read texts from the Bible and Mrs. Eddy's book. Christian Science, which has about 3,000 branches in 48 countries, publishes no membership figures. It maintains special radio and television programmes and an international daily newspaper of high standing, *The Christian Science Monitor.*

14.3. Religious Life Today

The characteristic feature of religious life in the U.S.A. is the diversity which history has produced. There are over 260 religions and sects in the U.S.A. The greatest diversity is found in California, where many esoteric and mystical Eastern cults were introduced by settlers from Asia. The host of religious and quasi-religious bodies in California today includes Hippie groups, whose creeds range from astrology to Christian revivalism. Charles Manson, who induced his adherents to ritual murder, referred to himself as Christ and Devil.

The full separation of Church and State compels the various congregations to support and govern themselves. This has imparted more vigour to their religious life than is normally found in state-supported churches. Moreover, the fact that no single religious group has ever gained considerable power has prevented the rise of the anti-clerical tendencies so strong in many countries with established churches.

The vigorous local groups have developed a 'religion of neighbourhood', which constitutes a strong force in the individual's life. Most churches have special rooms for various social activities, which bind their members' lives closely to their church.

The fact that the U.S.A. had early become a stronghold of liberty and safety from oppression infused into U.S. religion a strongly humanitarian element apparent in the crusades fought for the abolition of slavery, for temperance (leading in 1919 to Prohibition, unique in modern history), and in aid for countries shattered by war or natural catastrophes. Many a missionary has been the 'charity' of an individual congregation.

American itinerant preachers like Billy Graham and, recently, adherents of the Jesus People have made many converts, even in Europe. Graham's Tele-Evangelization EURO 70 was, according to his words, 'the greatest attempt in history to spread the 2000-year old message with all technical means available'. Even show business has profited from the evangelizing boom. The rock opera *Jesus Christ Superstar* (by English authors) held a record of Broadway performances in 1971.

The most recent revivalist movement is the Jesus People. It is estimated that since the beginning of the Jesus revolution in 1967 hundreds of thousands of drop-outs have flocked to the Pacific coast, the birthplace of the movement, letting themselves be baptized in the ocean and swimming pools. Innumerable street missionaries tour the country selling Bibles and issues of about 50 different Jesus magazines or records of pop music with religious themes, and gather their audiences in common prayer. Young people living in Christian Houses indicate their conversion by abstaining from drugs and sex, and wear plaques with inscriptions, such as 'The Messiah is the Message' or 'Smile, God loves you' or 'Drugs are out, Jesus is in'. There are hundreds of Christian telephone services for people in personal difficulties.

The Campus Crusade for Christ, with 3,000 missionaries, was founded by the millionaire Bill Bright, who hopes to conquer the U.S.A. by 1976 and the whole world by 1980 for the message of Christ.

The Jesus People share many of the characteristics of the Hippies, who were their first adherents in San Francisco. The fact that they are also known as Jesus freaks gives some indication of the unconventional aspects of the new religious 'style', as manifested for instance in the rock musical *Godspell*. The traditional Christian believer may feel alarmed if he sees biblical figures arrayed as clowns present the stories of the Gospel as if they were farces. He may feel still more amazed to see a sophisticated European audience listening in keen fascination. He is not likely to be convinced by the statement of Stephen Schwartz, who wrote the music and lyrics: 'When the world is in such a mess you can't take it too seriously; we make Christ into a music hall actor clowning about and doing a soft shoe dance with Judas. You simply have to like the man. Jesus amuses and delights you; he is the kind of character anyone would want to follow."

Whatever their aberrations from good taste, it is a fact that the Jesus People have offered an alternative to the defeatism of the Hippie groups and the social apathy of the establishment.

15. Phases of American Thought

15.1. Puritanism

In the 17th century, intellectual life was dominated by the Puritanism of New England, where the religious discipline of the colonial Bible commonwealths resulted in a distinctly religious culture based on Puritan morality. The political concepts inherited from English Puritanism gave rise to the first democratic governments. The conviction that success in life was a visible sign of God's grace favoured a pragmatic, utilitarian concept of life, the so-called 'work ethic', which resulted in an immense economic development.

15.2. Age of Reason

In the 18th century, orthodox Puritanism was challenged by Deism and Newtonian theories, which fostered interest in science. The belief in progress engendered by the Age of Reason became a characteristic feature of American thought. The rise of religiously tolerant Philadelphia as the intellectual capital marked the decline of Puritanism and the growing influence of Quaker liberalism and scientific progress (cf. Benjamin Franklin, p. 12).

Political thought in the revolutionary period was shaped by Puritan democracy at war with the despotism of the mother country, by John Locke's doctrine of natural rights, and by Montesquieu's concept of government with separate and balanced powers.

Thirteen years before the outbreak of the French Revolution, the American Declaration of Independence asserted 'that all men are created equal, that they are endowed by their Creator with certain unalienable Rights, that among these are Life, Liberty and the Pursuit of Happiness. That to secure these Rights, Governments are instituted among Men, deriving their just powers from the consent of the governed. . .' These ideas in their most radical form had entered America through the writings of the English revolutionary Thomas P a i n e. In his pamphlet *Common Sense,* Paine advanced the opinion that society 'promotes our happiness positively by uniting our affections', whereas 'government, even in its best state, is but a necessary evil; in its worst state an intolerable one'. His essentially deistic belief in a religion of humanity (while churches, to him, were 'set up to terrify and enslave mankind') was fundamentally shared by the Founding Fathers. Largely at the urging of Madison, who was convinced that religious establishments violated the free exercise of conscience, they provided for the complete separation of church and state. Thomas J e f f e r s o n ' s mystic faith in the common man, which was based on an inveterate belief in the universality of a moral sense that is essentially social has established itself as the abiding pattern of American thought.

15.3. Frontier Spirit

The continuing presence of a primitive life style on an advancing frontier had important effects on American attitudes. It perpetuated the American faith in making continual fresh starts, in redeeming a decadent world by building a better civilization. In early American literature, the influence of Rousseau and contact with the Indians favoured an aesthetic primitivism contending that the state of nature was superior to that of civilization. The noble savage was idealized by Philip F r e n e a u and later by Fenimore C o o p e r ' s *Leather Stocking Tales* and L o n g f e l l o w ' s epic poem *Hiawatha*. This literary romanticizing of the Indian, however, had little effect on the attitudes of the western settlers.

The glory and the problems of pioneer life found expression in W a l t W h i t m a n ' s poetry (cf. 'Pioneers! O Pioneers!'), in the novels of B r e t H a r t e and J a c k L o n d o n and Hamlin G a r l a n d. The historian F. G. Turner gave the classic statement of this side of American life in his essay 'The Significance of the Frontier in American History'.

The frontier gave rise to that rugged individualism, that love of freedom and that inventive pragmatism which influenced American thought right into the 20th century.

15.4. Transcendentalism

Transcendentalism (1830–60) was a philosophical and literary reaction against rationalism and Puritan orthodoxy. The name is derived from Kant's *Critique of Pure Reason*, transcendental knowledge being the mode of knowing things a priori. The movement was largely confined to New England, and the chief members of the Transcendental Club, Ralph Waldo Emerson, W. E. Channing and H. D. Thoreau lived in close contact in the vicinity of Boston and Concord. Transcendentalism was influenced by German idealism, communicated to America largely through the writings of Coleridge and Carlyle. The belief in the divine authority of the soul's intuitions resulted in the doctrine of self-reliance and individualism as well as the disregard of authority and tradition which life on the frontier had encouraged from the beginnings of American history. The desire for close communion with nature inspired the Transcendentalist co-operative experiment of Brook Farm and Thoreau's *Walden,* a narrative of two years spent close to nature in solitary contemplation on the woodland banks of Walden Pond. Their idealism and respect for the freedom of the individual made the Transcendentalists fervent supporters of the movement for the liberation of the slaves.

Transcendentalism found its classical expression in the essays of its foremost member Emerson. In *Nature,* which marked the beginning of the movement, Emerson encouraged man to trust the creative sources of nature rather than the wisdom of traditional schools. His later essays 'The Over-Soul' and 'Self-Reliance' expressed Emerson's romantic mysticism and his typically American belief in man's creative power of shaping the universe to his needs. In 'The Over-Soul' he speaks of 'that great nature, in which we rest as the earth lies in the soft arms of the atmosphere; that Unity, that Over-Soul, within which every man's particular being is contained'. And in another place: 'I am born into the great, the universal mind ... So come I to live in thoughts and act with energies which are immortal'. In 'Self-Reliance', Emerson scorns the American tendency to imitate European culture. 'Truly it demands something godlike in him who ... has ventured to trust himself for a taskmaster. High be his heart, faithful his will, clear his sight, that he may in good earnest be doctrine, society, law to himself'. In *The American Scholar* Emerson contends that even the scholar must rely not so much on books as on 'the resources to live', thus foreshadowing Dewey's pragmatism. By virtue of his clearer understanding of the world around him, the scholar is 'to cheer, to raise and to guide men by showing them facts amidst appearances', for he is 'the world's eye'.

15.5. Manifest Destiny

The opening up of the continent, symbolized in the slogan 'Go west, young man, go west!', engendered an unbounded confidence in the civilizing mission of the United States. The phrase 'Manifest Destiny' was first used in the *Democratic Review* in 1845 by John O'Sullivan, who expressed the national mood in the high-flown words: 'The far-reaching, the boundless future will be the era of American greatness. In its magnificent domain of space and time the nation of many nations is destined to manifest the excellence of divine principles. Its floor shall be a hemisphere, its roof the firmament of the star-studded heavens'. The new national optimism found its most telling expression in the poetry of Walt Whitman, who visualized the possibilities of a great national literature as an expression of the organic unity of American life and as an instrument for education. In his verse he propagated a new religion of comradeship and his belief in egalitarianism and world peace.

15.6. Social Darwinism

The creed of success engendered by America's Manifest Destiny was sustained by the ideas of Social Darwinism. Though conceived in England, it asserted itself nowhere so strongly as in the United States. The survival of the fittest became the new version of the Puritan doctrine of election, which could now be defined even more unrestrainedly in terms of material success. The new American creed as formulated by its major prophet William Graham S u m n e r, sociologist and economist, reads as follows: 'The truth is that liberty and property go together and sustain each other in a glorious accord, but only in the highest and best civilization which men have yet attained'. To Sumner, freedom was the product of civilization. 'Those who have the resources of civilization at their command are the only ones who are free. But the resources of civilization are capital; and so it follows that the capitalists are free ... The interdependence of wealth on civilization and civilization on wealth is the reason why all denunciations of the desire to increase or to win wealth are worse than childish' (from *Essays: 'Who is Free?'*).
The survival of the fittest can be guaranteed only by the liberal economic principle of laissez faire. Governmental interference with the free operation of competition would favour the survival and reproduction of the unfit and set back the progress of civilization. The oil magnate John D. Rockefeller expressed the creed of the 'gilded age' when he said in a speech: 'The growth of a large business is merely the survival of the fittest ... This is not an evil tendency in business. It is merely the working out of a law of nature and a law of God'. The steel king Andrew Carnegie proclaimed after reading Darwin and Spencer: 'Not only had I got rid of theology and the supernatural, but I found the truth of evolution. "All is well, since all grows better" became my motto, my true source of comfort'.
When, in the great coal strike of 1902, men were striking against gross abuses of power on the part of the owners, a spokesman for the latter declared: 'The rights and interests of the labouring man will be protected, not by the labour agitators, but by the men to whom God in his infinite wisdom has given the control and the property interests of this country and upon the successful management of which so much depends'.
There were few who tried to stem the tide, and they were not very effective. The economist H e n r y G e o r g e was more influential in Europe than in the U.S.A. With his remarkable book *Progress and Poverty: An Inquiry into the Cause of Industrial Depressions and of Increase of Want with Increase of Wealth* he led the revolt against laissez faire. From the conviction that poverty was bound to ensue as long as there was private property in land, he developed his single tax theory. If a tax were imposed equal to the annual use value of real estate according to productivity, so that land would have no capital value, progress would be orderly, and its fruits would be equitably shared.

15.7. Pragmatism

The last quarter of the 19th century was the heyday of American success in conquering a vast, scarcely explored continent. The struggle for survival on an open frontier of civilization, which had caused the Americans to respond so keenly to Darwin's theory of the survival of the fittest, now gave rise to a distinctly American school of thought, which considered practical experience through action as the ultimate source and test of all knowledge and value.

Charles S. Pierce, who introduced the term pragmatism in 1878, formulated the fundamental pragmatic tenet that an idea is a plan of action. Electricity for instance cannot be conceived except in terms of what it does, or through a plan of action to make it achieve a certain effect, e. g. illuminate a bulb.

Pragmatism, which was also called experimentalism and functionalism, was encouraged in its confidence in human possibilities by the development of science and technology operating for the improvement of social conditions and thus for the advance of modern society. For the pragmatist, human development was more important than the 'static aims' of classical rationalism. What counts is not what a thing is like but what it will be – what happens when subject and object interact.

The psychologist William James (1842–1910) introduced the functionalist approach to the problems of the mind. With James, psychology ceased to be a mental discipline and became a laboratory science. James created the first U.S. demonstrational psychology laboratory. He introduced the method of registering and classifying the instincts that constitute man's will. His chief work *The Principles of Psychology*, 1890, is still considered as one of the classic works of psychology. It represents a typically American approach to the problems of thinking and knowledge. 'The whole meaning of a conception expresses itself in practical consequences'. James even tested beliefs by their beneficial consequences on our conduct and temper. In *The Will to Believe* he conceived truth itself dynamically as man's will to believe, which makes a thing come true. Thus the willing subject is the initiator of thought as well as action. It is the primary event from which history dates. Individuals are the decisive factor in the formation and destruction of society. James's belief in a pluralistic universe, whose development depended on individual effort, and his concept that the belief which establishes a worth-while habit is a belief that creates a truth, were important contributions to modern thought. The theory of actions was the source of the later modification of pragmatism, the science of behaviourism, one of America's main contributions to 20th century psychology. The behaviourists replaced the current introspective method of psychology by defining psychological phenomena exclusively in terms of behaviour.

America's greatest pragmatist, John Dewey, who made wide-ranging contributions to the development of American thought, is chiefly renowned for his writings on education. He taught philosophy at the University of Chicago, where he became head of the combined departments of philosophy, psychology and educational theory, and established the University of Chicago's Laboratory School. For Dewey, thought had as its object the development of life, not the discovery of truth. He was a humanist and saw morality in terms of social values. 'When physics, chemistry, biolgy, medicine contribute to the detection of concrete human woes and to the development of plans for remedying them and relieving the human estate, they become moral.'

Dewey's preoccupation with the development of life explains the fact that his interests centred on education. He strove for the reform of a school system which, to him, was hopelessly cut off from the child's experience. Education should help the child to move in the world around him rather than teach him to think in abstractions and memorize tedious data. That meant an emphasis on activities as a means of 'thinking things out'. He defined the task of the Laboratory School, which he directed, as 'the problem of viewing the education of the child in the light of the principles of mental activities and processes of growth made known by modern psychology'. Children whose interest was actively engaged in their studies did not need a rigid code of behaviour.

Dewey developed from these views a philosophical basis for democracy and liberalism, which he set forth in his chief educational work *Democracy and Education*, 1916. He conceived of democracy not primarily as a form of government, but rather as a form of association which gives the members of society maximum opportunity for growth and activity. Dewey's ideas are still the most important influence operative in American education. Similarly, the behaviourist B. F. S k i n n e r, the foremost exponent of modern experimental and applied psychology, has become the father of programmed learning.

Just as Dewey made pragmatism the basis of education, his close friend, Oliver Wendell H o l m e s, introduced it into law. His book *The Common Law* begins with the sentence: 'The life of the law has not been logic, it has been experience'. To him, law contains the story of a nation's development through many centuries. But though it is based on precedent, its purpose is the building of a better future. *The Common Law* has become a legal classic, and the opinions Holmes formulated in his service on the Supreme Court constitute according to Justice Frankfurter 'the most comprehensive and philosophic body of American law for any period of history'.

15.8. The Lost Generation and Freud

World War I signalled the first serious crisis of the inveterate American belief in success and progress. The Puritan work ethic trying to counteract the fatalism inherent in the doctrine of predestination, the concept inherited from the Age of

Reason that man was called to build a better world, the frontier optimism with its belief in the infinite possibilities of the power of the human will: all were affected by the mood of depression of the post-war years. Failure had become a reality, which was stronger than personal effort.

It was in the twenties that the ideas of Sigmund Freud began to infiltrate into American thought. Frustration could be made bearable if failure and, for that matter, guilt were considered as a neurosis which psycho-analysis could relieve by making the patient conscious of its underlying causes. When information became available in 1955 that one in every 18 Americans suffered from neuroses, Congress ordered an investigation, which intensified the general interest in psycho-analysis. Although little notice was taken of them in Europe, Freud's ideas became a kind of secularized religion in 20th century America. They seemed to hold out the promise that by being made conscious of our mechanism for repressing our natural instincts we could be prevented from compensating our neuroses by aggression in politics, business, sex and other spheres of human relations. The horrors of the Hitler era seemed to bear out the theory that repressive principles of education lead to aggression and institutionalized cruelty. The impact of Freud's theories was felt especially in American education, where they favoured the development of anti-authoritarian principles. It may be argued that Freud's emphasis on the sexual motivation of human behaviour has helped to speed the sex revolution. At any rate it is significant that Europe, which had failed to put Freud's ideas into practice in education and medicine, received these new impulses via America.

15.9. The Beat Generation

The 'lost generation' after World War I and the 'beat generation' after World War II shared a pessimism born of the destructive experiences of war. However, unlike the lost generation, which fell into a mood of apathy, the beatniks were rebels in search of new life styles, deliberate drop-outs challenging the establishment in the underground. The term 'beat' was first used in the fifties by a literary group whose members called themselves 'beatniks'. In 1955, the San Francisco publisher and poet Ferlinghetti first published Allen Ginsberg's *Howl,* which became the creed of the beat generation. When Ginsberg, Jack Kerouac and Gregory Corso gathered in Greenwich Village, New York, which was already the principal focus of modern American trends in art and music, became a new literary centre as well. The aims of the movement were voiced by the underground paper *The Village Voice* and the action stage Living Theater. Kerouac's highly autobiographical novel *On the Road* tells of the breakout of young people from their bourgeois life styles into the vastness of the land. The road figures as a way of life, which leads the vagrant of our days on to new horizons; but the hero ends in disintegration and madness. Twelve years later, the experience of being on the road found a new bitter expression in the film *Easy Rider*, the heroes of which become the victims of a hostile society.

In the sixties, the cult of sex and narcotics provided new forms of inspiration and ecstasy. Their chief centres were the Hippie communes in California. The use of drugs reduced the 'trip' to an experience of the mind, to the psychedelic expansion of consciousness, which was also cultivated in meditations of Zen Buddhism.

Those who had not given up hope of regenerating social and political life received new impulses from the ideas of Herbert M a r c u s e, who adapted Marxist theories to the contemporary scene. After having fled from Hitler's Germany, Marcuse was confronted in the U.S.A. with a new form of aggression in the unbridled egotism of capitalist corporations. Like Karl Marx, Marcuse is convinced that institutionalized exploitation can only be brought to an end by revolution. In contrast to Marx, however, he does not believe in a revolution by the proletariat, whose initiative is paralyzed by the corporate state, which is able to satisfy the demands it creates for the sake of profit, and thus perpetuates its control over people. Most of the working class share the middle class instinct for stability. A revolution guided by the essential desire for 'liberation from the administered comfort and the destructive productivity of the exploiting society' would thus require a new type of consciousness. This new consciousness works for the concentration of radical political practices in active minorities among the middle class intelligentsia and the ghetto population. Marcuse warns the young generation against the 'repressive tolerance' of a society, which, by breaking down a few traditional taboos, ties them to their 'institutionalized fathers'.

Marcuse's ideas as laid down particularly in his *Essay on Liberation* provided the theoretical justification for the students' revolts, notably in California, where they inspired his most gifted student, Angela Davis, in her agitation for militant black power.

15.10. Pop Culture

The spirit of rebellion has created its own life styles and symbols. The dirty blue jeans, the long hair shunning the barber, the battered car (where hitch-hiking is not possible) – these are symbols accepted by many young people who wish to demonstrate at least some sort of progressiveness. The tendency, strongly supported by profit-seeking industries, to raise the most trivial objects to the level of cultural symbols and values, coupled with the predilection of the flower children for gay colours, has helped to create what is known as pop culture. Starting as popular art, (p. 174), it has now reached all spheres of modern culture. Fashion, stage decoration, advertising, dancing, music, literature have felt its influence. Its adherents are sociable and communicative, participants in rather than spectators of the scene. They delight in 'happenings', provocative fashions, shocking colours and noise. Their world is interpreted by the prophet of the electronic age, the Canadian Marshall McLuhan, who settled in New York, the centre of the pop scene. In his bestseller *The Medium is the Massage*, in which he enlarges on his earlier pronouncement that the medium ist the message, he establishes the theory that the mass media are a decisive factor in reshaping every aspect of our personal life, and unifying mankind. 'By encouraging unification and involvement, electric technology is replacing the alphabet and print technology of Gutenberg, which encouraged the fragmenting process of specialism and detachment'. The seventies are seeing a new vogue for the American sociologist Robert Nisbet, who, in his book *The Quest for Community* spelt out the need to treat man as a member of a social group rather than a self-contained individual. This longing for communication is in fact the common denominator of the many different groups: the drop-outs in the communes, the Hippies demonstrating for 'love not war', and the happy consumers of the blessings of mass society who congregate at pop festivals, in beatshops and discotheques, bearing out McLuhan's message of the unifying force of the world of sound.

16. Language

16.1. Foreign Vocabulary

It might be assumed that American speech has been greatly influenced by the fact that the U.S.A. has become the great melting pot of nations, absorbing vocabulary and phraseology from many European languages and Indian dialects. This, however, has not been the case. Apart from local and proper names and words connected with the Indian way of life like *wigwam* (tent), *tomahawk* (light axe), few Indian words have infiltrated into American speech. Nor have numerous Spanish, French or German words been absorbed into the American language.

Words that infiltrated from Spanish-settled southwestern areas belong either to the sphere of cattle-raising, such as *ranch* (cattle farm), *sombrero* (broad-rimmed hat), *stampede* (flight, rush), *corral* (pen for cattle); or they are geographical terms like *Arizona* (dry zone), *canyon* (deep valley), *piedmont* (foothills), *mesa* (a rock formation with a flat top standing out in a plain), *key*, as in the name of the island in South Florida, Key West, adapted from Spanish *cayo* (reef).

Words from French are also mainly topographical expressions like *prairie*, *butte* (in the U.S.A. usually an abruptly rising hill), and *levee* (river embankment) or *bayou* (river arm) in French-settled Louisiana.

Words taken from German often describe items of food, like *sauerkraut, pretzel,* while *kindergarten* suggests German influence on American education.

The languages of southern and eastern Europe exerted no influence on American speech, since Italian, Greek, Polish and Lithuanian immigrants came much later than settlers from western Europe and usually formed a poor, underprivileged class living in isolated urban ghettos.

16.2. Standard Speech und Regional Standards

Apart from taking over nouns such as the above-mentioned, however, the American language has, despite changes in intonation and pronunciation, remained singularly English in vocabulary and syntax. The forecast of America's great lexicographer Noah Webster that North America would, in the course of time, produce a language 'as different from the future language of England as the modern Dutch, Danish and Swedish are from the German or one another' did not materialize. However, with his dictionary and his *Spelling Book,* Webster made perhaps the most important contribution to his ideal of having 'a uniform national language to which all foreigners settling in this country should conform'. As a result, no American popular dialect differs widely from cultivated speech. Only in isolated communities, such as places in the Tennessee and Kentucky mountains where the general rule of American life, frequent mobility, does not apply, has the speech of the *'hillbillies'* retained an archaic character.

Of the three local types of speech – Northeastern, Southern and Western – which developed in the course of time, the speech of New England has been most influential in the literary sphere, because of the early predominance of New England in education and literature. The Yankee schoolmaster travelling through the Southern states, teaching the ABC from Webster's *Spelling Book,* and the New England grammar schools founded by law in every county town in the North established a usage that came to be recognized as the best English spoken in America, and has remained most akin to British English in pronunciation and intonation up to our own day. The abundant schools of oratory and vocal expression in the country are descended from Boston schools for cultivating language. The telephone was invented by a professor of speech physiology at Boston University.

As the centre of American life shifted to the West, a general or Western speech came to be spoken by the rest of the country. It is characterized by the notorious American drawl, greater nasalization of vowels as contrasted with speech in the East, and an 'unmusical' quality. On the other hand, the buoyant, adventurous character of life in the West has imparted to American speech a picturesqueness of expression not restrained by the conventional propriety which the ruling upper class established in post-Shakespearean England. The multitude of names that may be given to an undesirable fellow for instance shows the abundance of slang expressions: He may be a *bummer,* a *hoodlum,* a *rough neck,* a *hooligan,* a *scalawag* or a *rowdy.*

Contact with the Indians enriched the American language with a number of metaphors, such as the *pipe of peace, bury the hatchet, war path* and *war paint.*

16.3. Changes in Word Meaning

In the history of settlement, a number of English words took on a new meaning. Thus the *lot,* the method of portioning out the common lands in New England, came to designate a limited section of land. The word *corn,* in England another name for wheat, came to be used only for Indian corn, while the European term maize is not used in the U.S.A. The word *planter* has been restricted to the big plantation owners of the South. *Frontier* took on a wholly new resonance. In American history, the frontier has been an advancing border line between civilization and the Desert, cf. President Kennedy's *New Frontier* proclaimed as a new political challenge.

16.4. New Technical Terms

Political life produced a large number of technical expressions. Some have remained peculiar to the U.S.A., such as *caucus* and *primary* (meeting of the voters of a political party to nominate candidates for office), *floor* (legislative chambers), *filibustering* (obstructive tactics in legislatures), *gerrymandering* derived from a governor of Massachusetts, named Gerry, who engaged in political manipulation when rearranging constituencies, *platform* for the policy of a political party, to *run for President* (stand as a candidate). A *muckraker* is a person exposing political and other corruption. The word *lobby* for pressure groups in a legislature has become a common term in other countries too.

Considerable diversions from British English are found in the language of transport, the term transport itself being less frequently used than *transportation*, which, in England, more commonly refers to sending convicts to a penal colony. Americans speak of *railroad*, *truck* (lorry), *street car* (tram), *subway* (underground), *elevator* (lift), *freight train* (goods train). The term *baggage* occurs more commonly than luggage, *highway*, *throughway*, *expressway* are used for motorway. The American term *airport* has replaced the English *aerodrome* even in Britain.

In the sphere of trade and industry, the terms *lumbering* for wood felling, *lumberman* and *lumberjack* indicate the American preference for lumber to designate felled trees. *Packing*, originally used for preparing and packaging foodstuffs, is most commonly used in the term *meat-packing plant* in the Middle West. *Can* (in British English: *tin*) refers to containers for preserved food or drinks; hence *cannery* for the place where foodstuffs are canned, as in Steinbeck's novel *Cannery Row*. *Utility* is used for public services, such as a gas works or electric light system. *Power* is preferred to *energy* or *electricity*. For a place where things are sold, *store* is more commonly used than *shop*. The Americans go to the *movies* to see a *movie*, the English go to the *cinema* to see a *film*.

In the field of education, two terms differ considerably from the British use. *Public school* is definitely a school of the public system (instead of private), *grammar school* is a primary, not a secondary school. Wholly American is the term *campus* for the grounds on which the various university buildings stand, which has come to be used for university at large, e. g. 'opinion on campus'.

16.5. Group Designations

Certain expressions used to designate (groups of) people are wholly American. Such terms are *guy* (chap), *G.I.* for an enlisted soldier (from 'government issue' stamped on military equipment), *jet set* (fashionable, fast-travelling people), *Yankee*, which originally referred to inhabitants of New England, but has now

159

become the accepted nickname for all U.S. citizens throughout the world. *Uncle Sam* is used to designate the U.S. government.

16.6. Word Formation

The habit of forming nouns and adjectives from verbs + adverbs is more common in America than in Britain: e. g. *setback, comeback, set-up, drop-out* (person leaving the educational system either by choice or through failure), *take-over* (merger), *teach-in, sit-down* strike, *drive-in* movie, *cut-over* forest, *take-home* (net) pay. Compound words not linked by prepositions occur more frequently in American than in British speech: e. g. *consumer needs, career woman, moon shot.*
Adjectives are often formed by combining adjectives or nouns with participles: e. g. *foreign-born, high-powered, airborne, university-trained.*
Another characteristic feature is the use of adjectives as nouns taking an *-s* in the plural, which in England is limited to a few terms like *whites, ancients.* This total conversion of adjectives into nouns has spread from the language of business, above all in the field of advertising, e. g. 'All sizes, 35 to 54, to fit *regulars, shorts, longs* and *stouts*'. It occurs in *executive* (person employed in business organization), *alcoholic* (person suffering from alcoholism), *comic* (comic book or magazine), *commercial* (advertisement normally interrupting a television programme), *illiterate, documentary* (documentary film), *editorial* (leading article), and, in the field of music, *spiritual* (religious song), *blues* (melancholy jazz song), *musical.*

16.7. Grammatical and Idiomatic Characteristics

Forms of simplification are the more frequent use of the *-s*-genitive, e. g. *the car's speed, the earth's surface, a dream's end,* and, in slang, the dropping of the ending *-ly* in adverbs: to *act decent,* to *drive careless, real sorry, mighty dangerous.* Peculiarly American adverb formations are *maybe* (perhaps), *sort of* or *kind of* (rather), e. g. 'sort of busy', and *on all counts* (in every respect).
In slang, there is a tendency to substitute the object case of the personal pronoun for the subject case: '*me* and *her* were both late'. In the use of the interrogative and relative pronouns the form *who* for *whom* is almost universally heard. Questions like *Who did you meet?* have also become absolutely normal in Britain. Colloquial speech knows many verbs differing from British English: I *guess, reckon,* or *figure* for *assume,* to *loan* (lend), to *come by* (obtain), to *be through with* (finished with), *darn it!* for *damn it!*
Other typically American expressions are: *due to* (because of), *as though* (as if), *a couple of* (small number of), *aside from* (apart from), *so what?* (what does it

matter?). Popular American ejaculations are *my, gee, gosh*. The origin of *O.K.*, the American equivalent for *all right*, which is now used almost universally, is wholly obscure.

16.8. Spelling

The main differences in spelling are:
Words ending in *-our* drop the *u: labor, favor, endeavor, neighbor*.
Nouns ending in *-nce* take *-se: defense, offense*.
Nouns ending in *-re* have *-er: theater, center*.
Two-syllable verbs ending in *-l* do not double the *l* when taking an ending: *modeled, traveler*. On the other hand, adjectives formed with *ful(l)* retain the double *l* before *ful(l):* e. g. *skillful, willful*.

16.9. Pronunciation

Characteristic of American pronunciation as developed in the West are:
B. E. [ɔ] pronounced as A. E. [ɑ:] in words like *hot, God, lot*.
B. E. [ju:] normally pronounced as [u:] in words like *due, duty*.
B. E. [ɑ:] pronounced as [æ] before certain consonants, as in *ask, pass, after, chance, example*.
[r] in one-syllable words before an [e] or a consonant or at the end is retained in A. E., as in *there, lord, far, war*.
In all these cases the Northeastern speech has kept closer to British pronunciation.
As to stress, American English has a tendency in longer words to stress two syllables rather than shorten or even skip syllables in favour of strong emphasis on the first, or second syllable: e. g. *laboratory:* ['læbrə,tɔri] instead of British [lə'bɔrətri], *preparatory:* [pri'pærə,tɔri] instead of British [pri'pærətri].

16.10. Influence on European Languages

Although there is still a strong tendency among educated people in Europe speaking English to avoid Americanisms in pronunciation, it is a fact that American expressions and modes of speech have gained immense influence since the U.S.A. assumed a kind of leadership after World War II. This influence has led to the replacement of French with English as the language of international diplomacy. It has infused innumerable English or purely American terms into the languages of modern nations: in entertainment *(party, show, star, hit, happening, musical)*, in industry *(software, computer,* Offset-Druck), in business *(leasing, holding, marketing, dumping),* in publishing *(best-seller, thriller,* Werbe*spot),* urban development *(center),* clothing *(jeans, twin set, shirt, slip, home dress),* and in the terminology of drug addiction *(fixer,* take a *trip,* be *high, flip out).*

Words like *motivation, stress, test* used in modern American psychology have become universally established in the language of psychology and education. American English has become the international language of aviation, in which all pilots are trained.

The fact that American industry has established satellite plants in most big cities of Europe has created a kind of international business language, to which the advertising pages of any issue of a German newspaper may give evidence. Thus a copy of the "Süddeutsche Zeitung" offers jobs for *Phonotypistinnen, Datentypistinnen, Operatoren, Servicetechniker, Texter, Operational Auditors, Top Mitarbeiter.* Siemens wishes to employ a *Diplomingenieur für Industrial Engineering,* a furniture transporting firm (in U.S. slang, a *mover)* looks for an *Allroundman;* the Deutsche Verlagsanstalt for a *Cheflayouter;* an *Agentur für Marketing und Direktkommunikation* needs *Kontakter* und *Juniorkontakter; Public Relations Agenturen* and a *Manpower Informations-Center* offer a number of jobs.

Despite America's great loss of prestige through the Vietnam War, its pre-eminence in technology, business and many fields of science will continue to strengthen the influence of the American language in a world increasingly dominated by these forces.

17. The Media

The media are the main vehicles of that force in American life which has perhaps had the greatest impact on the modern world. American publicity in the fields of commerce, politics and culture has developed certain formulas and slogans which, through the media, have also come to influence the modes of communication and publicity in other countries.

It may even be argued that along with other American influences in building, fashion, food, music, show business and the arts, American methods of publicity have changed the face of modern and developing civilizations throughout the world.

Advertising in the U.S.A. has developed into a science. Commercials based on the latest findings of motivation research are allowed to interrupt television programmes at 12–13 minute intervals. In television debates between rival candidates during election campaigns, the studied gestures of the speakers often reveal the influence of clever managers versed in show business.

On the other hand, media in the U.S.A. are increasingly becoming aware of their responsibility towards the public. Investigative reporting by newspapers like *The New York Times* and *The Washington Post* or by the team of Ralph Nader ('Nader's Raiders') has not only served to expose abuses and corruption in politics and industry, but has also created a new reading public which has become aware of the individual's responsibility in public issues.

The *Reader's Digest*, which is published in 13 languages, has established the new type of periodical, which, through the simplified form in which it publishes information, makes the latest developments in modern civilization, in industry, the arts and science, accessible to a world-wide audience.

The comic, which seems to have become an indispensable part of children's diet all over the world, originated in America's yellow press.

17.1. The Press

17.1.1.

American journalism started in Boston, the intellectual centre of the colonies. The first American newspaper, *Publick Occurrences Both Foreign and Domestick,* which appeared in 1690, was instantly suppressed because it reported that English armed forces had allied themselves with 'miserable savages'. The printer of *The*

New England Courant, Benjamin Franklin's brother, was imprisoned for attacking the colonial government.

During the War of Independence, the press became an important influence in the formation of political opinion. Thomas Paine's periodical, *The American Crisis,* was one of the principal weapons in America's struggle against Britain. After the war had been won, the new Republic established the principle of the freedom of the press in the First Amendment to the Constitution.

17.1.2.

The 19th century saw the beginning of popular journalism. Papers providing fresh information on matters of immediate concern to the reader began to attract a wider public than party platforms and stale news from Europe.

The first paper to pave the way for the modern daily was the *The New York Sun,* founded in 1833. Its popularity was soon eclipsed by the *The New York Herald,* which was to become the best-known American paper. Its founder, James Gordon Bennett was the first to establish European correspondents, which made it possible for him to gather news quickly. He was a leader in the use of illustrations and introduced many innovations, such as financial news and theatre criticism.

Bennett was the first of a series of great editors, whose influence was often stronger than that of leading politicians. The major exponent of this 'personal journalism' was Horace Greeley, who founded the *The New York Tribune* in 1841. His campaign for the abolition of slavery, his excellent editorials, his introduction of book reviews and scientific reports had made the paper by 1865 the most distinguished in the country. In 1924 it merged with the *New York Herald* to form the *New York Herald Tribune.*

Another important representative of personal journalism was Henry James Raymond, who founded *The New York Times* in 1851. Raymond's aim was to bring news from all parts of the world 'clearly, honestly and impartially without bringing sympathies and antipathies into the discussion'. Thus today, *The New York Times,* much like *The Times* in Britain, has become a symbol of objective information with a somewhat conservative bias.

The constantly growing demand for news eventually ended the dominance of the individual in journalism. Big companies took over ownership and control of newspapers in enormous groups, supported by large-scale advertising. The printing process was accelerated by the invention of the rotary press. The gathering of news was facilitated by the use of the telegraph and telephone, and by big news agencies. The Associated Press was established in 1848. By the 1960s it was serving some 8,000 newspapers and a large number of radio and television stations. It has its own staff in key cities in the U.S.A. and throughout the world. It pioneered innovations, such as the typesetter (1951).

The new desire to reach an ever wider public gave rise to 'yellow journalism'. In 1883, Joseph Pulitzer, an immigrant of Hungarian descent, who had begun his career as a newspaper editor and liberal politician in Missouri, came to New York and bought the rapidly declining *World*. His paper, now the *New York World*, was enormously successful with its sensational news, striking headlines, numerous pictures, colour printing, and the comics, which became one of the main characteristics of the new American tabloids. The name 'yellow press' is derived from the hero of one of those comics, the Yellow Kid, who was presented in bright yellow clothes. Pulitzer gave $2 million to Columbia University for the foundation of a school of journalism and established the Pulitzer prizes awarded annually for literature, music and newspaper work.

His great rival, William Randolph Hearst, the son of a Californian pioneer, was even more successful in spreading the techniques of the sensational press. He bought the *The New York Journal*, which soon reached an unprecedented circulation. He bought newspapers in cities in every part of the U.S.A. and united them in the Hearst Concern. The 'chain papers' of his empire marked a new development in the American press. Hearst acquired several broadcasting stations and established news services to supply his papers with news.

17.1.3.

The period after World War II has added two new types of papers to those already existing: black journalism and the underground press, both including dailies as well as magazines.

The 'black' paper is not a new phenomenon. As early as 1827, the first paper for Negroes was issued; today such newspapers and magazines number some 20 at the national level. The civil rights movement of the sixties has radically altered these publications. Their aim is no longer to imitate the habits and ideals of the white middle classes, but to express a belief in the beauty, power and 'soul' of the blacks. Black papers, formerly regarded as charitable enterprises of well-meaning whites, have today become powerful rivals of the white press. The Johnson Publishing Co. Inc. in Chicago for instance issues a series of black magazines, including the weekly *Jet* and the monthly *Ebony*, which has a circulation of more than a million.

The underground press became the mouthpiece of the beat generation of the sixties, which voiced their criticism of the establishment and their ideas for an 'alternative society'. The first paper to appear was the *Village Voice*, to be followed by many others, such as *The Resistance Press, Liberation, East Village Other*. Today, the Underground Press Syndicate (U.P.S.) for North America claims more than 500 papers, which have become rather commercialized and have lost their original impromptu and apolitical character. Their correspondents are found in all major centres of political conflict, publishing news that is suppressed or slanted in the major papers.

The national unrest caused by the Vietnam War and the civil rights movement has revived an intense involvement in politics. It brought on a new struggle for the freedom of the press against the executive pressure which is brought to bear on papers publishing 'undesirable' news. In 1971, the Supreme Court rejected Nixon's plea to forbid the further publication of the secret Pentagon Papers, through which *The New York Times* and *The Washington Post* had revealed the government's dubious strategy in Vietnam. On the other hand, several journalists have been imprisoned since the Supreme Court ruled in 1972 that journalists did not have the right, under the First Amendment, to refuse to appear before grand juries or to protect the sources of their information.

17.1.4.

No American papers are party organs, one reason being that parties normally have no clear-cut ideological basis, and that their supporters tend to change sides according to changes in platforms or candidates. Broadly speaking, however, it may be said that until recently the American press reflected the conservative opinion of the great 'silent majority' in the nation, especially in the vast heartland of the Middle West. Since the Vietnam War, muckraking in Eastern papers by opponents of the government has encouraged a more liberal, even New Left bias.

17.1.5. Dailies

The question whether America has a national daily press must be answered in the negative. The very size of the country and its division into many partly autonomous states have prevented the development of national papers like Britain's *Times,* althouth *The New York Times* does have regional editions. – Each major city has its own papers, some with a high circulation. The *Chicago Tribune,* which until 1969 exemplified the militant patriotism typical of the Middle West, has recently dropped the slogan 'An American Newspaper for Americans' which it used to carry on the front page under the American flag, and has become much more liberal. Its former highly polemical reporting of events has given way to a more balanced approach, and it excels in investigative reporting, for which Chicago provides ample material. The *Los Angeles Times,* with its extensive staff of foreign correspondents and lively local news, has gained a considerable reputation. *The Washington Post* has come to the fore through its publication of the Pentagon Papers and its merciless reporting of the Watergate Scandal (p. 47), which roused the nation from its faith in the institution of the presidency. *The Christian Science Monitor* with its high standards, which is published in Boston, justifiably carries the subtitle 'An International Daily Newspaper'.

The centre of journalism, however, is still New York with its great printing industry and broadcasting stations, and its leading position as the centre of commerce, finance and cultural life. Here appear, besides *The New York Times*, such leading tabloids (small-format popular papers) as *The New York Daily Mirror* and the *New York Daily News*, which, within six years from its foundation in 1919, attained the highest circulation of all American papers.

The New York Times may be said to be the foremost high-quality daily. It has by far the largest staff of reporters and comprehensive coverage of commercial news, extensive reports on the arts and scientific advances and a prestigious book review section. Its 'Op-Ed' page has become an exemplary national forum for contrasting ideas. Its art reviews have a formidable influence, and a hostile review by a *Times* critic may kill a Boadway play. *The New York Times* has a high reputation for intelligent news coverage, and many of its reporters have won the Pulitzer prize. It was *The New York Times* which exposed the My Lai massacre in 1969.

Another important daily published in New York is *The Wall Street Journal*, which has long outgrown its classification as a financial paper. It ranks high in investigative reporting, and its editorial page is the country's most widely quoted source of conservative opinion.

The International Herald Tribune, published in Paris by *The New York Times* and *The Washington Post*, is the American paper with the highest international circulation.

17.1.6. Periodicals

The world's most widely read periodical is the *Reader's Digest* (founded in 1922), which is published in a large number of foreign editions in 13 languages. It reproduces informative articles on current issues from other periodicals in condensed and simplified form. Its multimillion circulation has made the periodical, which has a markedly conservative bias, a major social force. The news magazines *Newsweek* and *Time*, both with international editions, have gained a considerable reputation throughout the world. With their concise reports on politics, business, science, education and the arts, which are presented in fresh, colourful language, they are preferred by many readers to the heavier style of the standard dailies.

The intellectual magazines *Harper's* and *The Atlantic Monthly*, both with a wide range of articles on political, economic and cultural affairs, and the *Saturday Review*, which stresses educational subjects, are periodicals read by a more sophisticated public. The weekly *The New Yorker* is famous for excellent reviews and highly sophisticated cartoons. *The New York Magazine* gives extensive information on all problems of the Atlantic metropolis.

In recent years there has been a tendency towards a relative loss of ground by the large-scale circulation general magazines in favour of the more specialized or technical periodicals. The great illustrated magazines *Life* and *Look* have become victims of television. *Life*, the world's greatest illustrated magazine, which had developed a new and original style of picture journalism with magnificent photos and excellent texts, had to close down in 1972.

On the other hand, the American public supports a wide range of periodicals catering for readers who expect information on special subjects precisely gathered and documented, and presented in a condensed and interesting style. Thus *Psychology Today*, which was founded in 1967, soon became an astonishing success. *The New York Review of Books* is widely read in literary circles. Other specialized magazines having a high circulation are *Popular Mechanics*, *National Geographic*, *Science*, *Sports Illustrated*, *Outdoor Life*, *Vogue* (fashion). Circulation records are held by the men's periodicals *Esquire* and *Playboy* and by a number of women's magazines. *The Ladies Home Journal* has abandoned its conservative, patriotic bias for a freer, more up-to-date attitude appealing to the young, *Woman's Day* and *Good Housekeeping* give practical information and advice for the housewife.

17.2. Television

Meanwhile the influence of the press has been challenged by 'electronic' or 'broadcast' journalism. Broadcasting began after World War I; the first television licences were issued in 1941. Today almost 96 per cent of all homes have television sets. It has been pointed out that television has changed American society more profoundly than any other technical invention except the automobile.

Although American television is primarily concerned with entertainment, its news coverage has become unquestionably the most important source of information for the majority of the American public.

The television industry is dominated by three principal, sharply competing networks, the programmes of which are received through about 600 local channels: the Columbia Broadcasting System (C.B.S.), the National Broadcasting Company (N.B.C.) and the American Broadcasting Corporation (A.B.C.). In addition there are many independent stations with limited broadcasting range.

American television has two principal characteristics: Although the Federal Communications Commission (F.C.C.), which grants licences, may set certain basic requirements, the networks are not subject to public control. What is more, television is free of charge. The programmes are entirely financed by industry, which, in return, is allowed to interrupt programmes with commercials at irritatingly frequent intervals. As screen time is priced according to the size of the potential audience, the desire for mass appeal is apt to lessen the quality of the programmes. Thus one of the principal problems of television companies is reconciling the need for profits with the desire for prestige.

A general complaint about commercial television is that the day-time programme is chiefly filled with light entertainment, such as game shows and melodramatic serials – 'soap operas' – mainly directed at housewives who spend their entire day at home.

The need for educational and cultural programmes gave rise to public television, formerly known as NET (National Educational Television). This, however, suffers from the lack of funds, partially because the government is reluctant to finance programmes which are often critical of its actions. In comparison with commercial television it reaches a relatively small audience. Only four out of ten households watch some public television regularly.

In recent years, a source of general concern has been the encouragement of violence and crime through Westerns and crime shows. Another complaint is that television stations tend to push public-service spots like anti-smoking warnings, which TV must carry according to a ruling of the Federal Communications Commission, into off-peak periods, reserving the prime time for the profitable commercials.

Despite such dangers and the irritation caused by commercials, most Americans would not wish to change to a state-controlled system financed by the government and subscriptions such as exists in Europe.

18. The Arts

18.1. Painting

Art in America has been influenced more than any other aspect of cultural life by the conflict between imitation of European styles and the striving for an independent expression of native impulses. The European tradition has tended to introduce and naturalize classical elements, while the impressions produced by the exploration of a virgin continent have infused a fresh realistic element into painting. On the other hand, a tendency to glorify the history of a young nation has favoured history painting and allegory.

In the postwar years of the 20th century, American painting began to challenge European predominance, particularly in abstract art. New York has become the art capital of the world.

18.1.1. 17th Century

In its early stages, American art was handicapped by the absence of an indigenous tradition of craftsmanship, from which so much of European art had originated. Moreover, the Puritan mentality did not foster the delight in nature and human life that favours landscape and genre painting. But family feeling and personal pride in the early settlers gave rise to a primitive form of portraiture. More than 400 portraits of people born in New England and New Netherlands before 1700 have survived. Among the finest examples of an art which, in contrast to contemporary English art, valued grasp of character more highly than idealized beauty are portraits of Governor *John Winthrop,* Governor *Pieter Stuyvesant* and the first mayor of Albany, *Pieter Schuyler.*

18.1.2. 18th Century

In the 18th century, American art was strongly under the influence of European neo-classicism. It was therefore only natural that America's greatest artists left the country to achieve fame in Europe.

Benjamin West settled in England, where he became a celebrated representative of the Grand Manner. He received the title of Historical Painter to the King and was elected President of the Royal Academy. West's London studio became the first school for American artists. To these painters of the revolutionary period, the civic virtues of their leaders (especially Washington) became an inexhaustible subject.

In contrast to West, John Singleton C o p l e y, who hesitated for years before he settled in London, shows in his paintings qualities characteristic of the New World – a certain spontaneity and robust vitality. He is particularly successful when painting people in the setting of their daily lives, e. g. *The Boy with the Squirrel*. The most talented of West's American pupils was Gilbert S t u a r t. He became a master of the classical portrait style and 'made a fortune by Washington alone'. John T r u m b u l l, who served as aide-de-camp to Washington, painted battle scenes and murals for the Rotunda of the Capitol.

Among the finest examples of the neo-classical style are the portraits of historical figures by Charles Wilson P e a l e, whose belief in craftsmanship and training made him the organizer of the first art school in America. The leading role played by Philadelphia in the cultural life of the years after the Revolution was due to the inexhaustible artistic initiative of the Peale family as much as to the intellectual leadership of Benjamin Franklin.

18.1.3. 19th Century

In the 19th century, American art developed a greater independence from European influence.

18.1.3.1. Starting in 1811, the Pennsylvania Academy of Fine Arts in Philadelphia organized annual exhibitions. The New York Academy, later to become the American Academy of Fine Arts, followed suit, while Boston provided a cultural centre in the Atheneum, which served as a library and an art gallery.

18.1.3.2. From 1820, the rational attitude towards man and nature which neo-classicism had expressed in a lucid art of clear outlines and even lighting began to give way to a romantic intensity of feeling. The greatest representative of the first romantic generation was Washington A l l s t o n, whose landscapes (e. g. *Moonlit Landscape*) and narrative paintings (e. g. his famous *Belshazzar's Feast*) are dominated by mystery and gloom.

Though strongly influenced by the theory of an idealizing art, Samuel M o r s e (later inventor of the Morse Code) created in pictures like *Congress Hall* original works of documentary realism.

The romantic realism which Morse anticipated became characteristic of the new generation of American landscape painters, which produced the first 'school' in American painting, the Hudson River School. Its chief exponents were Thomas Cole and Asher Durand. C o l e's interpretation of the untamed loneliness of the American forest (e. g. *In the Catskills*) are a fine combination of imaginative realism and lyrical sentiment.

The greatest of the artists who made the frontier their theme was George Caleb

Bingham. *Raftsmen Playing Cards, Fur Traders Descending the Missouri* are pictures in which the figures, firmly drawn against the calm, beautiful background of the great river, convey an air of majestic solitude and hazy, luminous mystery. By far the most popular painter of this period was Albert Bierstadt, who preferred the melodramatic aspects of the western scene, e. g. *Thunderstorm in the Rocky Mountains.*

The Quaker Edward Hicks, who earned his living as a sign and carriage painter, is largely remembered for his *Peaceable Kingdom* illustrating the biblical prophesy of the lion lying down with the lamb; it is painted with a naive freshness.

One of the most brilliant painters of the period was George Innes. The appeal of his pictures, which are mainly interpretations of the eastern landscape, is based on harmonies of colour, which dissolve outline in atmosphere *(Peace and Plenty, Harvest Time).*

18.1.3.3. Until the eighteen seventies, American landscape painting developed comparatively independently from the fixed standards of European schools. This changed in the last quarter of the century when it became the fashion for artists to receive their training in European art centres – in Paris, London and Munich.

The greatest American expatriate painter, James McNeill Whistler, settled in London at the age of 21 and never visited his native country again. With his cosmopolitan leaning, his exoticism, his cult of bohemianism and 'art for art's sake', he became the head of a new movement in European painting, which was influenced by the colour harmonies of his *Nocturnes,* the decorative impressionism and refinement of his portraits (notably the famous portrait of his mother). The influence of Whistler is found in Homer Martin's *The Harp of the Winds,* once one of the best-known American paintings. Another American artist of considerable talent who settled in London was John Singer Sargent, whose cool, brilliant facility fascinated his generation.

In 1895, a group of New York and Boston painters, who exhibited together under the name of the 'Ten American Painters', formed a kind of academy of American Impressionism.

18.1.3.4. Despite their influence, the typically American objective realism persisted among independent painters like Winslow Homer and Thomas Eakins, who painted landscapes and scenes from the life of the people they were born among. Their monumental simplicity made them the greatest American painters of the late 19th century.

Winslow Homer had a genius for the beauty of the ordinary. He painted subjects such as Negroes in the South, soldiers in camp, children on farms. Thomas Eakins, whose pictures are marked by calm intensity and depth of tone, made the life of his native city Philadelphia his chief subject.

18.1.4. Twentieth Century

18.1.4.1. In 1908 an exhibition in New York signalized a revolt against the feeble aestheticism of the 'Ten American Painters'. The 'Eight American Painters', whose teacher and leader was Robert Henri, stressed the importance of American life and daily experience as artistic subjects. The Ash Can School, as they were called because of their humble subjects, brought a delight in the robuster aspects of life, as seen in the vitality of George Bellow's prize fight scenes or in John Sloan's humorous street scenes of New York.

18.1.4.2. The new European movements of Fauvism, Cubism and Expressionism were introduced by the Armory Show of 1913, organized by American artists who had studied in Paris. The show not only served to make the traditional techniques known to a wider American public but also paved the way for the acceptance of a new generation of American painters.
The dominant figure of the twenties was John Marin, who painted subjects like New York's skyscrapers and the coast of Maine in a dynamic style, in which he adopted original technical devices, such as the breaking of the vista into several compartments. Charles Demuth, whose favourite subjects were vaudeville and bar life, used water colour combined with clear, sharp pencil outline with great success.
Lyonel Feininger, who lived most of his life in Berlin until the rise of Nazism drove him back to America, and Charles Sheeler applied Cubist elements to architectural subjects. Joseph Stella, who was born in Italy and influenced by Italian Futurism, was inspired by New York's architecture to treat the beauty of technology in large, highly personal pictures. Georgia O'Keeffe's paintings and photographs of American architecture, of landscape, of bones and skulls convey a striking impression of silence and brooding loneliness. Stuart Davis painted greatly simplified objects in flat, brilliant colours in a poster-like style.

18.1.4.3. The discovery of folk art by Fauvism and Expressionism had its parallel in the U.S.A. in American Folk Art Exhibitions, which included the work of Eagle Bridge, who became known as Grandma Moses. The gaiety and simple humanity of her paintings made her a beloved national character.
A number of artists made it their aim to paint the rural life of the past in the regions where they lived. The best-known of these 'Regionalists', Grant Wood, painted his Iowan neighbours with the fidelity he had learned from the Flemish paintings and Gothic portraits in the Alte Pinakothek in Munich. His most widely known painting is *American Gothic*, a realistic, yet stylized picture of a farmer and his wife in front of a Gothic church.
The depression of the thirties turned out to have a beneficial effect on American painting in that it brought support from the federal government through the

Public Works of Art Project. Many artists who in preceding decades would have left America were given a start in newly established local art centres.

18.1.4.4. In the late thirties, a revolutionary step was taken toward the development of a more specifically American art. The Society of Abstract Artists, which was formed in New York in 1936, entrusted the creation of a picture to the spontaneous movement of hand and brush controlled only by unconscious inner forces. Being almost entirely limited to New York, the movement is sometimes called the New York School.

Arshile Gorky and Jackson Pollock were the painters who established Abstract Expressionism or Action Painting as the leading avant-garde movement after World War II. Gorky first began to convey intense emotional content in unpremeditated configurations without any reference to phenomenal appearance. Pollock invented a new technique of calligraphic expression. Spreading big canvases on the floor, he applied house paint and other pigments, sometimes pouring them directly from cans and letting them splash and run, or even dripping paint from sticks. By the rhythmic movement of his arm, combined with the beauty of his colour sequences, he gave his canvases an ordered complexity, and a fascinating lightness.

Other exponents of Abstract Expressionism are Hofmann, De Kooning, Kline and Motherwell. Hans Hofmann, a Bavarian, who studied in Munich and Paris, settled in America in 1933. He was the most influential teacher of painting in New York, and gave expression to the movement's aim: "Pictorial life is not limited life. It is, on the contrary, a created reality based on the inherent life within every medium of expression. We have only to awaken it". William de Kooning, who used paint with an unbridled violence, was the other notable leader. His dynamic handling of the brush exercised a stronger influence on the new generation than Pollock's elegance.

From the fifties, the creative impulses in painting and sculpture have come from New York and London rather than from Paris. For the first time, American pictures started to bring high prices on European art markets.

18.1.4.5. In the sixties, New York again became the centre of a new art, which had started in London in 1955 when the Independent Group began to discuss the subject of 'popular culture'.

Pop art has substituted for the idealistic theories of traditional art a new realism experimenting with the materials and techniques of the industrial and technological world surrounding the artist. Pop art is the elevation of the trivial to aesthetic value. It is closely related to all the other concrete phenomena of a consumer age, to mass-produced art, Walt Disney art, teen-ager art, and to the world of Westerns, which have influenced youthful fashions. The first to aim at bridging the gulf between life and art was Robert Rauschenberg, who combined painting with objects from every day life: newspaper cuttings, clothes, tires. Rauschenberg's followers, because of their unconventional materials salvaged from junkyards and rubbish heaps, have been called Neo-Dadaists, although their art is more optimistic than the gloomy protest voiced by the Dadaist war generation of 1916.

The new artists in New York were interested in the 'uncommitted act', 'the unpremeditated happening', trying to keep artistic activity free from drab custom. Andy Warhol, Roy Lichtenstein and Claes Oldenburg prefer to use the sharp contours of advertising techniques. In an interview at an exhibition of his works in London, Roy Lichtenstein observed: 'Instead of looking like a painting, pop art seems to be the actual thing' and 'One of the things a cartoon does is to express violent emotion in a completely mechanical and removed style.' Lichtenstein contends that American 'industrial painting' will become universal as industrialization spreads from America to the whole world. Closely related to this concept of art is photo-realism, which tries to reproduce the uncommitted objectiveness of the photograph in painting. Chief representatives of photo-realism are Paul Sarkisian and Don Eddy.

18.2. Modern Sculpture

18.2.1.

The most imposing examples of American sculpture, which are viewed by crowds of tourists every year, are the colossal statue of Abraham Lincoln by D. C. French in the Lincoln Memorial in Washington D.C., and 'the largest sculptures in the world' of four American presidents, which Gutzon Borglum carved in the granite of Mount Rushmore in the Black Hills long before 'land art' was discovered.

18.2.2.

In the forties, a development comparable to that of Abstract Expressionist painting occurred in the discovery of welded and brazed metals, partly caused by the shortage and expense of bronze during the war years. Alexander Calder was the first to use metal and wire as materials for his 'mobiles' and 'stabiles'. José de Rivera's chromium surfaces are fascinating in the sinuous movement of their contracting and expanding spirals on revolving turntables.

Herbert Ferber, David Smith and Seymour Lipton eliminated the last vestiges of figural expression and created abstract forms of great symbolic power. Sculptors like Louise Nevelson and John Chamberlain search junk heaps and car dumps for materials whose special qualities can be turned to new purposes. Chamberlain's immense constructions of crushed car parts are striking comments on the murderous power of machines.

18.2.3.

The recent international exhibitions of modern art, the Biennale in Venice and the Documenta in Kassel, have given evidence of the leading role of America in a number of new movements to which the sixties gave rise.

Minimal art, which reduces sculpture to the arrangement of simple geometrical shapes (cubes, pyramids, hooks) to form carefully conceived patterns, is represented by Donald Judd and Robert Morris. The artists prefer the smooth surfaces of industrial materials, conceiving their art as just one of the many expressions of a technologically organized world.

Object art, whose most notable representative is Edward Kienholz, arranges objects to represent 'environments'.

What is called land art or earth art is anything from seeding fields in prescribed patterns to bulldozing earth to change the face of the landscape. M. Heizer's *Nine Nevada Depressions* exploit the features of the desert. Smithson constructed his *Spiral Jetty* in the Great Salt Lake. The project of the Californian Walter de Maria to sink a 300-foot airshaft (nicknamed 'Denkloch') through the hill built up of air-raid rubble on the site of the 1972 Olympic Games in Munich was rejected by the Olympic Committee.

18.3. Architecture

In contrast to South America and Mexico, British North America never made Indian arts an ingredient of its architectural and artistic tradition. While the Spaniards in New Mexico and California followed the stone and adobe building techniques of Indian pueblos, blending native materials and craftsmanship with Spanish baroque (as seen in their famous chain of missions along the coast of California), the British colonists built their houses and churches in the styles to which they had been accustomed at home.

In New England, the steepled churches and gabled wooden houses with their white-washed clapboard siding are still the most characteristic feature of the rural towns.

In the aristocratic South, the elegant plantation houses were built in the neo-classical Georgian style. The chief decorative effect of these mansions is the colour contrast between the brick of the walls and the white stone of the columns of the gabled porticos. Variations of the Southern Georgian style may be found in *Mount Vernon*, George Washington's estate, and in *Monticello*, the home of Thomas Jefferson, which he himself designed. Other examples are the 18th century houses and churches of Annapolis and Charleston as well as the tidewater plantations of South Carolina and Virginia.

The most aristocratic of the colonial traditions was that of Virginia, as seen in the buildings of the University of Virginia, which was designed by Jefferson, and in *Williamsburg* with its *Capitol*, its *Governor's Palace* and its *College of William and Mary*. Williamsburg was restored in the 20th century as a national monument according to the original plans.

L'Enfant's planning of Washington in the monumental manner of Versailles as the capital of the new Republic set the pattern for town planning throughout the country, much as Jefferson's design for the State House of Virginia in the style of a Roman temple set a pattern for government buildings in America. Jefferson's admiration for the Roman Republic made him a fervent believer in the appropriateness of the Roman style for official buildings in the American Republic.

Less spacious and aristocratic in conception were the official buildings in New England. Here the early predominance of private over public investment can be seen in the pretentious porticos of many banks, which were copied throughout the country.

As in Europe, architects in the 19th and the first part of the 20th century made indiscriminate use of the Gothic and neo-classical styles for public buildings without regard to function. Outstanding examples of this period are the neo-Greek *Lincoln Memorial* in Washington, 1915, the neo-Gothic *Woolworth Building* in New York, 1916, and the *Chicago Tribune Building* 1922.

The rapid expansion westward led to a characteristically American development – the tradition of 'do-it-yourself' home building. By the middle of the 19th century, there already existed many cheaply printed books full of plans for easily erected wooden houses in every conceivable 'style' for families of all sizes and means. The explosive growth of the cities created a need for quickly erected, inexpensive structures. Standardization and rationalization of the building process became early characteristics of American architecture. The prefabrication of building components had made it possible by the 1890s to order certain standardized buildings and facades from catalogue firms in New York, who delivered them all over the country.

With the growth of America's big cities, the value of their commercial sites increased so much that architects had to find new means of utilizing the limited space. This gave rise to a new type of building, the skyscraper. Since the first skyscrapers were built in Chicago and New York in the 1890s, the office buildings of big cities, with their strictly geometrical character, have become a major feature of modern architecture. The most striking landmarks of 20th century building, such as the *Empire State Building*, the *World Trade Center* and the *Rockefeller Center* in New York are the result of private rather than public investment.

From the thirties onward, a number of remarkable European architects migrated to the U.S.A. Eliel Saarinen with his son Eero came from Finland, Ludwig Mies van der Rohe and Bauhaus director Walter Gropius from Hitlers's Germany, which did not favour revolutionary ideas in building. Their contributions hastened the acceptance of progressive European design in the U.S.A.

America's most important native architect, Frank Lloyd Wright, first became known as a propagator of the modern American ideal of the detached single-family home in a rural setting. In his writings, he describes the principle of 'organic architecture': the necessity of an adequate consideration of the environment, the expression of the character of the building, the respect for special qualities of materials. One of the most famous examples of this theory is *Falling Water*', the residence he designed in 1935 for E. J. Kaufmann in the mountains of western Pennsylvania. The house was named after its picturesque setting on a series of rock terraces over a stream and a waterfall. The *Guggenheim Museum* in New York, which Frank Lloyd Wright designed, is one of the most unconventional and fascinating of contemporary buildings.

Since many of the leading architectural schools are associated with institutions of learning, especially in the East, many of the advanced structures are found in connection with universities. The most striking of these buildings is Eero Saarinen's skating rink with its continuously curvilinear plan and elevation, which he designed for Yale University. One of the special achievements of American build-ing is its many bridges, from the first suspension bridge across the East River in New York to the gigantic *Verrazano Narrows Bridge* that spans the entrance to New York Harbour and the *Golden Gate Bridge* across San Francisco Bay.

In contrast to such great achievements of modern architecture, the U.S.A., like all industrial nations, suffers from the devastating effects of rapid commercial and industrial development: the decay of the inner core of its cities, the uncontrolled growth of the suburbs, the defacement of the countryside by unscrupulous con-tractors, the infinite repetition of only a few basic designs of a split-level or ranch-style house.

18.4. Films

18.4.1.

For about 60 years, America's film production has centred in Hollywood, a suburb of Los Angeles. Its film companies have grown into giant corporations (Metro Goldwyn Mayer, Paramount, Columbia Pictures, Rank Organization), whose great producers (e. g. Billy Wilder, Orson Welles) have made Hollywood the world's film capital.

Within America itself, Hollywood has become 'the mythology that Americans have in common', which explains the fact that film stars have always been more important to the public than directors. Hollywood has created certain human types and patterns of behaviour which embody the ambitions and dreams of the American population. The American Westerns gave a sophisticated world a new romance, in which adventure and violence blended with sentimentality and the moral satisfaction of seeing the villain punished and the virtuous hero rewarded. Despite criticism of the fact that they stimulate violence, despite many new developments in film production, the Western has more than any other type of film held its place in cinemas and on television all over the world.

American crime shows, which developed chiefly in the thirties when the U.S.A. was plagued by big crime, have had less permanent international success, perhaps because of England's tradition of a more subtle detective literature.

In the fifties, the Micky Mouse films of Walt Disney introduced the entirely new genre of animated cartoons, which became particularly popular for shows of all kinds for children. The fifties also saw remarkable films produced from famous novels, e. g. Edna Ferber's *Giant* or Steinbeck's *East of Eden*.

When the competition of television made itself felt, Hollywood producers attempted to hold the public's attention with ever more extravagant productions. Box office sensations like *Ben Hur* and *El Cid* employed casts of thousands. Such productions also include films on religious themes (*The Ten Commandments, The Greatest Story Ever Told*, and, recently, *Jesus Christ Superstar*).

18.4.2.

By the late fifties, independent small producers had begun to challenge Hollywood's dream factory with entirely new types of experimental films, often produced with the most primitive means. In 1960, these 'underground' film makers joined in the New American Cinema Group and founded the Film Makers' Cooperative to support film producers and arrange performances. They distributed film cameras in the black ghettos, encouraging Negroes to interpret their appalling social conditions under the motto 'Shoot your way out with the camera'.

The foremost representatives of the underground cinema include Jonas Mekas, Stan Brakhage and the all-round artist and pop idol Andy Warhol. With pornographic films like *Flesh* and *Trash*, Warhol has meanwhile shot his way through to become a millionaire himself.

The new films lay stress not on the story as much as on the psychological problems arising from it – which is in keeping with the contemporary preoccupation with Freud. 'Our search goes within; and this leads some of us to the regions of the irrational, the religious and mystical. We leave the superficial problems of materialism and consumer civilization behind us in order to find within ourselves new conceptions and a new freedom' (J. Mekas). Many of these abstract films are highly surrealistic, expressing mystical states of mind or visions produced by drugs; others

179

produce fleeting impressions of colour, form and movement through elaborate montage techniques, e. g. Brakhage's *Songs* and *Art of Vision*.

18.4.3. The result of this new conception was that in the sixties Hollywood's 'one-man autocracies' began to employ young directors more in touch with the developments of the avant-garde.

The new films produced by these men tend to focus on human moods and passions rather than on plot. Like the most provocative literature, they attempt to treat subjects that were once considered shocking. Thus *Chappaqua* treats the life of drug addicts, *Reflections* homosexuality, *The Heat of the Night* racial hatred. The *Graduate* deals with the sexual experiences of a college graduate. John Wayne's film *The Green Berets* gives a merciless picture of the horrors of war, although it is not free from a nationalist bias. The most successful of recent films were *Bonnie and Clyde* and *The Godfather*, perhaps because they blended the old-time crime show with the new trend of drawing the audience into sympathy with their anti-heroes. *Easy Rider* (p. 155) is one of the best interpretations of the new counter-culture.

An old and continuing trend in film-making has been the thriller, the movie designed to shock, to frighten and finally leave the audience in a state of emotional exhaustion. The earliest of these films were based on classical horror stories, such as Mary Shelley's *Frankenstein* and Bram Stoker's *Dracula*. Later, Alfred Hitchcock manipulated deep-seated emotions and fears in such well-known films as *Psycho* and *Frency*. This striving for emotional effects has achieved new heights in *The Exorcist*, which became an international hit within a few weeks after its first production.

The demanding subject matter of many modern films has tended to attract chiefly younger people, while the middle-aged usually prefer the lighter fare of American television.

18.5. Music

18.5.1. Music in Colonial America

The first impulse for musical activity was provided by the churches of New England. Versified psalm texts set to music and manuals published by Massachusetts ministers provided the material for the singing schools which represented the main musical activity in colonial times and often developed later into choral societies.

Secular music was cultivated outside New England in New York and in the Southern cities. Charleston had its own concert hall, in which the St. Cecilia Society (founded in 1762 and existing until 1912) gave fortnightly concerts with a professional orchestra. Charleston also held the first performance of a ballad opera in the colonies. In the 18th century, musical societies founded in the coastal cities encouraged choral music, which enriched songbooks with glees and catches.

18.5.2. Patriotic Music

The Revolution provided a powerful impulse to create a national American music. It produced rallying songs for the troops (e. g. 'Yankee Doodle'), the national anthem, 'The Star-Spangled Banner', and more ambitious compositions. Benjamin Carr's *The Archers* in the ballad-opera style expressed the American situation in terms of the Wilhelm Tell legend. W. H. Fry wrote the first American 'grand opera' *Leonora*, G. F. Bristow an opera *Rip van Winkle*. The German immigrant Anton Philipp Heinrich tried to create a characteristically American music with his oratorios *The Pilgrim Father, Yankee Doodliad* and *National Memories*. He helped in organizing the Philharmonic Society of New York (1842), America's oldest permanent orchestra.

18.5.3. Hymns and Negro Spirituals

Hymnody received a new impulse from the Methodist revival. John Wesley published his first hymns at Charleston in 1737, even before Methodism gained a footing in England.
As the Great Revival reached the Negro slaves in the South, it produced a musical expression that has since affected almost every kind of music in America. What the slaves inherited from West African music – the call-and-response pattern of West African work chants and the African tradition of melodic improvisation – blended in their spirituals with the intensity of revivalist hymns. The Negro spirituals with their Christian content – the hope for salvation and the expectation of the Promised Land – became symbols of the Negro's hope for freedom (e. g. 'Swing Low, Sweet Chariot, Coming for to Carry Me Home' and 'When Israel Was in Egypt's Land, Let My People Go').

18.5.4. Minstrelsy and Folksong

In contrast to the spiritual, so-called Negro minstrelsy was really white enter-tainment drawn from the experience of the strolling players of the early 19th century and their notions of Negro life. 'They paint their faces black, sing Negro songs, dance and jump about as if possessed' wrote a contemporary musician. When real Negro minstrel troupes began to appear, the entertainment they offered was but an imitation of the white men's shows.
But this period of minstrels and sentimental songs founded the American folksong. The two best-known composers of this time represented both traditions. Stephen C. Foster's plantation songs 'Swanee River' or 'Carry Me Back to Ole Virginny' embodied the sentimental tradition. Dan Emmet's minstrel song 'Dixie', which the Confederate troops sang when marching to battle, has been called the anthem of the South.

18.5.5. Festivals

The eighteen-sixties saw the first music festivals. In 1868, the Handel and Haydn Festival was established in Boston as a triennial event. Musical conventions in Worcester, Mass., became an annual festival, in which twenty towns and villages participated. By 1900, festivals had sprung up in many cities of the Middle West. The most spectacular mass performances were organized by the composer of the famous song 'When Johnny Comes Marching Home', P. S. Gilmore, in 1869 and 1872. A building was erected in Boston to house an audience of fifty thousand. The enormous Jubilee of 1869 to celebrate the country's regained unity offered everything from military bands to organ music and massed choruses of 10,000, mobilized from all over New England. It lasted five days and drew visitors from as far as California. At the World Peace Jubilee of 1872, 'The Battle Hymn of the Republic' brought an audience of 20,000 to its feet shouting 'the jubilees, the jubilees forever!' From that time on, amateur bands replacing the regimental bands of the Civil War became indispensable to the festivites of American communities.

18.5.6. Musical Life in Boston and New York

Professional musical education began in 1833, when the Boston Academy of Music was founded, followed by the Academy of Music in New York in 1854 and, in the sixties, by conservatories in the Middle West. In 1881, the Boston Symphony Orchestra was founded. Toward the end of the 19th century, Boston became the headquarters of a number of composers known as the Boston group. Frederick Converse's opera *The Pipe of Desire* and Horatio Parker's *Mona* were produced by the Metropolitan Opera in New York, the first operas by American composers to be accorded this distinction. By the beginning of the 20th century, New York had become the nation's musical metropolis, where the captains of finance and industry, the Morgans, Vanderbilts and Rockefellers generously supported the Metropolitan Opera (founded in 1883) and the New York Symphony Orchestra. In 1911, Joseph Pulitzer left a million-dollar endowment to establish the New York Philharmonic Orchestra and another bequest to provide scholarships for promising composers. The International Composers Gild, organized in New York, saw to it that major works by foreign composers, such as Arnold Schönberg, Igor Stravinsky, Paul Hindemith, Bela Bartok were performed even before they came to live in America. These works helped to bring to the public new musical departures with which an American composer, Charles Ives, was already experimenting. Ives was at first dismissed as an eccentric, but later hailed as an innovator who brought new spontaneity and expressiveness to music. His Third Symphony was awarded the 1947 Pulitzer Prize.

In the twenties, New York became the centre of national broadcasting when the National Broadcasting Company was established in 1926 and the Columbia

Broadcasting System in 1927. Experimentation with 'synthetic sound', also begun in the twenties, led to the establishment of an Electronic Music Center at Columbia University in 1953.

The Rockefeller Center houses the headquarters of the Radio Corporation of America, the studios of the National Broadcasting Company and the Radio City Music Hall. The Lincoln Center for the Performing Arts contains the Philharmonic Hall, the Metropolitan Opera and the Juilliard School of Music.

The New York City Ballet performs at the New York State Theater in the Lincoln Center. Many of its works were created by George Balanchine, whose *Slaughter on Tenth Avenue*, a pioneer work and his first big Broadway hit, established ballet as an art permanently on Broadway. In 1972 he performed his most recent works in Munich during the Olympic Games.

18.5.7. George Gershwin

When, in 1924, the popular band leader Paul Whiteman planned his famous concert that was to be an 'Experiment in Modern Music', he commissioned for the programme a piece for piano and jazz orchestra. This piece was *Rhapsody in Blue* by George Gershwin (1898–1937), America's best-known composer. Gershwin's earliest ambition was to be a great popular song composer, an aim which he achieved as a composer of musical comedies and, later, films. The success of his *Rhapsody in Blue* led the composer to continue writing serious music in this style, e. g. *An American in Paris* and his folk opera *Porgy and Bess* (1935) depicting Negro life in a Southern city. This work, which combines successfully the form of grand opera and folk elements from popular music, achieved tremendous success and was soon produced in Latin American and European countries.

18.5.8. Musical Comedy

Already by the 1890s, the topical song and dance comedy in the British music-hall style had taken the place of the minstrel shows in New York theatres, which set the tone for the American musical stage. The first to experiment with the idea of expanding the usual brief variety sketches into full-length musical comedies was G. M. Cohan. His *Little Johnny Jones* (1904) contained two songs that have become part of American folklore: 'Give My Regards to Broadway' and 'The Yankee Doodle Boy'. With his musical plays Cohan created a native entertainment with fast moving action and colloquial speech, which moved musical comedy out of the world of imaginary Balkan principalities into modern everyday life.

Jerome Kern's *Show Boat* (first produced in 1927) drew its plot from American literature. It integrated music and characterization, song and drama with a realism that distinguished it from operetta, in a popular idiom that distinguished it from opera. After the Second World War, Leonhard B e r n s t e i n ' s *West Side Story*, a modern Romeo and Juliet story set against the background of racial conflict and gang warfare in New York, became a world-wide success. In musicals like *Kiss Me, Kate*, *South Pacific*, *The King and I* and *My Fair Lady*, the synthesis of play and music had developed so far that the line between musical and opera became difficult to define. The sixties added a large number of new musicals to the original hits, e. g. *Hello Dolly*, *Fiddler on the Roof* and *Zorba*. In recent years, *Hair*, which voices the ideals of the American counter-culture and its protest against war, rapidly became an international hit.

Today the Broadway musical is perhaps America's most widely understood and appreciated art-form.

18.5.9. Jazz

Jazz is a form of band music chiefly determined by melodic and rhythmic elements from Negro folk music, which originated at the beginning of the 20th century. Since its characteristic feature is improvisation, jazz depends greatly on the personality of the players and has therefore in the course of time given rise to many notable soloists.

The three roots from which modern jazz sprang were Ragtime, New Orleans jazz and Dixieland jazz.

Ragtime, which originated in the cabarets and saloons of Western cities and railway camps, was piano music integrating the banjo tunes of plantation Negroes and the rhythm of Negro marches and dances with shanties and other popular melodies in a new syncopated style. Its rhythmic freedom and irresistible spontaneity revolutionized social dancing and became a national craze.

New Orleans jazz: Actual jazz, which blended the traditional musical forms of the South – the Negroes' melancholy folk songs known as 'blues', their spirituals, work songs and field cries – was played first in New Orleans, where countless festivals, carnivals and riverboat excursions offered ample occasions for band music. New Orleans jazz, which was played by white as well as Negro bands, was characterized by three melodic lines played by three wind instruments (cornet, trombone and clarinet) supported by rhythmical instruments (usually drum, banjo, guitar, or piano). The first recordings were made by a white band, the Original Dixieland Jazz Band, which made *Dixieland* another name for 'white' music from the South. Pieces like 'The Original Dixieland One Step' and 'Tiger Rag' became hits throughout the country. The father of Dixieland jazz, which embodied the unproblematic gaiety of the period before World War I, was 'Papa' Jack L a i n e.

When, in 1917, the entertainment district of New Orleans, Storyville, was closed as a result of the country's entering the war, band musicians began to migrate to the North and West, disseminating jazz through the rest of the country. Most musicians went to Chicago, where 'King Oliver' and Louis Armstrong formed their famous bands. New Orleans jazz saw its heyday in the Chicago of the twenties. Ensemble playing was now interrupted by more extended solos. The saxophone became a symbol of jazz.

Swing: In the thirties the freer rhythms of popular swing branched off from the traditional two-beat jazz. 'King of Swing' was the clarinettist Benny Goodman, whose famous swing concert in Carnegie Hall in 1938 signalled the acceptance of popular music as concert music.

Bebop: When swing declined into overscored music for oversized bands, the spirit of jazz was recovered in a deliberately rebellious-sounding music called bebop (or bop), which began to be heard in Harlem's jazz clubs toward the end of World War II, and was played in smaller groups. In the late forties bop began to merge into 'cool jazz'. Instead of the explosive outburst of bebop, cool-jazz musicians preferred a relaxed, flowing line. The dominant figure was Miles Davis, whose note of resignation and sadness reflected the situation of the postwar period. The 'funky' style which he initiated found a new approach to the original blues, which was played slowly and heavily to a strong beat.

Of the many 'kings of jazz', Louis Armstrong and Duke Ellington have become the most famous.

Louis Armstrong, who was trumpet virtuoso, singer, showman and comedian all in one, was like so many of his race a self-taught musician. His ingenious improvisation soon raised him above collective band performances and made him America's star soloist. Despite his brilliant career, he basically remained a primitive with an incomparable boldness of approach.

Duke Ellington was, in contrast to him, a trained musician, who had never been in New Orleans. The 'grand old man' of big-band jazz was also a successful composer, whose many popular melodies and larger compositions often reflect the history of his race, e. g. *Harlem; Black, Brown, Beige,* or *New World a-Comin'* – the dream of a better world with no race discrimination. He created the 'jungle style' with its growl effects of trumpet and trombone reminiscent of voices in the jungle at night. He exercised an immense influence on the development of jazz, both in sound and in instrumentation.

Free jazz: Since 1960, jazz has tended to abandon all limitations of 'classical' jazz, indulging in a cult of intensity not bound to rules of harmony or rhythm, which are given up in favour of the shock effects of frantic noise. Music is no longer conceived as an arrangement of sounds in a given rhythm, but as an effective presentation of anything that may be heard, much as modern pictorial art achieves effects by indiscriminate collages of objects and materials presenting themselves to the artist's imagination. A major exponent of this latest development of progressive jazz is Stan Getz.

18.5.10. Pop Music

There is considerable disagreement as to whether popular American music is a form separate from jazz. It may in fact not be a distinct form at all. Pop music ranges from the more melodious folk-tune style derived from the blues and plantation songs of the Negroes through the strong, emotionally stimulating rhythms of 'soul music' to the aggressive force of rock. To the young generation, the harsh sounds of rock are expressive of their protest against a civilization, which, while producing beautiful music, also conducted bloody wars and committed atrocities. Questioned about the pleasure derived from such music, they interpret in Freudean terms the substitution of mere force of sound for the principle of harmony inherited from classical music. In the discotheques, the ego is 'drowned' in the atmosphere of frantic noise and the anonymous mass of young people seeking freedom from the inhibitions of the preceding generation. Teenage aggressions and pent-up emotions can be released in energetic dancing.

Big business has taken advantage of the fact that the young generation has begun to form a considerable part of the consumer market and therefore has given them a voice, even though it may be an 'angry' one.

Electronic reproduction has revolutionized the entire position of music within culture. The American today is exposed to it almost continually, from the piped-in 'muzak' in the elevators and supermarkets to the ubiquitous car radio. At home he certainly has his own record player. The demand for new music is practically limitless, and American composers have continually sought new sources of inspiration. Not only Arab and Indian music but also electronic manipulations of sound, and, more recently, drugs have all assumed importance in the development of American music. And American music itself has now replaced the film as the country's chief cultural export.

Bibliography

General Information on Contemporary America

Adam, R.: *Die USA* (Olzog, München, 1965)
von Borch, H.: *Amerika – Die unfertige Gesellschaft* (Piper, München, 1964) [English Translation: *America – The Unfinished Society* (Hawthorn Books Inc., New York, 1962)]
Breitenstein, R.: *USA heute* (Econ, Düsseldorf, 1971)

History

Adams, J. T.: *The Epic of America* (Little, Brown and Co., Boston, 1943)
Beard, C. A. and M. R.: *New Basic History of the United States* (Doubleday and Co., Garden City, 1960)
Klose, N.: *American History*, 2. vols.; I. Am. Hist. to 1877, II. Am. Hist. since 1865 (Barron's Educational Series, Inc., Woobury, 1970)

Geography (Physical and Economic)

Compton's Pictured Encyclopedia: The U.S.A. – Its Land, Its People, Its Industries (F. E. Compton and Co., Chicago)
[German Translation: *USA, Das Land, seine Bevölkerung und Wirtschaft* (Westermann, Braunschweig, 1961)]
Mead, W. R. and Brown, E. H.: *The United States and Canada – A Regional Geography* (Hutchinson Educational Ltd., London, 1962)
Paterson, J. H.: *North America – A Geography of Canada and the United States* (Oxford University Press, London, 1965)
White, C. L. and Foscue, E. J.: *Regional Geography of Anglo-America* (Prentice Hall, Englewood Cliffs, 1954)

Economic Life

Galbraith, J. K.: *The Affluent Society* (Penguin Books Ltd., Harmondsworth, 1967, first published 1958)
Galbraith, J. K.: *The New Industrial State* (Houghton Mifflin Co., Boston, 1972, first published 1967)
Lilienthal, D. E.: *Big Business – A New Era* (Harper and Brothers, New York, 1953)
Lilienthal, D. E.: *TVA – Democracy on the March* (Pocket Books Inc., New York, 1944)
Mintz, M. and Cohen, J.: *America Inc. – Who Owns and Operates the United States* (Dell Publishers Co., New York, 1972)
Packard, V.: *The Hidden Persuaders* (van Rees Press, New York, 1962, first published 1957)
Servan-Schreiber, J. J.: *The American Challenge* (Avon Books, New York, 1968)

Social Life

Broom, L. and Glenn, N.: *Transformation of the Negro American* (Harper and Row, New York, 1967)

Cook, B.: *The Beat Generation* (Charles Scribner's Sons, New York, 1971)
Gorer, G.: *The American People. A Study in National Character* (Norton and Co., New York, 1964)
Hagan, W. T.: *American Indians* (The University of Chicago Press, Chicago, 1970)
Mills, C. W.: *The Power Elite* (Oxford University Press, London, 1959)
Muse, B.: *The American Negro Revolution – From Nonviolence to Black Power* (Indiana University Press, Bloomington, 1968)
Reich, C.: *The Greening of America* (Penguin Books, Harmondsworth, 1971)
Whyte, W. H.: *The Organization Man* (Simon and Schuster Inc., New York, 1972, first published 1956)
[German Translation: *Herr und Opfer der Organisation* (Econ, Düsseldorf, 1958)]

Government and Law

Griffith, E. S.: *The American System of Government* (Methuen and Co., London, 1969)
Levine, E. L. and Cornwell, E. E.: *An Introduction to American Government* (The Macmillan Company, New York, 1971)
Ogg, F. A. and Ray, P. O.: *Essentials of American National Government* (Appleton-Century-Crofts/Prentice Hall, New York, 1969)
Ogg, F. A. and Ray, P. O.: *Essentials of American State and Local Government* (see above)

Education

DeYoung, C. A. and Wynn, R.: *American Education* (McGraw-Hill Book Co., New York, 1972)
Hechinger, F.: *Das amerikanische Bildungssystem auf neuen Wegen* (Education Editor der New York Times für den US Information Service)
McGhee, G. C.: *Die Rolle der amerikanischen Universität im Leben der Gemeinschaft* (Ansprache vor Gästen der Hannoverschen Hochschulen, 1967)

Religion

Hudson, W. S.: *American Protestantism* (University of Chicago Press, Chicago, 1966)
Marty, M. E.: *The New State of American Religion* (Harper and Brothers, New York, 1959)
Smith, J. E.: *Religion im heutigen Amerika* (Amerikanische Gelehrtenwoche 1961, Ludwig-Maximilians-Universität, München, 1962)
Sperry, W. L.: *Religion in America* (The Macmillian Company, New York, 1946)

American Thought

Curti, M.: *The Growth of American Thought* (Harper and Row, New York, 1964)
Marnell, W. H.: *Man-made Morals – Four Philosophies that Shaped America* (Doubleday and Co., Garden City, 1968)
Smith, J. E.: *Der philosophische Pragmatismus Amerikas* (Amerikanische Gelehrtenwoche 1961, München, 1962)

American Language

Krapp, G. P.: *The English Language in America*, 2 vols. (Frederick Ungar Publ. Co., New York, 1966)

Kirchner, G.: *Die syntaktischen Eigentümlichkeiten des amerikanischen Englisch*, 2 Bde. (Enzyklopädie/Hueber, Leipzig/München, 1970, 1972)
Galinsky, H.: *Amerikanisches und Britisches Englisch* (Hueber, München, ³1975)

Art

Hamilton, G. H.: *Contemporary American Architecture, Painting and Sculpture* (Amerikanische Gelehrtenwoche 1961, München, 1962)
Richardson, E. P.: *Painting in America* (T. Y. Crowell Co., New York, 1965)
Rose, B.: *American Art Since 1900 – A Critical History* (Thames and Hudson, London, 1967)

Music

Behrendt, J. E.: *Das Jazzbuch – Von New Orleans bis Free Jazz* (S. Fischer, Frankfurt/Main, 1971)
Sablosky, I. L.: *American Music* (The University of Chicago Press, Chicago, 1969)

Readings in American Studies

Boorstin, D. J. (ed.): *An American Primer* (The University of Chicago Press, Chicago, 1966)
Heffner, E. D. (ed.): *A Documentary History of the United States* (The American Library, New York, 1965)

Reference Books

The American Almanac – The U.S. Book of Facts, Statistics and Information (Grosset and Dunlap, New York, 1972)
Encyclopedia Americana (Encyclopedia Americana Co., New York, 1972)
Encyclopædia Britannica (Encyclopædia Britannica Inc., London, 1972)
Friebel, I. and Händel, H. (eds.): *Britain – U.S.A. A Survey in Key-Words* (Moritz Diesterweg, Frankfurt, 1968)

Newspapers and Periodicals Used

Newsweek (International Edition: Germany, Frankfurt/Main)
Time (Atlantic Edition: Netherlands, Amsterdam)
The Reader's Digest (The Reader's Digest Association, Pleasantville, N. Y.)
Süddeutsche Zeitung (Süddeutscher Verlag, München)
Die Weltwoche (Weltwoche-Verlag AG., Zürich)

Index

Please note the following for the use of this index:
1. All acts and treaties are listed under one reference respectively.
2. Where reference is made to a list, the number of the page is printed in *italics*.

C

Aktuelle Übungs- und Lesebücher zur Amerikakunde

Hartwig Isernhagen

The U.S. from Within

A Workbook for Students

1975, ca. 190 Seiten, kart., Hueber-Nr. 2176

Ein neuartiges landeskundliches Lese- und Arbeitsbuch. Es werden um einzelne Schwerpunktprobleme amerikanische Originaltexte thematisch gruppiert. Diese Textgruppen sind mit ausführlichen *Workpoints* zur Diskussion und schriftlichen Erarbeitung versehen. Dadurch wird eine intensive Auseinandersetzung mit dem Amerikabild der Amerikaner wie mit unterschiedlichen sozialen und stilistischen Sprachebenen erzielt.

Albert Schmitz

A Look at the Press: Britain and the USA

1973, 112 Seiten, kart., Hueber-Nr. 2163

Dieses Arbeitsbuch für die Klassen 10–13 bietet eine Einführung in das Pressewesen Großbritanniens und der USA sowie im Anschluß daran eine Artikelauswahl aus 27 englischen bzw. amerikanischen Zeitungen. Die Artikel wurden in der für das Blatt typischen Form übernommen, mit Originalzeitungskopf, Schlagzeilen, Zeichnungen, Cartoons, usw.

Die Länge der Beiträge ist so gewählt, daß man sie, je nach Intention, auch in einer Unterrichtsstunde bewältigen kann.

Neben der Tagesberichterstattung (Streik, Preiserhöhungen, Bezahlung, Alkoholausschank, Schiffsunglück) werden in den Artikeln der Bau des Kanaltunnels, das Fernsehen, Vorstadtprobleme, die Umweltverschmutzung, Minoritätenprobleme, Nordirlandfrage sowie andere Themen aus den Bereichen Kultur, Politik, Medizin, Naturwissenschaft und Sport behandelt.

Es wird hier Material geboten für: Konversations- und Diskussionsübungen, landeskundliche Information, Textaufgaben, Wortschatzerweiterung, stilistische Übungen, Sprachbetrachtung.

 Max Hueber Verlag · Informationsabteilung
D–8045 Ismaning/München, Krausstr. 30, Tel. (0 89) 9 62 31

Appendix

Fig. 1: Physical Divisions

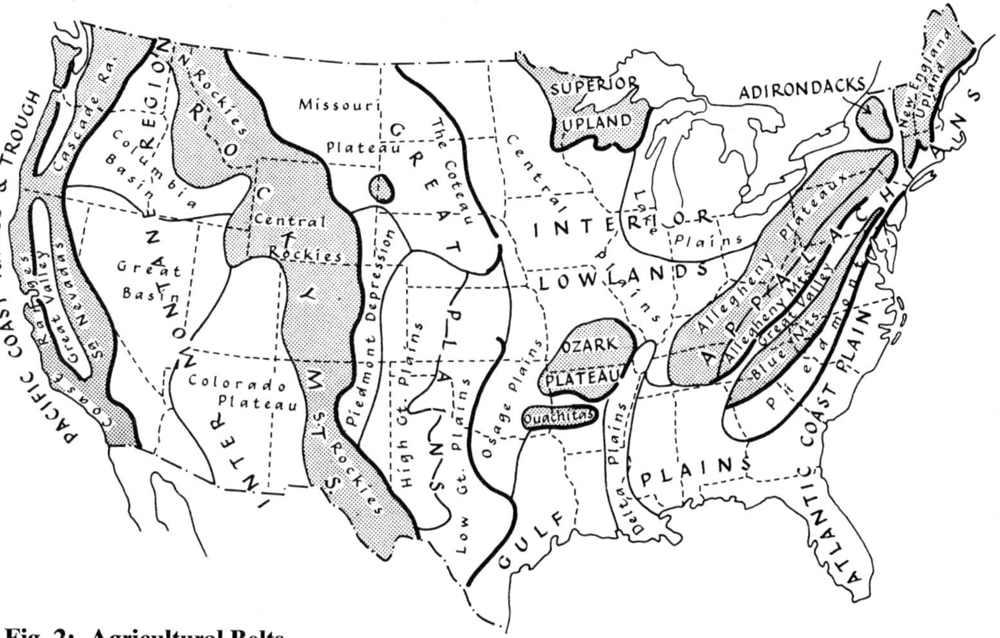

Fig. 2: Agricultural Belts

Fig. 3:
Physical and Topographical Map
of the U.S.A.

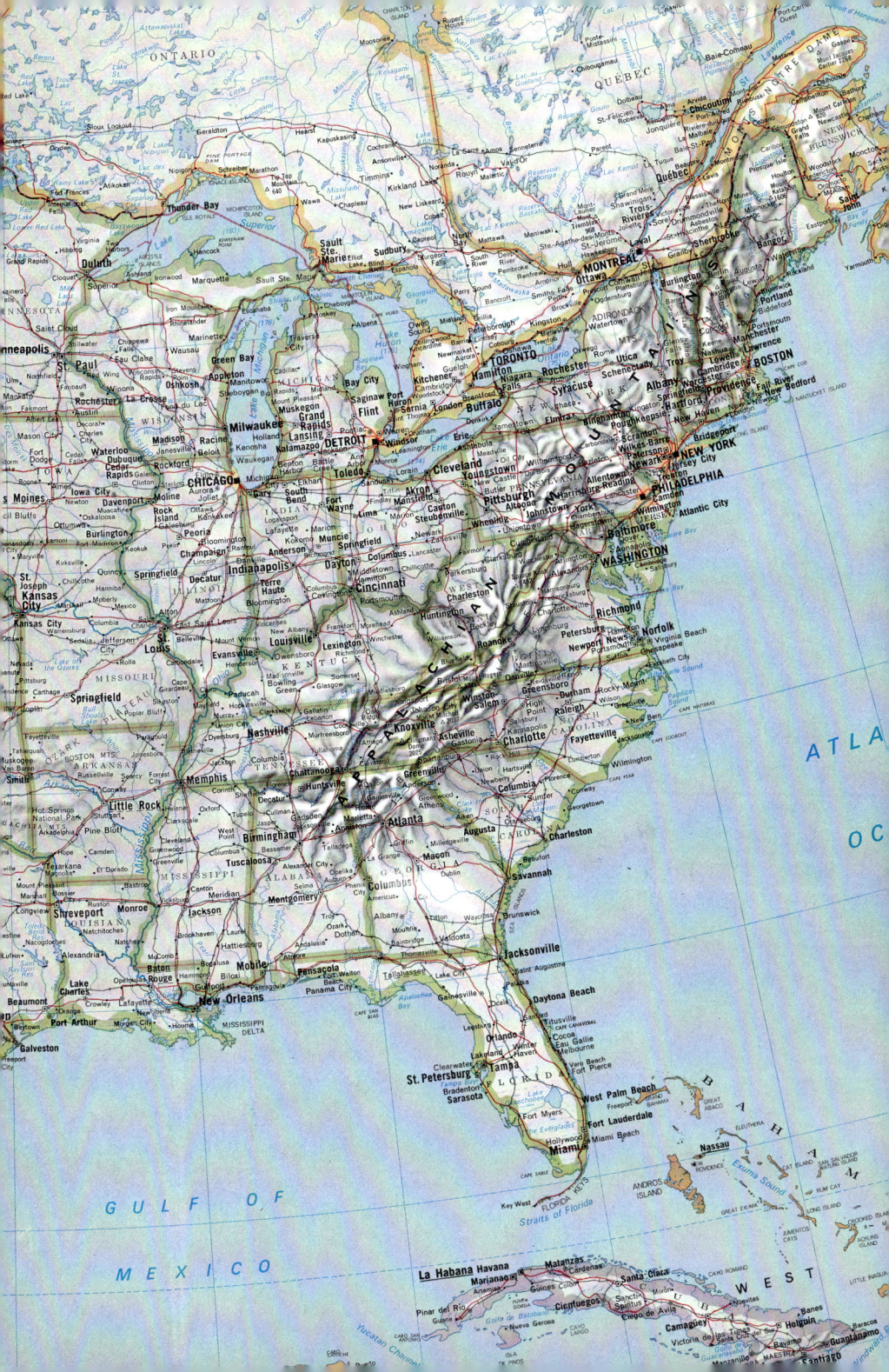

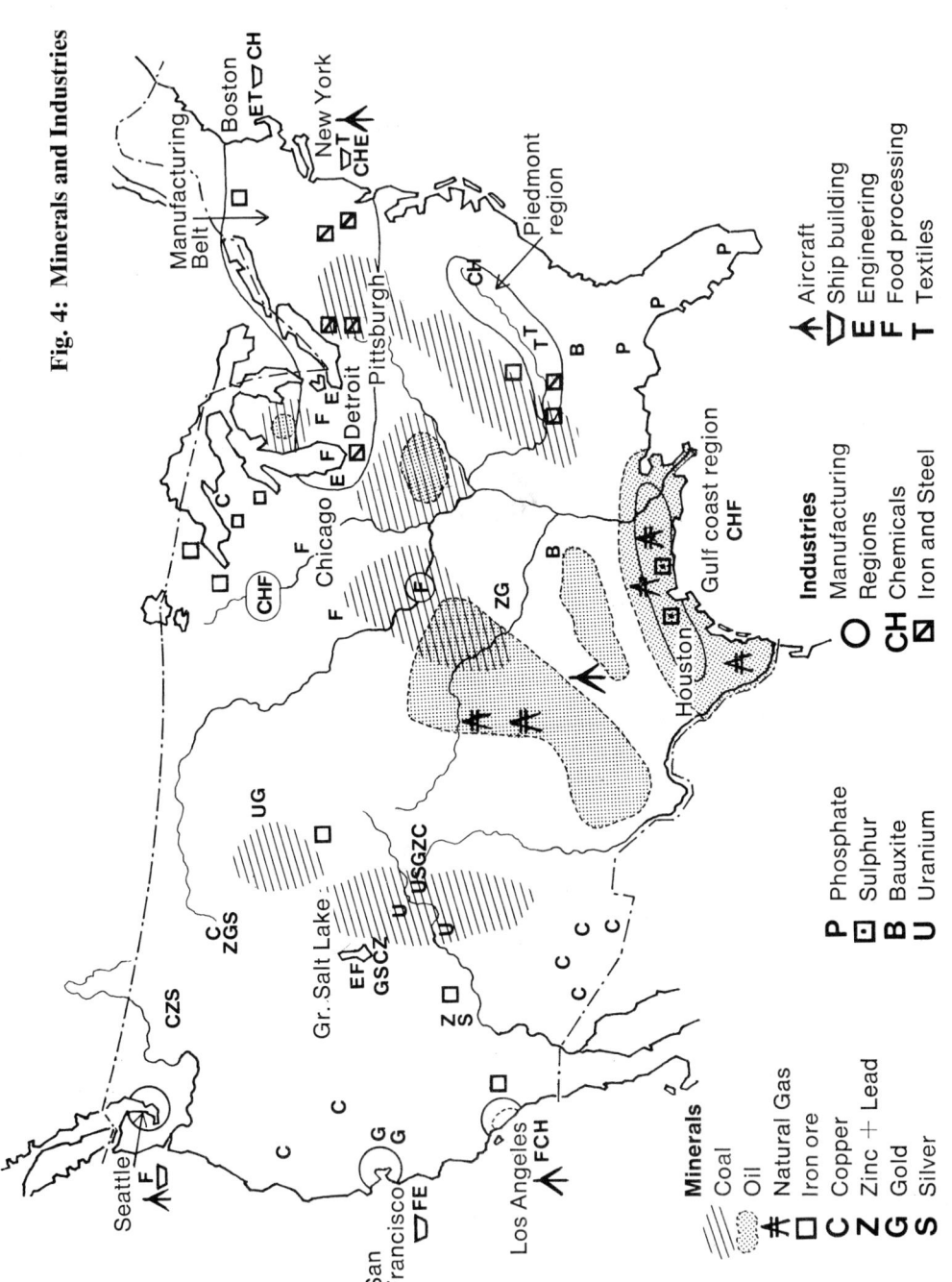

Fig. 4: Minerals and Industries